THE CABAL

Mr. Secretary Coventry: Would know what the meaning of the CABAL is.
Mr. Garroway: That is so great a mystery, that he would know it above
all things.

Report of a debate in the House of Commons, January 14, 1674

UNIVERSITY OF ILLINOIS PRESS, URBANA, 1965

THE CABAL

Maurice Lee, Jr.

For Helen

Acknowledgments

Like all scholarly books, this one would not have been possible without the cooperation and assistance of many people and institutions. My grateful thanks are owing to the following: the University of Illinois for its generosity with time; the John Simon Guggenheim Memorial Foundation for a fellowship which made a year's research in Great Britain possible; the following libraries: University of Illinois Library, Princeton University Library, New York Public Library, Public Record Office (London), British Museum, Scottish Record Office (Edinburgh), National Library of Scotland (Edinburgh), and their uniformly helpful and courteous staffs; the earl of Jersey for his kindness in allowing me to quote from the Commonplace Book of the duke of Buckingham; my former student, Dr. James O. Richards, for his exemplary diligence during his year as my research assistant; my friend Professor Frederick C. Dietz, who read Chapter 4 to its considerable benefit; and my other colleagues at the University of Illinois, who have listened patiently, given me the benefit of their advice, and saved me from several errors; they are in no way responsible for those that remain.

I should also like to thank the National Portrait Gallery for their permission to publish the illustrations, and Mrs. Carolyn McConnell of the University of Illinois Press for her care and skill in seeing this manuscript through the press.

Contents

A Note on Dating and Other Technicalities

The dating throughout this book is Old Style; letters written with New Style dating are provided with the Old Style date as well. Except in the poetry, spelling has usually been modernized, and punctuation occasionally supplied. The following abbreviations have been used throughout in the footnotes:

B.M.—British Museum
H.M.C.—Historical Manuscripts Commission
N.L.S.—National Library of Scotland, Edinburgh
P.R.O.—Public Record Office, London

Chapter 1

The End of Clarendon

Prologue

How can this nation ever thrive
Whilst 'tis governed by these five:
The Formal Ass, the Mastiff Dog,
The Mole, the Devil, and the Hog? [1]

S o runs a squib circulated in the streets of London in the early months of the third Dutch war. The five so ful-somely described are the famous Cabal—Clifford, Arlington, Buckingham, Ashley, and Lauderdale. They were not the first group of English politicians to have the epithet "cabal" applied to them, nor the last for that matter, but because of the accident that the first letters of their names spell out the word, the label has stuck.

To call these men a cabal is really very misleading. The word suggests a group of conspirators; nothing could be further from the truth. They were seldom united in support of any policy; more often than not, they were plotting against each other. The period of their greatest influence, the years between 1667 and 1674, was marked by vicious political intrigue, as they competed among themselves and with other aspiring politicians for the favor of King Charles II. None of them ever succeeded in achieving a position of preeminence, as Lord Chancellor Clarendon had before them, and as Lord

[1] Quoted in John H. Wilson, *A Rake and His Times* (New York, 1954) , p. 216.

Treasurer Danby was to have, to a lesser degree, in the middle of the
1670's. Cross-purposes and disharmony characterize the surface of
politics during the Cabal period. Below that surface the skillful
manipulator who sat on the English throne was in fact making his
own policy.

Charles II is one of the most striking figures in the annals of
English royalty. Everybody knows about him—his mistresses, his
bastards, his spaniels, his wit. It is all epitomized in the lines of the
earl of Rochester,

> Restless he rolls about from Whore to Whore,
> A Merry Monarch, scandalous and poor,[2]

a couplet which inevitably brings to mind the saw about the pot and
the kettle. What "everybody knows" is accurate enough, of course.
Charles did have mistresses and bastards, etc., etc., and he and his
women—the virago Castlemaine, Mistress Stewart, beautiful but
dumb, and pretty, witty Nell—will always be popular with what has
been called the "bedspring and chamber pot school" of historical
writing. There is general agreement, too, on many facets of Charles's
character—his charm, his intelligence, his knowledge of men, his
fundamental unscrupulousness—and on his central political objective: to be his own master, independent of restriction by Parliament.
What has provoked dispute is the intensity with which Charles
pursued his political ambitions and the nature of his ultimate moti-
vation.

The traditional picture of Charles is taken mainly from the pages
of Bishop Gilbert Burnet, the loquacious Scotsman who wrote the
most famous contemporary account of the Restoration period.
Burnet portrays the king as a cynical, selfish, and indolent absolutist,
who admired the government of his cousin Louis XIV, but would do
nothing which might lead to his going on his travels again. "The
king loved the project in general," wrote Burnet of a suggestion that
Charles emulate the king of Denmark and establish a despotism by a
coup d'état, "but would not give himself the trouble of . . . managing it."[3] He would not give himself the trouble: here is the key to
this interpretation of Charles. To what might be called the revision-

---

[2] George deF. Lord, ed., *Poems on Affairs of State* (New Haven, 1963)
I (1660–78), 424.

[3] Gilbert Burnet, *The History of My Own Time* (ed. Osmund Airy,
Oxford, 1897–1900) I, 487.

ists, on the other hand, the king's indolence and lack of purpose were simply surface appearances, deliberately designed to mask a deep political drive. To his admirers, like C. H. Hartmann and Sir Arthur Bryant, he was a wise and farseeing patriot; to others, like David Ogg, his true objectives were revealed by the reactionary regime of the years after 1681, when, says Ogg, "the cynical monarch" was "comfortable at last."[4]

Whether Charles's ultimate goal was patriotic or selfish, whether his pursuit of it was continuous or sporadic, the obstacle was always the same: Parliament. Charles never forgot that Parliament had put an end not only to his father's attempt at absolutism but also to his life, and that, if sufficiently provoked, it might well try to do the same to him. Parliament's power to do this, its power to influence policy, either positively or negatively, had to be broken if Charles was really to rule in England. As Burnet put it, "he did not think he was a king as long as a company of fellows were looking into all his actions, and examining his ministers as well as his accounts."[5] Charles had learned the lessons of the last twenty years well enough, however, to realize that a return to the policy of Charles I was impossible. The politically minded classes in England would never stand for the complete abolition of Parliament. The problem for Charles, therefore, was not how to get along without Parliament, as many historians have said; rather, his problem was how to make Parliament pliable.

In the story of Charles's struggle to free himself from the influence of Parliament the significance of the years from 1667 to 1674 is crucial. It was during these years that Charles made his great effort to achieve power on the terms he preferred. The attempt was necessarily made in large part behind the scenes, and it ultimately failed. Consequently it has been frequently overlooked, the more so since Charles later did achieve a kind of absolutism, under very different circumstances. The violence engendered by the Popish Plot, and one of the Plot's consequences, the Exclusion Bill, virtually compelled Charles to act in defense of the principle of hereditary right to which he owed his throne. His apparent acquiescence in Danby's leadership in the years between the failure of the policy of the Cabal

[4] David Ogg, *England in the Reign of Charles II* (2nd ed., Oxford, 1955) II, 651.
[5] Burnet, *History* II, 3.

period and the outbreak of the Popish Plot and his attitude in the Plot's early stages have led some historians to suggest that Charles might never have acted at all if his hand had not been forced—and even then, his action took the form chiefly of masterly inactivity. It is possible to argue, with Ogg, that at this stage of his career comfort was indeed the king's chief objective. But at the time of Clarendon's fall this was not so. In 1667 Charles was thirty-seven years old, in the prime of life. He had absorbed a great deal of useful information about human nature and politics in the drab years of exile and in the more comfortable days since his Happy Restoration. He was now prepared to make his great effort to become supreme in his kingdom. The chief supporting figures in his grand design, whether they knew it or not, were the five members of the Cabal.

II

Early in 1664 the French ambassador in London sent this rather self-consciously intellectual appraisal of the English political situation to his master: "If Aristotle, who attempted to define even the smallest things pertaining to politics, were to come again to this world, he could not find words to explain the manner of this government. It has a monarchical appearance, as there is a king, but at bottom it is very far from being a monarchy. . . . Whether this is caused by the fundamental laws of the kingdom, or by the carelessness of the king, herein lies the difficulty."[6] The ambassador's perplexity is understandable, and was widely shared, both at the time and since. The exact nature of the restored regime is by no means easy to define. In fact, to talk about "the Restoration" is almost as misleading as to talk about "the Cabal." It was impossible, in 1660, to turn the clock back to 1641, much less to 1640. What was restored were forms: government by king, lords, and commons, and the rest. But no amount of formal restoration could disguise the fact that the situation of 1660 was utterly unprecedented and that a great deal of experimenting would have to be undertaken if a stable settlement was to be achieved.

The great political crises of the Restoration period were to revolve around four interrelated questions: the religious policy of the government and the religious proclivities of the king, the conduct of

[6] J. J. Jusserand, *A French Ambassador at the Court of Charles the Second* (London, 1892), p. 106.

foreign policy, the financial problem, and, underlying them all, the question of the nature of the English kingship. Of these four, one was not legally affected by the change of regime. Foreign policy had always been a matter for the executive, and in 1660 control of foreign affairs, including the power to decide on questions of peace and war, reverted to the crown as a matter of course. Religion and finance were the subject of specific legislation as a part of the settlement. Much less clear-cut were the powers of the restored kingship.

The legal position of the crown, in one respect at least, was clear enough. Those acts of the Long Parliament which had received the assent of Charles I were valid; the others were not, nor were the laws of any Interregnum government. This general principle was subjected to modifications in detail almost as soon as it was adopted. In those areas, such as economic policy, in which what was wanted was continuity rather than "restoration," this was achieved by the re-enactment of some of the economic legislation of the Interregnum, especially the Navigation Act, and by the employment of former Cromwellians in important financial offices. The most prominent of these was Anthony Ashley Cooper, who in 1661 became Baron Ashley and chancellor of the exchequer.[7] Conversely, that legislation of 1641 which was generally admitted to have gone too far was either repealed, like the act excluding bishops from the House of Lords, or modified—the Triennial Act, for example, was replaced in 1664 by a much milder version which was deliberately designed to be a dead letter. The Triennial Act was the only major limitation on the power of the crown accepted by Charles I which was not maintained, however. The others still stood, which meant that important institutions and powers which had been available to his father, notably prerogative courts and prerogative taxation, were denied to the restored king. The area in which the crown might act was not clearly defined after 1660, but the area in which it might *not* act was far larger than in 1640.

The circumscribed legal position of the crown was offset to some extent in 1660 by a tremendous wave of enthusiasm for monarchy as

[7] On the general question of continuity before and after 1660 see Charles Wilson, *Profit and Power* (London, 1957), chap. VII. Louise F. Brown, *The First Earl of Shaftesbury* (New York, 1933), pp. 100–101, points out that the old Cromwellians who became privy councillors after 1660 were most heavily represented on the economic committees of the council.

an institution. This was in large measure the result of the execution of Charles I, who was a martyr in the eyes of many in 1650 and of far more in 1660. Even the withering scorn of John Milton could not destroy the enormous popularity of *Eikon Basilike, the Pourtraicture of His Sacred Majesty in His Solitudes and Sufferings,* which went through edition after edition in spite of the Interregnum governments' efforts to suppress it.[8] The martyr's son was king by hereditary right; his reign began on January 30, 1649, the day of the martyrdom. Now, in the happy year of 1660, the twelfth of his reign (the statutes of this year are so dated), King Charles II, himself miraculously preserved after his military debacle at Worcester, was miraculously come into his own again, without bloodshed, now that the Devil had taken away Old Noll, his servant. The popular intoxication with the mystique of kingship was at its height in 1660; whether it was widespread and intense enough to have permitted a repeal of all the limiting legislation of the Long Parliament and a return to the days of an untrammeled prerogative can never be known, since the attempt was never made, probably owing to the caution of the earl of Clarendon.

Charles was well aware of the value of this sentimental cult of kingship, and in some ways he sedulously fostered it by such things as touching for the King's Evil. He was seconded by the leaders of the restored Church of England, who did what they could to emphasize the divinity that doth hedge about a king and to turn it to practical use by advocating the doctrine of nonresistance. In time, however, as was bound to happen, the popular fervor began to wane. This was not entirely Charles's fault. No one could have answered to all the expectations of that Restoration summer, and some of Charles's supporters did him a serious disservice by endowing him with far more virtue and wisdom than he, or most other mortals, had.[9] The various provisions of the Restoration settlement, though equitable enough in most respects, inevitably disappointed many people, especially those loyalists who felt that they had some claim to the king's gratitude. Charles could soften the blow for many of

[8] Godfrey Davies, *The Early Stuarts 1603–1660* (2nd ed., Oxford, 1959), p. 159.
[9] As two samples among many, see Sir William Davenant, *Poem upon His Sacred Majesties Most Happy Return to His Dominions* (London, 1660), and Sir Samuel Tuke, *A Character of Charles the Second* (London, 1660).

these men by the exercise of his personal charm, but he could not keep them from feeling aggrieved and, somehow, cheated. As one contemporary, looking back, remarked, "What was termed in years following 'Whigism' [sic] . . . really sprang by degrees from the discontent of noble families and of many good families of the first gentry in the Counties whose ancestors were sequestered, decimated, and what not on account of their steadfast loyalties."[10]

In one important respect, however, Charles himself greatly contributed to the weakening of the cult of kingship, and this was in his personal behavior. This was not merely a matter of immorality. Englishmen did not expect their king to be perfect, but they did expect him to be kingly—dignified—just as nowadays they expect him to be middle class. What lowered Charles in the eyes of the politically minded Englishman was not his womanizing but his frivolity. Henry VIII's messy marital career did not notably diminish the awe in which he was held, or even his popularity, because Henry always carried himself in a manner rather larger than life. But Charles did not. Charles was a wit. He told jokes—imagine Henry VIII, or any Tudor for that matter, telling a joke! Charles was believed to be lazy and neglectful of business, as the pages of Pepys bear witness. And as for his behavior: one of the most familiar anecdotes about Charles is the story recorded by Pepys in his *Diary* in the black days of June, 1667. The Dutch fleet was in the Thames, the outer ring of London's fortresses was being bombarded, the defenses had been enfeebled by corruption and theft on the part of government officials, the great city itself trembled in anticipation of assault—and Charles, in these desperate days, was having supper with Lady Castlemaine and chasing a moth around the dinner table.[11] The story may not be true, but that does not matter. The mere fact of its being told is evidence that by the later 1660's the luster was beginning to wear off. Charles never lost his personal popularity, in large measure because he was universally regarded as infinitely preferable to his brother James, the next heir. The cult of the royal martyr continued to flourish, and kingship as an institu-

---

[10] W. E. Buckley, ed., *Memoirs of Thomas, Earl of Ailesbury, Written by Himself* (Roxburghe Club ed., Westminster, 1890) I, 6.

[11] *The Diary of Samuel Pepys,* June 21, 1667. The H. B. Wheatley edition (London, 1926) is the one I have used; references will be by date, to facilitate referral to other editions.

tion was never in jeopardy; there was no desire to repeat the republican experiment. This was a permanent gain for the crown. But by 1667 the sentimental enthusiasm which had surrounded the beginning of the reign, which had led to the election of the Cavalier Parliament in 1661, and which had sent Pepys and countless other Londoners into the streets to get drunk on coronation day had evaporated.

The honeymoon was over, but the ambiguity in the crown's position still remained. The prerogative, as employed by Charles I, had been struck down by Parliament, but prerogative power as such had not been destroyed, and, indeed, could not be as long as the king was king by indefeasible hereditary right. Such a right was not within the power of any Parliament to bestow; as long as it was the basis of kingship, the royal prerogative was potentially and theoretically still in existence. What remained to be determined was whether this prerogative power could still be used at all, and if so, whether it could be used, in combination with the king's executive authority, in such ways as to give Charles a fighting chance to free himself from his dependence upon Parliament.

One obvious road to the restoration of the independence of the crown was closed to Charles: he could not use force. If there was one point on which all shades of English opinion were agreed, it was that there must be no standing army. To Cavaliers a standing army conjured up the awful vision of Oliver and his major-generals; former Commonwealthmen were reminded of Black Tom Tyrant and the Popish despotisms of the Continent. This very seriously limited what Charles could do. He dared not follow a policy which would provoke general resistance, and in fact his ends could best be served if he could succeed in creating the impression that he was not doing anything at all. It is this circumstance which makes so much of the history of Charles's reign obscure and difficult to follow.

A tentative experiment with the prerogative was made in 1662 in connection with religion. The Church of England was "restored," just as government by king, lords, and commons was, but the church of the 1660's resembled that of the 1630's in theory rather than in fact. In the eighty-odd years of its existence prior to 1640 the Anglican Church had theoretically been a comprehensive church. Queen Elizabeth's objective had been to make the official religion tolerable to as many shades of opinion as possible, even at the expense of doctrinal consistency, and she had succeeded moderately well. As time went on, however, the official church became less and less satisfactory to more and more people; during the regime of William Laud only a minority of Englishmen could conscientiously support it. But until its overthrow in the Puritan Revolution it remained in theory the church of all the people of England, and penalties for nonconformity were severe. The restored Church of England in the 1660's revived this theory of the church. A new Act of Uniformity was passed. The legal position of the church reverted to what it had been in 1640. Penal legislation was revived, though the Court of High Commission was not. Ostensibly the old comprehensive church had been resurrected—but it was a resurrection which was now utterly at variance with the facts of English religious life. The church settlement was made in large measure by the disciples of Laud,[12] but they knew perfectly well that the Laudian vision, of a uniformity to be created by a combination of coercion and ritual, had been shattered forever by the events of the past twenty years. Coercion there was to be, but with a crass political motive. Nonconformists were to be harried by the law, not to save their souls but to prevent them from stirring up sedition. Control in the restored church lay in the hands of men who had been in exile, and like so many emigrés, they were suspicious and bitter. The latitudinarian *Irenicum,* published in 1660 by Edward Stillingfleet, a cleric who had not emigrated, was exceptional among Anglican pamphlets. Far more common was the view of the author of a distressingly bad poem, "The Fortunate Change":

> For if to Heretick in Church or State
> You give an inch, they'l take an Ell, and prate
> Their wild Opinions to the Multitude,
> Who'l know no reason, but from hand that's rude.[13]

No concessions were made to the Presbyterians or to anyone further to the left in the religious spectrum. The established church was

---

[12] For the most thorough recent study of the church settlement see R. S. Bosher, *The Making of the Restoration Settlement: The Influence of the Laudians 1649–1662* (New York, 1951) .

[13] Quoted in F. Bate, *The Declaration of Indulgence, 1672* (London, 1908) , p. 18.

purposely made narrowly exclusive, and nonconformity was equated with sedition and republicanism—with what was called, bitterly now, the Good Old Cause.[14]

This deliberately uncompromising settlement, which was epitomized in the persecuting legislation known, rather unfairly, as the Clarendon Code, was far from reflecting the true mind of the king. Charles's religious views have been widely misunderstood. Far too much has been read into his deathbed acceptance of Catholicism; with respect to personal faith, he was indifferent. A bright young man of his court, one of the group of wits who collected around Buckingham and the rakish earl of Rochester, called Charles a deist: "And this uncommon opinion he owed more to the liveliness of his parts, and carelessness of his temper, than either to reading or much consideration; for his quickness of apprehension at first view could discern through the several cheats of pious pretences; and his natural laziness confirm'd him in an equal mistrust of them all, for fear he should be troubled with examining which Religion was best."[15]

Charles may have had an opinion as to "which Religion was best." He certainly felt considerable sympathy and gratitude to the English Catholics, who had been staunch supporters of the Stuart dynasty during the civil war and who, at considerable personal risk to themselves, had helped him to escape from the country after his defeat at Worcester. He had no enthusiasm for the Laudian sort of church which emerged; at first he inclined to a genuinely latitudinarian solution, until the rigid attitude of the Presbyterians demonstrated to him how difficult it would be to arrange such a settlement and how little the Catholics would gain from it.[16] In the last analysis, though, Charles was prepared to adopt whatever religious policy

[14] See, for instance, the vituperative tract of 1663 justifying the Act of Uniformity in Lord Somers, *A Collection of Scarce and Valuable Tracts* (2nd ed., ed. Walter Scott, London, 1812) VII, 567–86, which makes the dissenters talk of "our good friends the catholiques" and which, paradoxically, makes them sympathetic both to France and to anabaptism and republicanism.

[15] John Sheffield, earl of Mulgrave, quoted in John H. Wilson, *The Court Wits of the Restoration* (Princeton, 1948), p. 17. "Deist" is here being used in the seventeenth-century sense of "indifferentist."

[16] H. C. Foxcroft, ed., *A Supplement to Burnet's History of My Own Time* (London, 1902), pp. 69, 71. John Stoughton, *History of Religion in England from the Opening of the Long Parliament to 1850* (4th ed., London, 1901) III, 113–15. E. W. Kirby, "The Reconcilers and the Restoration," *Essays in Modern English History in Honor of Wilbur Cortez Abbott* (Cambridge, Mass., 1941), pp. 49–79. Arthur Bryant, *King Charles II* (rev. ed., London, 1958), pp. 99–100.

seemed most likely to enhance his political power. In this matter, as in so many others, the example of France was always before him: a state church under royal control, where the conditions of toleration of dissenters were determined by the king alone. Charles certainly envied the amount of power possessed by Louis XIV, and he made some remarks which led the French ambassador to report that Charles was convinced that no religion was as suitable for an absolute monarch as Roman Catholicism.[17] In one respect, however, Charles's position was superior to Louis': he was the unquestioned head of his church and not subject to outside interference, such as Louis suffered at the hands of Innocent XI during the controversy over the Gallican Liberties. On the other hand, Louis could determine the fate of the Huguenots by edict. Charles wanted to wield the same power. Since the established church, with the Parliamentary majority behind it, was persecuting and exclusive, Charles's attempts to assert such authority inevitably came to revolve around the question of toleration.

Charles's attitude toward religious toleration is more complicated than has usually been supposed. It does not follow that, because Charles was religiously indifferent, he was therefore tolerant. Charles was not bloodthirsty and did not believe in "capital and sanguinary punishments" in religious cases.[18] But he did not subscribe to any theory of toleration, and he did not like dissenters— witness his well-known remark to Lauderdale that Presbyterianism was not a religion for gentlemen. He did want to help the Catholics. But if there was greater political power to be had by supporting a persecuting Anglicanism, then Charles would do this, as he did during the last ten years of his reign, after the failure of his earlier policy had been obviously demonstrated. That earlier policy had been, in essence, one of imitating Louis XIV and creating toleration by royal prerogative, in the interest of his own authority and to relieve his Catholic subjects.

The keystone of the Restoration's religious settlement was the Act of Uniformity, which became law in the summer of 1662. It was not particularly palatable to the king and his advisers. Clarendon

[17] Apr. 13, 1663, Cominges to Lionne, in Jusserand, *French Ambassador*, p. 206.

[18] See his speech to Parliament on February 18, 1663, given in Arthur Bryant, ed., *The Letters, Speeches, and Declarations of King Charles II* (London, 1935), pp. 139–40.

thought it vindictive; to the king, it was a measure which was burdensome to Catholics and, if left unchallenged, amounted to acknowledgment of Parliamentary supremacy in religious questions. There was also some fear in government circles that the religious discontent it would evoke would lead to seditious outbreaks: Charles and his advisers, like most returned emigrés, were very nervous about plots.[19] So for all these reasons Charles, in December, 1662, issued a declaration of indulgence. The document was the work of four men, the chancellor of the exchequer, Lord Ashley, who believed in toleration on principle and held that religious persecution was bad for business, the Catholic earl of Bristol and the Presbyterian Lord Robartes, who were seeking to serve the interests of their co-religionists and, possibly, to undermine the position of Clarendon, whom they disliked, and finally, Sir Henry Bennet, the future Lord Arlington, the new secretary of state, whose first important act in domestic politics this was. Clarendon, who was laid up with the gout, was kept informed of what was going on by Bennet; his attitude was ambiguous at best, as he was not convinced that such a measure was politically necessary at this time.[20]

The declaration was exceedingly cautious on the subject of the prerogative: Charles and his advisers were feeling their way. The declaration of Breda, issued by Charles in April, 1660, before his restoration, had promised liberty to tender consciences; the Act of Uniformity had stultified that promise. Therefore, said Charles, "we shall make it our special care . . . without invading the freedom of Parliament, to incline their wisdom at this next approaching sessions to concur with us in the making some such Act . . . as may enable us to exercise with a more universal satisfaction that power of dispensing *which we conceive to be inherent in us*" (italics mine).[21] In other words, Parliament was to be asked to concur in Charles's

[19] Bosher, *Restoration Settlement*, pp. 281–82. Edward, Earl of Clarendon, *A Continuation of His History of the Great Rebellion* (Oxford, 1857) I, 557. W. C. Abbott, "English Conspiracy and Dissent 1660–1674," *American Historical Review* XIV (1908–9), 515–16.

[20] G. R. Abernathy, "Clarendon and the Declaration of Indulgence," *Journal of Ecclesiastical History* XI (1960), 55–73, attempts to show that Clarendon favored the declaration. The argument is not entirely convincing. Cf. for this and for the two earlier attempts at indulgence in 1662 Bosher, *Restoration Settlement*, pp. 250–53, 259–64, 269–70.

[21] Andrew Browning, ed., *English Historical Documents 1660–1714* (New York, 1953), p. 373.

exercise of a power which in the nature of things he already possessed.

It is unlikely that Parliament would have approved of this in any case, but the chance of approval was reduced to the vanishing point by the king's frankness in stating that he intended to use his powers in behalf of the Catholics. This was a bad tactical blunder, since it alienated much nonconformist opinion; many of them, like the Presbyterian leader Richard Baxter, were so afraid of Popery that they preferred suffering themselves to showing the slightest leniency to Catholics. So, when Parliament reconvened in February, 1663, there was strenuous objection to the indulgence, although not on constitutional grounds. The Commons declared that they could not be bound by the declaration of Breda, that toleration was politically very dangerous, and that to dispense with the Act of Uniformity would establish schism by law and bring the authority of the church into contempt. They were not moved by the argument put forward by Bennet and Ashley, in a paper explaining the government's position, that the charge of favoring Popery was the same complaint used by the "malignants" against Charles I.[22] So the king recoiled, as he almost always did when faced with vehement and determined Parliamentary opposition; a bill introduced by Robartes to give effect to Charles's declaration was dropped, and the king, putting the best face on it that he could, made a conciliatory speech to the Commons when they sent a deputation to him to explain their opposition to his policy. Charles's first attempt to mitigate the religious settlement, and at the same time to strengthen his prerogative, was a failure. Pepys heard that the king was really angry at his defeat, "which I am sorry for, and fear it will breed great discontents."[23]

"Great discontents" were also bred on all sides by financial problems, though for utterly different reasons. In no area was it less possible to turn the clock back in 1660. Some of the financial devices of the Parliamentary regimes were retained, such as the excise; the

[22] D. T. Witcombe, "The Cavalier House of Commons: The Session of 1663," *Bulletin of the Institute of Historical Research* XXXII (1959), 181–83. For Baxter, see his *Fair-Warning, or, XXV Reasons Against Toleration and Indulgence of Popery* (London, 1663).

[23] Pepys, *Diary*, Mar. 3, 1663. There is a good account of the politics of this indulgence controversy in V. Barbour, *Henry Bennet, Earl of Arlington* (Washington, D.C., 1914), pp. 60–68.

last of the king's sources of revenue as feudal overlord was swept away, with the confirmation of the Commonwealth's abolition of all feudal burdens on land tenure. Indeed, there was nothing else to be done; such burdens had not been enforced for the past fifteen years, and land had been bought and sold with no feudal obligations attached.[24] But in one very pernicious respect there was a "restoration": the old distinction between ordinary and extraordinary revenue was revived. Parliament proposed to give Charles an income of £1,200,000 a year, which would pay for the ordinary costs of government. Only in the event of an extraordinary situation, such as war, was he supposed to have recourse to additional taxation. This antiquated theory demonstrated its inadequacy almost immediately. The sources of revenue provided by Parliament, chiefly customs duties and excise taxes, described as "the pillars of the revenue," produced nothing like £1,200,000 a year. The king from the beginning was saddled with his father's debts, for which Parliament made no special provision, The system of collection was inadequate, and no satisfactory means of raising loans in anticipation of revenue was devised in the first few years of the Restoration. The result was ever-mounting debt and ever-mounting interest rates.

In this situation Charles, Clarendon, and the honest but incompetent lord treasurer, the earl of Southampton, lived from hand to mouth. The very unpopular sale of Dunkirk to France in 1662 was caused by financial hardship; the government was so short of cash that one chest of the Dunkirk money had to be pledged for a loan of £1,000 to buy machinery to recoin the rest. Equally unpopular was the enactment of a hearth tax in 1662, which fell very heavily on the poor; local officials were most uncooperative about assisting in its collection.[25] Thus the government was caught between an inadequate revenue and collection machinery and an antiquated theory of taxation, complicated by a slump in consumer-goods industries which reduced customs revenues. The king's behavior did not help matters any. The hoary legend that Charles squandered all his money on his mistresses has been exploded, but they certainly cost

[24] J. R. Tanner, *English Constitutional Conflicts of the Seventeenth Century 1603–1689* (Cambridge, 1928) , p. 221.
[25] A. E. Feaveryear, *The Pound Sterling* (Oxford, 1931) , p. 96. L. M. Marshall, "The Levying of the Hearth Tax, 1662–1689," *English Historical Review* LI (1936) , 628–46. Andrew Browning, *Thomas Osborne, Earl of Danby and Duke of Leeds* (Glasgow, 1951) II, 29–30.

something, and they caused the king to appear extravagant and irresponsible. Here was the answer to Southampton's plaintive question on the subject of loans to the government. "Why will they not trust the king as well as Oliver?"[26] The answer was obvious enough: the sobersided and businesslike protector inspired confidence in the hard-bitten goldsmith-bankers who were the only sources of large sums of ready cash; the lover of Lady Castlemaine did not. So the goldsmiths charged the government very high rates of interest, when they lent at all. Pepys, who was ready enough to be critical of the king in most matters, was on his side in this case; his own job in the admiralty made him aware of the extent of the government's financial difficulties. The goldsmiths' charges were "a most horrid shame, and . . . must not be suffered."[27] But for the moment there was no alternative.

The second Dutch war, which began in 1665, generated new and extreme financial pressures and some new solutions, largely the work of Sir George Downing, an old Cromwellian, whose dislike of the Dutch did not prevent him from imitating their fiscal methods. Downing's proposal, which was adopted by Parliament in the fall of 1665, was to appropriate the new levy of tax money specifically for the war. This would make it easier to get people to make the necessary anticipatory loans to the government and thus enable the government to borrow at lower interest rates, since the goldsmiths could be partially bypassed. As an added attraction, loans made to the government would be registered and repaid *seriatim;* the borrower would receive a warrant, which would be transferable on endorsement. If sufficient confidence could be generated in these warrants, this would amount to an emission of paper money.[28]

Downing's scheme was moderately successful; it might have been more so if it had had the wholehearted support of his official colleagues. Clarendon and Southampton were dubious; so were lesser

[26] Pepys, *Diary,* Apr. 12, 1665.
[27] Pepys, *Diary,* Jan. 19, 1663. A good general account of the goldsmiths can be found in Dorothy K. Clark, "A Restoration Goldsmith-Banking House," *Essays . . . in Honor of Wilbur Cortez Abbott,* pp. 3–47.
[28] John Beresford, *The Godfather of Downing Street, Sir George Downing 1623–1684* (London, 1925), pp. 206–7. W. A. Shaw, "The 'Treasury Order Book,'" *The Economic Journal* XVI (1906), 33–40. All students of the period will recognize the debt these paragraphs owe to the work of Shaw, especially his *Calendar of Treasury Books.* The introductions to these calendars are useful but have to be treated with caution.

men. Samuel Pepys, for instance, was convinced that it would not work. Downing sought him out, patiently explained the act to him, and told him to go raise loans on it, "which vexed me more than all the pleasure I took before," said Pepys, who never liked Downing very much anyway.[29] But of course Downing's device was a stopgap. It would not increase the king's income; at best it would do no more than slow down the growth of his debts.

Among those who had reservations about Downing's scheme when it was first mooted was the busy chancellor of the exchequer. Ashley felt that the bankers might be offended by it and therefore reluctant to lend; this was, perhaps, more important to him than the consideration that the appropriation of money for a specific purpose was an encroachment on the royal prerogative. A more serious encroachment was to follow. Parliament's attitude was that it had provided amply for the king's needs and for the war, and so, if Charles was short of funds, it must be owing to mismanagement. By the middle of 1666 the government's financial embarrassment was apparent; loans were almost impossible to arrange, even at 9 per cent; Charles had even had to borrow small sums from his own servants, from Arlington to Will Chiffinch, his chief backstairs agent.[30] This situation, combined with the administration's failure to supply any financial program or leadership to Parliament in the fall of 1666, led the House of Commons to decide to appoint a committee to look into the government's accounts and take testimony on them. This was clearly an invasion of royal rights; the Commons controlled supply, but the king unquestionably controlled expenditure. The House anticipated resistance in the Lords, and so it tacked the measure onto a revenue bill, which by immemorial custom the Lords were not supposed to amend. The government did its best to defeat this maneuver; the king sent around to the theaters and bawdy houses, where his supporters were apt to be found, to urge them to suspend their customary pursuits long enough to go to Westminster and vote for the prerogative.[31] In vain; the tack was successful. It "hath

[29] Pepys, *Diary*, Dec. 12, 1665.

[30] Beresford, *Downing*, pp. 209–11. Brown, *Shaftesbury*, pp. 122–23. Clarendon, *Continuation* I, 575. W. G. Hiscock, *John Evelyn and His Family Circle* (London, 1955), p. 59. A. B. Hinds, *et al.*, eds., *Calendar of State Papers, Venetian* (London, 1864–1947) XXXIV, xi, 133. Abbott, "English Conspiracy and Dissent," *A.H.R.* XIV, 703.

[31] Pepys, *Diary*, Dec. 8, 1666.

surprised us to observe the plurality of voices concurring in it" wrote Arlington the next day.[32] Charles could save himself only by appointing his own committee of inquiry and by killing the Commons' measure by a prorogation.

In financial questions, then, the king was on the defensive. It was utterly impossible to raise money to eke out his inadequate revenues by means of the prerogative; the civil war and what followed had settled that question once and for all. Even in its most effusively loyal moments Parliament was tightfisted, partly, at least, because heavy taxation, such as a general excise, was reminiscent of Oliver and the bad old days.[33] Such revenues as Charles was entitled to could not be efficiently collected, because local officials and local courts were not cooperative and because there was no armed force at the king's disposal for this purpose or for anything else. The most that the king could hope for was that, somehow or other, economic expansion and prosperity and peace might combine to swell his income from customs and excise and cut his expenditures to the point where he could some day make ends meet. In the middle of the second Dutch war that day appeared to be the Greek calends. In the meantime the best that could be done was to fight off Parliamentary invasions of the prerogative on this score and to see what could be accomplished by better administration. The death of Southampton in May, 1667, opened the door. No new lord treasurer was named; instead, a five-man commission was appointed, four of them to do the hard work, and one, General Monck, now duke of Albemarle, as window dressing. Among the four were Ashley and Clifford. The appointment of this commission, dominated as it was by men who were impatient with existing governmental policies and practices, was a definite indication of change. It marked the first stage in the downfall of the Lord Chancellor Clarendon and the emergence of the Cabal.

III

"It is strange," wrote Samuel Pepys a month or so after the Dutch raid up the Thames, "how . . . everybody do now-a-days reflect upon Oliver, and commend him, what brave things he did, and

[32] Thomas Brown, ed., *Miscellanea Aulica* (London, 1702), p. 431.

[33] On this point see E. Hughes, *Studies in Administration and Finance 1558–1825* (Manchester, 1934), p. 122.

made all the neighbor princes fear him; while here a prince, come in with all the love and prayers and good liking of his people . . . hath lost all so soon, that it is a miracle what way a man could devise to lose so much in so little time."[34] The failures of the Dutch war, so damaging to Charles's prestige, had to be blamed on somebody; Clarendon was the inevitable victim.

The war was the occasion rather than the cause of Clarendon's fall, however; a change of men and of measures had been in the cards for some time. It is true that as the head of a wartime government Clarendon was worse than useless. He had not approved of the war in the first place, and during the conflict his attitude was one of deliberate aloofness: he would not meddle with an undertaking of which he disapproved. In his memoirs he actually boasted of his inactivity: "nor throughout the whole conduct of the war was he [Clarendon] ever known to presume to give an advice." Not only would he not act himself, he would not permit anyone else to act either without his approval. It was this almost total immobility and his widespread unpopularity which led to the clamor for his dismissal.[35]

It is difficult to be entirely fair to the earl of Clarendon. He had a certain breadth of vision, but his vision was that of an idealized Elizabethan past, in which crown, privy council, and Parliament all cooperated harmoniously together. This was an attitude widely shared by the generation which had come politically of age under Charles I; it was held, in rather different form, by Oliver Cromwell.[36] Clarendon, like Cromwell, did not understand how the Elizabethan governmental machine actually worked; like Cromwell, he did not see that even a correct application of Elizabethan methods would no longer suffice in the changed circumstances of the mid-seventeenth century, and so his system, like Cromwell's, proved to be unworkable.

Clarendon proposed to govern through the privy council. "The body of it is the most sacred, and hath the greatest authority in the

---

[34] Pepys, *Diary*, July 12, 1667.

[35] Clarendon, *Continuation* II, 371. Pepys, *Diary*, Sept. 2, 1667. Aug. 31, 1667, Arlington to Ormonde, T. H. Lister, *Life and Administration of Edward, First Earl of Clarendon* (London, 1838) III, 470.

[36] On Cromwell see the suggestive essay by H. R. Trevor-Roper "Oliver Cromwell and His Parliaments," R. Pares and A. J. P. Taylor, eds., *Essays Presented to Sir Lewis Namier* (London, 1956) , pp. 1–48.

government of the state next the person of the king himself," he wrote.[37] But it was not the Elizabethan privy council that he had in mind. Elizabeth's council was consultative only; the queen was the executive. Clarendon's council was to be the executive as well. The various departments of the government were to report to the council and to take their orders from it, and Parliament would accept guidance and leadership from the councillors who sat therein, as it had a hundred years before. Clarendon completely failed to realize that Parliament could no longer be dealt with in this paternalistic way. As early as 1663 his control had broken down, and he had been forced to admit some dangerous rivals to the council committee on Parliamentary management: William Coventry, the duke of York's secretary, Sir Henry Bennet, and Bennet's protégé, the hot-tempered Thomas Clifford, M.P. for Totnes, who thus made his appearance in high politics.[38] The chancellor's methods of executive administration came to be more and more displeasing to Charles. The king was not a traditionalist and had no attachment to Elizabethan methods of government as such—as Clarendon ruefully put it, "the objections of novelty rather advanced than obstructed any proposition."[39] Charles did not care for the chancellor's cautious attitude on the prerogative. Furthermore, Clarendon was not a good administrator, and neither were his friends, with the possible exception of the duke of Ormonde in Ireland. The council was too big to act as an administrative board itself and too big to insure secrecy. It also removed the king's hands from the levers of power; policy decisions were hammered out in council, and the king was presented with a *fait accompli*. All the threads of government passed through the king's hands, to be sure, but they passed through Clarendon's first, and this meant that Clarendon, not Charles, determined the relative strength of each thread. Had Clarendon been able to use his monopoly of power skillfully, all might have been well. But Clarendon was no more adept at the conduct of policy, particularly foreign policy, than he was at managing Parliament. "In all the king's foreign negotiations he meddled too much, for I have been told that he had not a right notion of foreign matters," wrote the not unsym-

[37] Clarendon, *Continuation* II, 297.
[38] Witcombe, "The Cavalier House of Commons," *Bulletin of the Institute of Historical Research* XXXII, 189–91.
[39] Clarendon, *Continuation* II, 226.

pathetic Burnet. "He took too much upon him and meddled in everything, which was his greatest error."[40]

Under these circumstances it is surprising that Clarendon stayed in office as long as he did. He was not popular in Cavalier circles; as John Evelyn said, "he made few friends during his grandeur among the royal sufferers, but advanced the old rebels that had money enough to buy places."[41] Clarendon was helped by the disunion of his opponents, who disliked each other quite as much as they did him, and by the ineptness of some of their attacks, notably that of the earl of Bristol in 1663. His status as the duke of York's father-in-law was some use to him; so, too, was the increasingly warm support of the bishops, as his religious outlook became more conservative. After 1663 Clarendon gave free rein to his Laudian proclivities. Toleration of dissenters no longer seemed necessary or desirable, and he opposed a scheme concocted by Bennet and Ashley in 1664 to sell liberty of conscience to nonconformists, a plan which, in the opinion of its authors, would have the double merit of bringing something in to the treasury and of keeping the dissenters quiet during the anticipated war with the Dutch. To Clarendon this plan was "Ship-Money in religion, that nobody could know the end of, or where it would rest; that if it were passed, Dr. Goffe or any other apostate from the Church of England might be made a bishop . . . here, all oaths and subscriptions being dispensed with."[42] The king was not pleased, and for a day or two it was thought that Clarendon might fall. But he did not; it was the failures of the war, of a war he had not wanted, which at last brought the chancellor down.

Of the five future "members" of the Cabal, only one had nothing much to gain in 1667 by Clarendon's fall. This was Ashley, who had profited from the death of Southampton to become the central figure on the five-man treasury commission. The creation of this commission had effectively deprived Clarendon of his control over finance,

---

[40] Foxcroft, *Supplement to Burnet's History*, pp. 54–55. For Clarendon's methods of government see E. I. Carlyle, "Clarendon and the Privy Council 1660–1667," *English Historical Review* XXVII (1912) , 251–73.

[41] E. S. DeBeer, ed., *The Diary of John Evelyn* (Oxford, 1958) III, 493–94.

[42] Clarendon, *Continuation* II, 93–98. Stephen Goffe had been a chaplain of Charles I and had been used by him on several confidential missions. He had subsequently become a Roman Catholic and at the time of Clarendon's remark was chaplain to Henrietta Maria.

and the reorganization which the new commissioners proposed was under way by the time of Clarendon's fall. So, when the final attack was launched, Ashley actually defended Clarendon. He had no enthusiasm for the chancellor's opponents, and he believed that his own prospects of rising higher, as an energetic second under a tired chief, were greater if Clarendon remained. The other four members of the Cabal all stood to gain from the chancellor's fall. Clarendon had always been hostile to Lauderdale and had done his best to keep Scottish affairs out of Lauderdale's hands, only to be baffled by the utter ineptitude of Lauderdale's Scottish opponents. Bennet, who became Lord Arlington in 1665, and his follower Clifford both hoped for more power and influence once the chancellor was out of the way, and they, along with Sir William Coventry, led the opposition inside the government. But the focus of the opposition and the barometer of its success was the fifth member of the Cabal, the duke of Buckingham.

Clarendon and Buckingham had hated each other for years; they were alike in nothing, in character or principles or personality. Buckingham was not in the government; he was the only member of the Cabal who never held a great office of state. Yet he was as important as most ministers of state, because he was the king's friend. He and Charles were almost of an age; they had been brought up together as boys. More important than this, they had the same tastes and the same pastimes. They both dabbled in science; they both loved the theater, and actresses; they were both immensely witty. Buckingham was such a wonderfully entertaining companion that Charles, in spite of the duke's frequently outrageous behavior, could never bring himself to cut the last ties between himself and his childhood playmate.

Buckingham's dislike of Clarendon was well known. As early as July, 1661, Pepys was reporting the rumor that "my Lord Chancellor is much envied, and that many great men, such as the duke of Buckingham . . . do endeavor to undermine him." The duke's method was to poke fun at Clarendon and to make him look ridiculous, which, with a man as pompous as Clarendon, was easy enough. But it was not sufficient to pull Clarendon down. Charles might laugh until his face was wet at Buckingham's imitations of the chancellor at their convivial supper parties, but, as Pepys went on to say, "the king (though he loves him [Clarendon] not in the way of a companion, as he do these young gallants that can answer him in his pleasures), yet cannot be without him, for his policy and service."[43] With the war, however, Clarendon's "policy and service" began to seem far less useful or desirable. At the same time Buckingham hit upon a much more effective device for eliminating his rival: he would organize the discontented members of Parliament, constitute himself their spokesman, and make it obvious that none of the king's business would be done in Parliament until the hated minister was dismissed.

The duke proceeded to make a terrible nuisance of himself in the Parliamentary session which began in September, 1666. He organized an opposition group in the Commons, especially among the Yorkshire M.P.s, among whom he had great influence thanks to his extensive estates there. He harassed Clarendon's friend Ormonde by his support of the bill which prohibited the export of Irish cattle to England and almost fought a duel with Ormonde's son in consequence. He brawled with other peers who were supporters of Clarendon and twice was sent to the Tower briefly to cool off. He introduced what Pepys called a "wild" motion in the Lords that all those who cheated the king be declared traitors and felons. Ashley mildly pointed out to him that proof would be hard to obtain, but Buckingham went ahead anyway. "He is now hard at it," wrote Clifford rather sourly to Arlington, "drawing up his bill and has nothing else in his head."[44] He went so far, in fact, that he seriously provoked the king, who was inclined to agree with Clarendon that the duke was responsible for "all the ill humour which had been in both houses of Parliament in the last session."[45] So, early in 1667, Clarendon and Arlington concocted a charge against the duke, to the effect that he had consorted with a crackbrained astrologer named Heydon to cast the king's horoscope, which was a treasonable offense, since it amounted to compassing or imagining the king's death. The duke's situation looked serious for a while; Pepys believed that "this silly lord" was now utterly ruined.[46] Just the reverse was true; as the war went more and more badly, the duke became more and more

[43] Pepys, *Diary,* July 27, 1661.
[44] M. A. E. Green, *et al.,* eds., *Calendar of State Papers Domestic, Charles II* (henceforth *C.S.P.D.*) (London, 1860ff.) VIII, 185–86. Pepys, *Diary,* Oct. 5, 1666.
[45] Clarendon, *Continuation* II, 432.
[46] Pepys, *Diary,* Mar. 3, 1667.

popular, as a symbol of opposition to a discredited regime. After the Dutch raid up the Thames and after a proclamation had gone out summoning Parliament back into session, Buckingham, who had been evading arrest for some months, judged that the time was ripe to surrender. He did so and on his way to the Tower was treated like a conquering hero by the London crowds. He disposed quickly enough of the formal charges against him, which were quite unprovable; when he was taxed with his real fault, that of courting popularity as an opposition leader, he replied that anyone would be popular who was thrown into prison by Clarendon or Arlington.[47] So Buckingham was released; he celebrated by taking his wife and his mistress to the theater and getting into a brawl with one of his mistress' disappointed pursuers.

Buckingham's release was immensely popular. "People do speak kindly of . . . Buckingham, as one that will enquire into faults; and therefore they do mightily favor him," wrote Pepys,[48] and with his release and with the signing of peace with the Dutch, it was evident that Clarendon's days were numbered. The discontent that was abroad in the land was taking a more ominous turn. There were rumors that the king intended to raise a standing army and to govern without Parliament. These stories cropped up in every serious crisis in Charles's reign, and are normally evidence that popular dissatisfaction was reaching a dangerous pitch. And, as is usual at moments of crisis, there were other, contradictory hopes and fears— for instance, one of Pepys's acquaintances assured him that there would soon be a commonwealth again, because of the extravagance and inefficiency of the present government, by contrast with Oliver's.[49] The chancellor might have saved himself for a brief time by accepting Buckingham's offer of a coalition directed against Arlington, whom Buckingham regarded as the principal contriver of the trumped-up astrology charge, but Clarendon knew perfectly well that, once Arlington was ruined, Buckingham would turn on him, and he refused the duke's overtures. But he refused to resign, in spite of heavy pressure to do so,[50] possibly because he believed that resignation would be tantamount to a confession of inadequacy. So, on

[47] *Ibid.*, July 17, 1667.
[48] *Ibid.*, July 22, 1667.
[49] *Ibid.*, July 29, Aug. 9, 1667.
[50] Aug. 27, 1667, Arlington to Ormonde, Lister, *Clarendon* III, 468.

August 30, 1667, the inevitable happened; the king sent him an order to surrender the seals.

Clarendon's removal from office was not enough for Buckingham; he was afraid that the fallen chancellor would someday return to power, and so he urged Charles to support an impeachment. The king, who was certainly weary of Clarendon but not vindictive, agreed to do so because Buckingham convinced him that otherwise Parliament would never vote a supply. Clarendon's chief opponents within the administration, Arlington and Coventry, cared very little for this policy. Coventry frankly opposed it; Arlington eventually went along with it, probably because he was afraid that if he did not, Buckingham would urge Parliament to make him as well as Clarendon the scapegoat for the failures of the war. But his acquiescence was reluctant at best; quite apart from everything else, the impeachment occupied everybody's attention, and "in the meantime the king's business stands, and no measures can be taken in it, which is a perplexity I hope we shall not long labor under."[51] For the sake of his future career, Arlington was wise to acquiesce; Coventry by his opposition lost his influence with the king, and in due course, in March, 1669, lost his offices as well. Other opponents of impeachment suffered less severely. Ashley, for instance, did not lose his job, but his hopes of influence were seriously deferred.

The impeachment of Clarendon served its immediate purpose. The old man, distracted by his fall, by the recent death of his wife, and by the report that he would be tried by a court presided over by Buckingham, fled to France in November, 1667; he was destined to spend the rest of his life in exile, where, like so many fallen statesmen, he attempted to justify himself by writing his memoirs. The impeachment nevertheless turned out to be an error which did not augur well for the king's future plans. It was not enough to insure supply: Charles had to concede, and did concede, what he had previously fought against, the appointment of a commission to examine his accounts and report to Parliament about them. Buckingham evidently favored this concession and had a hand in naming the commissioners, one more evidence of his great influence at this

---

[51] Nov. 5, 1667, Arlington to Ormonde, *ibid.* II, 425–26. In October, 1667, when the impeachment was introduced in the Commons, Arlington was in difficulties there owing to his role in the order for the division of the fleet in May, 1666, which led to the English defeat in the Four Days' Battle in June. Oct. 31, 1667, Williamson's Journal, P.R.O., S.P. 29/231, f. 71.

moment, since his utter incapacity in financial questions was well
known. A story told by Pepys implies that the duke's motive was to
make himself politically indispensable by increasing the authority of
Parliament, which he had undertaken to manage.[52] Charles's confidence in Buckingham's ability to control Parliament was sadly mis-
placed; Parliament's mood was such that the question of supply was
not even raised.

Not only was there no additional revenue, there was also no
impeachment. Clarendon had not governed well, but he was guilty
of blunders rather than crimes. His prosecutors were floundering
badly when he saved the situation for them by his flight. The
impeachment was promptly dropped, and an act of banishment was
passed, decreeing lifelong exile and permanent disbarment from
public office. But the failure of the impeachment proceedings was
manifested even before Clarendon's flight, when the Lords, to Buckingham's chagrin, refused to commit the fallen chancellor to the
Tower on the ground that such an action was not warranted by a
general charge which lacked specific accusations. It was apparent to
everyone that the charges against Clarendon were not believed by
their chief supporters and that this was merely a move in the political game, a device to insure office and influence by permanently
wrecking a political rival. Such a device enhanced the authority of
Parliament. Attacks on the king's ministers in Parliament now
looked like a stepping-stone to office, and Parliamentary cooperation
was necessary to seal a victory over a fallen opponent. Furthermore,
Parliamentary investigation of the proceedings of the king's officials
in fields which had hitherto been exempt from interference had
been conceded.[53] Buckingham's whole design of bringing Clarendon
down by whipping up public opinion, using Parliamentary pressure,
and then keeping him down by the same means was certain to
weaken the power and independence of the crown in the long run.
Buckingham, who very seldom saw beyond the end of his nose, was

[52] Pepys, *Diary*, Nov. 17, 1667, reports that Buckingham, when asked
why he allowed Charles to acquiesce in the investigation, replied, "I do suffer him
to do this, that I may hereafter the better command him." See W. A. Shaw, ed.,
Calendar of Treasury Books 1667–1668 (London, 1905), pp. li–liv, for the commission.

[53] For a good discussion of the impeachment see C. Roberts, "The
Impeachment of the Earl of Clarendon," *Cambridge Historical Journal* XIII
(1957), 1–18.

hardly the man to understand this or even to care very much, as long as his immediate objective was attained and his own greatness enhanced.[54] The king saw a bit further: Clarendon was dismissed when Parliament was not in session. But then Charles gave way to Buckingham's importunities when it was recalled and allowed the impeachment in the hope of disarming public hostility and of making Parliament more amenable to his future requests for money, without seeing the long-range implications of what he was doing.

"If you look upon our condition here as it is reported by common fame, I do confess you have reason to have those apprehensions you mention," wrote Charles to his sister Henrietta on November 30, 1667. "The truth is, the ill conduct of my Ld. Clarendon in my affairs has forced me to permit many inquiries to be made which otherwise I would not have suffered the Parliament to have done, though I must tell you that in themselves they are but inconvenient appearances rather than real mischiefs. . . . I am sure I will not part with any of my power."[55] It would be too much to say that Charles was whistling in the dark in writing this, but certainly the prospect which stretched before him and his circle of advisers was anything but bright. The war had been a failure, punctuated by the great natural disasters of plague and fire and climaxed by a national disgrace. Owing to the war, the nation's finances were in an appalling mess. The war had even helped to set off a revolt, in Scotland, which was caused also in large measure by religion, and religious discontent was by no means confined to the northern kingdom. The gilt and the glory of 1660 were faded and gone; the accumulated failures of the past seven years had made men reflect upon Oliver and had made the loyal Cavaliers elected to Parliament in 1661 sound ominously like the followers of Sir John Eliot by 1667. It might not be long before they began to sound like the followers of Pym.

Charles, in his optimistic way, believed that these many problems could be solved; not only that, he believed that they could be solved

[54] See, for instance, the protest he, Arlington, and twenty-five other lords drew up against the refusal of the House to commit Clarendon for treason without a specific charge. J. E. T. Rogers, ed., *A Complete Collection of the Protests of the House of Lords* (Oxford, 1875) I, 34–36. If high officials could be committed for treason by Parliament without specific charges, orderly government would become virtually impossible.

[55] C. H. Hartmann, *Charles II and Madame* (London, 1934) , p. 196.

in such a way as to enhance his own power. Hitherto his authority had been cast into shadow by the power of Parliament and by the Clarendonian governmental system. Now, Clarendon was gone, and gone with him was his system of government by privy council. Bab May spoke more truly than he knew when, on learning of Clarendon's fall, he fell on his knees before Charles and called him king for the first time.[56] Now, the king was his own chief minister, taking advice from different men on different subjects, and making the decisions himself.

Clarendon was gone, but Parliament remained. The chancellor's fall seemingly strengthened its position. The king might be making policy himself now, but his personal prestige was not what it was in 1660, and the men from whom he now took advice inspired little respect, in part because of the mishandling of the impeachment. "You will have the advantage of coming into a Court where there is not one man of ability," wrote Viscount Conway to Sir John Finch in February, 1668. In the same month Pepys wrote of Parliament, "Oliver would have dissolved them for half the trouble and contempt they have put upon the king and his councils."[57] The achievement of untrammeled authority, which was the dearest object of Charles's ambition, had been made considerably more difficult by the blunders and failures of the Clarendon era.

The situation was by no means hopeless, however. The king still had certain as yet unexploited advantages, Scotland, for one. There had been a revolt in Scotland, to be sure, but it had been owing to the pursuit of a Clarendonian policy there which the king's chief confidant on Scottish affairs had always insisted was mistaken. Now that Clarendon was gone, that policy would be changed. Furthermore, the constitutional checks on the royal power in Scotland were virtually nonexistent. Might it not be possible, somehow, to use Scotland as a base from which to weaken or undermine the power of Parliament and thus to accomplish his grand design? The idea was worth exploring. And Charles had the perfect instrument at hand, in John Maitland, second earl of Lauderdale.

---

[56] Pepys, *Diary*, Nov. 11, 1667. Bab May was keeper of the privy purse, one of those men who, as David Ogg says of Will Chiffinch, "performed a great and honourable service to the Stuarts by *not* writing his memoirs." *England in the Reign of Charles II* I, 331.

[57] *C.S.P.D.* VIII, 258–59. Pepys, *Diary*, Feb. 17, 1668.

Chapter 2

Launching the Grand Design

Lauderdale

This haughty Monster with his ugly claws
First temper'd Poison to destroy our Lawes
Declares the Councel Edicts are beyond
The most authentick Statutes of the Land,
Sets up in Scotland alamode de France,
Taxes Excise and Armyes dos advance.
This Saracen his Countryes freedom broke
To bring upon our Necks the heavier yoke: . . .
Of all the Miscreants ever went to hell
This Villin Rampant bares away the bell.[1]

John Maitland, second earl and only duke of Lauderdale, is a man whose character and career after the Restoration have prompted very little controversy among historians. If "haughty monster" and "villain rampant" seem a bit strong, it is only because scholarly language nowadays is milder and more polite than the epithets of the seventeenth century. Lauderdale is the "hog" of the quatrain at the beginning of Chapter 1; when Henry Savile, one of the witty young men who lightened the king's leisure hours, supported one of the many attacks on Lauderdale in the Commons and temporarily lost his bedchamber post in conse-

---

[1] Anon., "An Historicall Poem," c. 1680. H. M. Margoliouth, ed., *The Poems and Letters of Andrew Marvell* (Oxford, 1952) I, 204.

quence, he wrote to his friend Rochester that he had been "sacri-
ficed to that filthy dog Lauderdale."[2] The earl was always unpopular in England—the common fate of Scottish politicians in the
seventeenth century—and he, in common with other members of
the Cabal, has suffered in the eyes of posterity from the attacks and
innuendoes of his political opponents.

Here, for instance, is the opinion of the earl of Ailesbury:
"[Lauderdale] had learning and endowed with a great memory,
as disagreeable in his conversation as was his person, his head was
towards that of a Saracen fiery face, and his tongue too big for his
mouth, and his pronunciation high Scotch, no highlander like him,
uttering bald jests for wit, and repeating good ones of others, and
ever spoiled them in relating them, which delighted the good king
much. . . . I am sorry to say it, but he was of a most abject spirit
when kept down."[3]

The impression Ailesbury leaves is that Lauderdale was a coarse
and obsequious buffoon, hardly the sort of man one would expect
Charles to entrust with high office for twenty years. One explanation
is supplied by Gilbert Burnet, whose description of Lauderdale is
well known and is the one most generally accepted, because Burnet
was a Scot, who was originally a friend and supporter of the earl and
later broke with him, as did so many of Lauderdale's Scottish allies.

He was the coldest friend and the violentest enemy I ever knew. . . . His
great experience in affairs, his ready compliance with every thing that he
thought would please the king, and his bold offering at the most desperate
counsels, gained him such an interest in the king, that no attempt against
him, nor complaint of him, could ever shake it, till a decay of strength
and understanding forced him to let go his hold. He was in his principles
much against popery and arbitrary government; and yet, by a fatal train
of passions and interests, he made way for the former, and had almost
established the latter.[4]

Arbitrary government is the charge most frequently laid at
Lauderdale's door. It is easy, of course, to be wise after the event; in
1673 Burnet dedicated a book to Lauderdale in fulsome language,

---

[2] John H. Wilson, *The Court Wits of the Restoration* (Princeton,
1948), p. 83.
    [3] W. E. Buckley, ed., *Memoirs of Thomas, Earl of Ailesbury, Written
by Himself* (Roxburghe Club ed., Westminster, 1890) I, 14–15. This habit of
spoiling jokes in the retelling may have been what Buckingham had in mind
when he said that Lauderdale had a "blundering understanding." Gilbert Burnet,
The History of My Own Time (ed. Osmund Airy, Oxford, 1897–1900) I, 184.
    [4] Burnet, *History* I, 185.

praising his learning and judgment as having contributed to the
happy settlement of the kingdom.[5] And not all the considered verdicts on Lauderdale were unfavorable. Roger North called him "the
best and wisest statesman that ever England had," and a Covenanting minister, Robert Law, wrote of him, "He was truly a man of a
great spirit, great parts, great wit, a most daring man, and a man of
great success . . . a man very national, and truly the honor of our
Scots nation for wit and parts."[6]

"A man very national": here is the key to Lauderdale's behavior,
the consistent thread that runs through his long and complicated
political career. He came by his patriotism naturally enough: he was
the grandson of John Maitland of Thirlestane, the chancellor and
political mentor of James VI, and a grandnephew of William Maitland of Lethington, the famous Secretary Maitland of Mary, Queen
of Scots. He was born in 1616 and was thus the oldest member of the
Cabal. His political career began early; from the beginning of the
civil war he was deeply and prominently involved in Scottish relations with England—fitting employment for a Maitland—and became a member of the Committee of Both Kingdoms. He was a
Covenanter, but not a fanatic: what he objected to in the policy of
Charles I was the king's obvious intention of forcing English religious practices on Scotland, of governing Scotland without regard to
her interests. His hope was that defeat in war would bring the king
to his senses; the failure early in 1645 of the negotiations at Uxbridge, the Scots' great effort to persuade the king to compromise
while there was yet time, was a grievous disappointment to him. The
consequences of that failure created an awkward dilemma for
Lauderdale, a dilemma which he resolved, in common with most
of the moderate Scottish Presbyterians, by gradually shifting to the
king's side. He never had any illusions about the character and
intentions of Charles I, but the prospect of the domination of the
Independents was still worse. "The Independents," he wrote, "intended the ruin of the monarchy, and the destruction of the king
and his posterity."[7] Charles, with all his faults, was a Stuart, the

[5] M. A. E. Green, *et al.,* eds., *Calendar of State Papers Domestic,
Charles II* (henceforth *C.S.P.D.*) (London, 1860ff.) XVI, 73.

[6] Roger North, *Examen* (London, 1740) , p. 79. J. G. Fyfe, ed., *Scottish
Diaries and Memoirs 1550–1746* (Stirling, 1928) , p. 261.

[7] Quoted in W. C. Mackenzie, *The Life and Times of John Maitland,
Duke of Lauderdale* (London, 1923) , p. 83.

successor of Fergus; government by Cromwell and his friends would completely snuff out Scottish independence and also the privileged position of Lauderdale's class; Cromwell had said, after all, that he "hoped to live to see never a nobleman in England"—and, no doubt, in Scotland as well.[8]

So Lauderdale became the prime mover in the treaty of Carisbrooke, the so-called Engagement, signed in December, 1647. By its terms the king was bound to confirm the Covenant in both kingdoms by act of Parliament, though it was not to be forcibly imposed on the unwilling, to adopt Presbyterianism for three years, and to suppress the sectaries. Union between the two kingdoms was to be consummated; if this was not feasible, all the trading privileges of each kingdom were to be extended to the other. Charles went further; he privately promised the duke of Hamilton to consent to the incorporation of Westmoreland, Cumberland, and Northumberland into the northern kingdom.[9]

This was an extraordinarily unrealistic treaty, and it led to the disaster of the second civil war. Such an agreement could command no support in England, and it produced a deep split in Scotland, as Lauderdale speedily discovered. In spite of Lauderdale's urging, Charles had not personally accepted the Covenant, and the extreme Presbyterians would have nothing to do with an un-Covenanted king. Not for the last time, Lauderdale underestimated the strength and depth of Scottish opinion when it differed from his own, especially in matters of religion. It was a failing strikingly reminiscent of his granduncle, the secretary.

Lauderdale was not a personal participant in the catastrophe which followed; early in 1648 he was sent on behalf of the Scottish estates to negotiate with Prince Charles, his future master, now eighteen years old. It was a momentous meeting, because there sprang up between the two men a personal affection of a kind which Charles never felt for any other Scot, and which, on Lauderdale's side, turned into deep devotion. The earl's career to this point demonstrates that he had no inherent tendency to obsequiousness to kings in general. But the events of the 1640's had made him into a political Royalist, and his affection for the young Charles gradually ripened into an undeviating personal loyalty, as great as his loyalty

[8] *Ibid.*, p. 107.
[9] *Ibid.*, pp. 124–27. Burnet, *History* I, 59.

to his native land. After 1660 his attitude toward the king often appeared to be that of a toady, "qui se range toujours . . . du côté où il voit pencher son maître," as the French ambassador put it in 1670. This verdict has been echoed by later historians. Lauderdale was a "grand vizier" to Osmund Airy, a "palace minion rather than a minister of state" to W. L. Mathieson.[10] This does Lauderdale considerably less than justice. For one thing, he was anything but a mindless sycophant; he was an intellectual, a genuinely learned man, to whom Sir George Mackenzie could write, "You are yourself the greatest statesman in Europe who are a scholar, and the greatest scholar who are a statesman." This might be dismissed as the flattery of an underling, but Burnet testifies that "He was very learned, not only in Latin, in which he was a master, but in Greek and Hebrew. He had read a great deal in divinity, and almost all the historians, ancient and modern."[11] His house at Highgate, which belonged to his first wife, was in danger of collapsing in 1670 because he kept such a large library in the top story.[12] The earl was a courtier but not a toady; he was a man with a policy, a policy which became inextricably bound up with his personal devotion and his personal gain, so that he could sincerely write in 1669 to his master, "all your commands are to me above all human laws,"[13] because he believed that those commands embodied his interest and the king's and Scotland's.

The practical results of Lauderdale's first meeting with his future sovereign were not very happy, however. The disaster at Preston and the execution of Charles I were followed by the curious gamble of 1650–51, when Charles, now a king without a kingdom, attempted to recover what his father had lost by making his own bargain with the Scots, a bargain which entailed his acceptance of the Covenant. Sir

[10] Osmund Airy, ed., *The Lauderdale Papers* (London, 1884–85) I, xi. W. L. Mathieson, *Politics and Religion, a Study in Scottish History from the Reformation to the Revolution* (Glasgow, 1902) II, 203. July 4/14, 1670, Croissy to Louis XIV, F. A. M. Mignet, ed., *Négociations relatives à la succession d'Espagne sous Louis XIV* (Paris, 1835–42) III, 216–17.

[11] A. Lang, *Sir George Mackenzie, King's Advocate of Rosehaugh, His Life and Times* (London, 1909) , p. 148. Burnet, *History* I, 184.

[12] Sept. 22, 1670, Countess of Lauderdale to Lauderdale, Airy, *Lauderdale Papers* II, 203. In this letter Lauderdale was urged to get the books down from the top floor, and to see to the necessary repairs, "since your books has [sic] been the occasion" of the damage.

[13] *Ibid.,* p. 141.

Edward Hyde was outraged, but Lauderdale insisted and carried his point, because only a Covenanted king could command any support at all in Scotland at this juncture. Throughout the whole long series of negotiations Lauderdale made it clear that he was unalterably opposed to meddling by Englishmen in Scottish affairs: Charles must be guided by Scottish advice only—an attitude not calculated to please Hyde.

Military disaster again followed, at Dunbar and Worcester. The immediate consequence was the forcible amalgamation of Scotland with England by Cromwell. More important in some ways was the impression made upon Charles himself by his unhappy experience as a Covenanted king. The political folly of the Scottish clerical leadership was compounded by their subjecting the king to as many as six sermons a day and by their insistence that he sign a statement "lamenting his own sins, his father's opposition to the Covenant, and his mother's 'idolatry.' " "I think I must repent, too, that ever I was born," remarked the harassed young man.[14] About the only recreation allowed to Charles was golf, a game he evidently did not like. The result was the growth in Charles's mind of hatred and contempt for the Covenant and all that the Covenanters stood for, the good as well as the bad, the belief in Scottish independence as well as the intolerant and theocratic Presbyterianism to which he was subjected. "It contributed not a little," wrote Burnet, "to beget in him an aversion to all sort of strictness in religion."[15] He never returned to Scotland after his departure in 1651; after 1660 the welfare of his ancestral kingdom did not concern him. Scotland might be a factor in his political calculations, but of and for itself it was never to be an object of his attention or his sympathy. There was nothing there worthy of either.

Could he have known of it, Charles would have wholeheartedly endorsed Dr. Johnson's opinion as to the noblest prospect a Scotsman ever sees, but the road which Charles took to England, accompanied by Lauderdale, led to Worcester. The earl was captured by Cromwell's forces and spent the next nine years in prison in various places: the Tower, Portland Castle, Windsor Castle. He apparently passed the time largely in reading; he was able to get what books he

[14] Mackenzie, *Lauderdale*, p. 180. H. W. Chapman, *Great Villiers* (London, 1949) , p. 65.
[15] Burnet, *History* I, 94.

wanted and was even allowed once to spend a day in Eton searching
for one. He corresponded with people like Richard Baxter and
worked with him on the translation of French theological treatises.
He also contrived, somehow, to keep in touch with his exiled master.
For him there could be no compounding with Cromwell, even had
he wanted to, and he did not want to. Whatever his views may have
been before, when he emerged from his prison in March, 1660, he
was a convinced monarchist. Lauderdale was nothing if not logical—natural enough, perhaps, for a man brought up on Calvinist
theology—and he now saw the logic of revolution: Independency in
religion and republicanism in politics, and the subjection of Scotland to alien military rule behind a constitutional façade. Cromwell's union was bitterly unpopular north of the Tweed, and
Lauderdale knew it. As time was to show, Lauderdale's Presbyterianism sat ever more lightly on him; what interested him was order,
order in both church and state, and preferably an orderly polity
willingly accepted by the people. Lauderdale subscribed to the common seventeenth-century belief in the uniformity of civil and ecclesiastical institutions; in his own lifetime he had seen the failure of
several attempts to create such Anglo-Scottish uniformity, with a
subsequent resort to force. The policy of Charles I had led to
disorder; in the early 1640's Lauderdale, in his inexperience, had
worked for the uniformity he cherished by means of the abolition of
episcopacy.[16] He had now learned that the Scottish tail could not
wag the English dog. Cromwell's version of uniformity was successful, but only because it was based upon military occupation and
dictatorship. Only a monarchical framework could preserve order
without the use of force, and so the monarchy must be restored and
its power enhanced. Within this framework, provided a moderate
religious settlement were made, England and Scotland both could be
made to fit.

Lauderdale was convinced that this could be done only by a policy
which was acceptable to the Presbyterians in Scotland and probably
in England as well. He had, in a sense, committed himself to such a
solution, after his release from prison, by helping to win over Richard Baxter and the other English Presbyterians to active support of

[16] See his remark to the French agent in England at the time of the
Uxbridge negotiations, cited in Mackenzie, *Lauderdale*, p. 67.

the king's return.[17] Lauderdale could not hope to influence the settlement in England, nor did he try. He held consistently to his view that, as a Scot, he must not meddle in English domestic politics, save as they affected Scotland;[18] by the same token, he steadily opposed any interference by Englishmen, Hyde in particular, in the Scottish settlement.

As soon as he could after his release from prison, Lauderdale, like so many others, betook himself to the Netherlands to pay court to Charles. He was fortified by a friendly letter the king had written him on the news of his release,[19] and he had high hopes that his advice on Scottish affairs would once again be followed. But he found that matters had greatly changed in ten years. Charles was glad to see him, but had little time for Scottish business, and Hyde, who disliked him intensely, was virtually all-powerful in Charles's councils. The earl paid assiduous court to the future earl of Clarendon and made light of his Covenanting past, and not without some success, as Clarendon admits. "In sum, all his discourses were such as pleased all the company, who commonly believed all he said, and concurred with him."[20] His gifts as a courtier gained him one immensely important advantage on which he was to build his future career: appointment, over Clarendon's opposition, as secretary of state for Scotland, which guaranteed his constant attendance on the king. He was by far the best man for the job; it is reasonable to suppose, however, that it was equally important that he was the only Scottish politician Charles really liked.

Lauderdale got the office he coveted, but not the settlement in Scotland. "Restoration" north of the Tweed meant something quite different from what it meant in England; in Scotland it meant an abrupt turning-back of the clock, best exemplified by the Act Rescissory of 1661, which at one stroke annulled all the acts of Parliament passed since 1633, including those of 1641, a Parliament at which

[17] Louise F. Brown, *The First Earl of Shaftesbury* (New York, 1933), pp. 92–93. See also A. Robertson, *The Life of Sir Robert Moray* (London, 1922), pp. 102–4.

[18] See, for instance, June 25, 1663, Moray to Lauderdale, Airy, *Lauderdale Papers* I, 136–38.

[19] The letter is in *ibid.*, p. 13.

[20] Edward, Earl of Clarendon, *A Continuation of His History of the Great Rebellion* (Oxford, 1857) I, 366.

Charles I had been personally present. There was no serious consideration given to maintaining the Cromwellian union. Clarendon, in his account, hints that he rather favored retaining it, and well he might have, since it entailed the subjugation of Scotland to English rule. "It might well be a question," he wrote, "whether the generality of the nation were not better contented with it, than to return into the old road of subjugation. But the king would not build according to Cromwell's models."[21] And, indeed, as Lauderdale pointed out, Cromwell's models were extremely unpopular in Scotland. Even those few Scots who had felt some sympathy for Cromwell's policy had been alienated by the protector's heavy taxation. The Restoration, on the other hand, was immensely popular; as one disapproving Covenanter wrote, it "made people not only drunk but frantic."[22] Lauderdale insisted that Scotland must be governed by Scotsmen, and that all traces of English domination be extinguished, especially the English garrisons, "those badges of our slavery," as he called them.[23] Clarendon wanted to keep the soldiers there until the settlement was completed, but even the chancellor's Scottish allies would not support him on this point, and the garrisons were withdrawn. "So," concludes Burnet, "he [Lauderdale] became very popular in Scotland."[24]

There, however, Lauderdale's successes ended. The earl was the leader of the Scottish moderates, many of them ex-Covenanters like himself; his principal allies were the earls of Tweeddale and Kincardine and Sir Robert Moray, a distinguished scientist who became the first president of the Royal Society. His opponents were extremists, including some vehement ex-Covenanters, and it was they who, thanks to Clarendon, got most of the important posts in the Scottish administration. The earl of Middleton became the king's commissioner; Glencairn got the chancellorship; the rather flabby Rothes,

[21] *Ibid.*, p. 362. Cromwell's Scottish policy was popular in England, says Clarendon, owing to English dislike of Scots. *Ibid.* II, 35.

[22] Mathieson, *Politics and Religion* II, 176. See also D. Nobbs, *England and Scotland 1560–1707* (London, 1952), p. 127. A Scottish tract of 1660 includes, among the other iniquities of the Interregnum, "the ignominious surrender of the liberty of the nation into the hands of strangers." Lord Somers, *A Collection of Scarce and Valuable Tracts* (2nd ed., ed. Walter Scott, London, 1812) VII, 490.

[23] July 18, 1663, Lauderdale to Moray, Airy, *Lauderdale Papers* I, 160.

[24] Burnet, *History* I, 194–95. See also June, 1661, Sharp to Primrose, T. H. Lister, *Life and Administration of Edward, First Earl of Clarendon* (London, 1838) III, 132–33.

quite possibly the worst speller ever to achieve high political office, became president of the privy council. Only one major office went to a friend of Lauderdale: the staunchly Presbyterian earl of Craw-ford, who had been Lauderdale's fellow-prisoner in the 1650's, be-came treasurer. The lesser offices fell to Clarendonians too: men like Archibald Primrose, who became clerk register and who reportedly suggested the Act Rescissory "half in jest."[25]

Lauderdale did not like the Act Rescissory; it was far too sweep-ing.[26] Nor did he approve of the financial generosity of the Parlia-ment, which voted Charles an annual revenue of £40,000 sterling, to be raised by customs and excise duties; he called this "an inconsid-erate act of prodigality or cowardliness."[27] Still less did he like what the Act Rescissory portended: the restoration of episcopacy. The act had passed so easily because Charles had promised to maintain the church "as by law established"; with the act in effect, that legally established polity was episcopalian. Lauderdale fought as hard as he could to stave off what was both an act of bad faith and, more important, a serious political error. The sudden imposition of epis-copacy would shake the perfervid loyalty which it was obviously to Charles's interest to preserve in case he had trouble in England. His own cautious attitude to the religious problem was illustrated by his arranging to have a Presbyterian and an Episcopal minister share the pulpit in his home parish of Haddington; people could attend whichever service they chose.[28] He argued against the immediate restoration of the bishops before "the lords of the English council who were appointed to sit with the Scots"[29]—another of Claren-don's devices to secure English influence in Scotland—and he argued it brilliantly, as even Clarendon admitted.

Lauderdale began by repeating his denunciation of the Covenant and assured the assemblage that he believed in episcopacy and wanted it instituted in Scotland, but not yet. Public opinion was not yet prepared; too many of the leading men "were still so infatuated

[25] Burnet, *History* I, 214.

[26] It affected him personally: he had to secure passage of a special act of Parliament validating all grants to him which had depended on the rescinded acts. Mackenzie, *Lauderdale*, p. 212, n. 1.

[27] *Ibid.*, pp. 210–11.

[28] Burnet, *History* I, 195–96. T. E. S. Clarke and H. C. Foxcroft, *A Life of Gilbert Burnet* (Cambridge, 1907), p. 61.

[29] Clarendon, *Continuation* I, 370.

with the Covenant, that they would with equal patience hear of the rejection of the four Evangelists, who yet, by conversation, and other information . . . might in time be wrought upon." Presbyterians were still being encouraged to hope for favor in England: why should they be thus maltreated in Scotland? Such action would simply strengthen the hands of the Presbyterian extremists, including the marquis of Argyll, who had been the dominant political figure in Scotland during the Interregnum and was now destined for punishment. It would be better to concentrate now on indemnity for the past, securing the prerogative, and disposing of Argyll. This argument was impressive and impressively delivered, "with more advantage of elocution than the fatness of his tongue, that ever filled his mouth, usually was attended with," and the king hesitated. But Middleton and the rest pointed out that Lauderdale had not lived in Scotland for ten years; they knew the temper of the people better than he, and they assured the king that the people were eager to throw off the hated Presbyterian yoke.[30]

So Lauderdale's policy of gradualism was discarded in favor of a policy of reaction which Clarendon would not have dared to attempt in England. Middleton and his cronies, flushed with their success— and, no doubt, with the quantities of alcohol they were famous for consuming[31]—now decided to destroy Lauderdale completely. They hated him with the rancorous hatred of the emigré for all those who at any time had wavered even slightly in their loyalty to the *ancien régime*, much less openly opposed it, and who compounded their former treachery by venturing to differ with the triumphant loyalists. Their attitude was made obvious from the beginning. In September, 1660, a formal burning of the Covenant was being planned. Lauderdale disliked this; Middleton's reaction was that "it mattered not if it [the Covenant] were hanged about his neck, if he favored it."[32] Middleton's first device for eliminating Lauderdale was to require an oath abjuring both the Covenants, in the hope that Lauderdale would refuse to take it. Lauderdale's friend, the scrupu-

[30] The account of Lauderdale's speech and the quotations are in *ibid.*, pp. 370–76.

[31] As Burnet puts it in concluding his account of the session of Parliament in 1661, "It was a mad, roaring time, full of extravagance; and no wonder it was so, when the men of affairs were almost perpetually drunk." *History* I, 220.

[32] *C.S.P.D.* I, 260.

lous earl of Crawford, did resign on account of this, but Lauderdale professed himself willing to "swallow a cartload of such oaths," adding that he was never bothered by lies as such, but only by "damn'd insipid lies."[33]

Having failed with this ploy, Middleton and his friends next bethought themselves of the Act of Indemnity, which Lauderdale had insisted upon as a piece of political justice, and as a means of preventing Middleton and his friends from lining their pockets at the ex-Covenanters' expense. The king was persuaded, over Lauderdale's opposition, to approve a clause which would bar from public office a number of persons, not to exceed twelve. Middleton now arranged to have the twelve chosen by a process called "billeting," a secret ballot by the members of Parliament. Lauderdale and Sir Robert Moray were billeted: when the earl told the king of this, Charles was furious. So too was Clarendon, at the ineptitude Middleton had shown in trying to get rid of Lauderdale in this disingenuous way. It was Middleton who fell; in March, 1663, Charles deprived him of his post as commissioner.[34]

Lauderdale followed up his victory by going to Edinburgh in the summer of 1663 to overawe his remaining opponents, notably Archbishop Sharp, who now fawned upon Lauderdale as he always did on those in authority, and the earl of Rothes, who had turned against Middleton at the proper moment and was rewarded by succeeding him as commissioner. The king rather liked Rothes, who was an amusing drunk, and so Lauderdale had to put up with him, although he did not trust him. The Scottish Parliament, as always, proved compliant; the billeting act was annulled, and a further measure provided for an army of 20,000 foot and 2,000 horse, to go anywhere in the king's dominions "to oppose invasions, to suppress insurrections, or for any other cause in which his authority, power, or greatness were concerned."[35] Lauderdale's purpose here was not to impose military dictatorship, but rather to strengthen the prerog-

[33] Burnet, *History* I, 255–58.
[34] An account of the billeting business can be found in Mackenzie, *Lauderdale*, pp. 249–58.
[35] Burnet, *History* I, 367–68. Parliament's compliance was made absolute by the revival of the Jacobean method of electing the Committee of the Articles, a method which guaranteed governmental control of that committee, which itself controlled Parliament. For a discussion of the committee see R. S. Rait, *The Parliaments of Scotland* (Glasgow, 1924), chap. IV.

ative by a show of force and to demonstrate the loyalty of Scotland to its ancient dynasty.[36]

Lauderdale's power in Scotland was now seemingly established, especially when he succeeded Middleton as governor of Edinburgh castle early in 1664 and obtained the restoration to his estates of the son of the executed marquis of Argyll. Lauderdale, wrote Pepys, "hath got the whole power of Scotland into his hand," and "is never far from the king's ear nor council . . . he is a most cunning fellow." Pepys was not well acquainted with the earl; a visit he paid to Lauderdale's house must have put him off. He found the company odd and disliked the Scots music played on the violin during supper. His host was not a music lover; Lauderdale remarked that "he had rather hear a cat mew, than the best music in the world; and the better the music, the more sick it made him; and that of all instruments he hates the lute most, and next to that the bagpipe."[37]

Pepys exaggerated the extent of Lauderdale's control in Scotland. Clarendon remained, and until he was gone, the earl's power would never be secure. Lauderdale was now the ally of his fellow-secretary Sir Henry Bennet;[38] he may have had hopes of the attack made on Clarendon in 1663 by Bennet's former patron, the earl of Bristol, but, like Bennet, he carefully dissociated himself from it. Bristol had called the removal of the English garrisons from Scotland treason, and, wrote Lauderdale, "no rational man will believe me so little a Scot as to be consenting to a paper with that into [sic] it."[39] The major substantive issue between Lauderdale and Clarendon was religion. Episcopacy was now reestablished in Scotland, with the turncoat James Sharp—"Sharp of that ilk," Cromwell had called him—as primate and the narrow-minded persecutor Alexander Burnet in the archbishopric of Glasgow. Lauderdale had no illusions as to the quality of the Scottish episcopate or its popularity. The opinion of many Presbyterians is epitomized in the pathetic letter Lauderdale received from his old friend Robert Baillie, in

[36] See the instructions he sent Moray in July, 1663, Airy, *Lauderdale Papers* I, 169.

[37] *The Diary of Samuel Pepys* (ed. H. B. Wheatley, London, 1926), Feb. 22, Mar. 2, 1664, July 28, 1666.

[38] See Bennet's letter to Ormonde in November, 1663, in Thomas Brown, ed., *Miscellanea Aulica* (London, 1702), p. 330.

[39] July 18, 1663, Lauderdale to Moray, Airy, *Lauderdale Papers* I, 160–61.

April, 1661: "I tell you that my heart is broken with grief. . . . What needed you do that disservice to the king? . . . Is it wisdom to bring back upon us the Canterburian times? The same designs, the same practices, will they not at last bring on the same horrible effects, whatever fools dream? . . . If you have gone with your heart to forsake your Covenant, to countenance the introduction of Bishops and books . . . I think you a prime transgressor, and liable among the first to answer to God for that great sin. . . . I will continue to pray for you, do what you will."[40]

Lauderdale did not want to bring back the Canterburian times, as Baillie mistakenly assumed, but he fully expected the bishops and their supporters to make a mess of things. After the turmoil of the past twenty-five years there was a chance that a moderate and gradually introduced episcopal structure could have won general acceptance, and in fact many Presbyterian clergy did accept the new system; nonconformity was largely concentrated in the southwest.[41] Lauderdale, however, was determined that his judgment should be vindicated, and so he allowed the prelates and their Clarendonian supporters a free hand, contenting himself with an occasional protest for the record. In 1664, for example, Archbishop Sharp proposed the creation of a special commission to enforce religious legislation. "Lord Lauderdale saw that this would prove a high commission court: yet he gave way to it, though much against his mind." When Burnet protested about this, Lauderdale explained: it was the policy of enough rope. "He was persuaded he [Sharp] would ruin all: but he said he was resolved to give him line, for he had not credit enough to stop him. . . . Things would run to a height, and then the king would of himself put a stop to their career."[42] And so, indeed, it turned out. After the event, Sir Robert Moray wrote to congratulate Lauderdale on his wisdom and skill. "These seven years past you have constantly walked with singular tenderness in all matters, both as to the State and the Church, wherein the consequences might any wise reflect upon you. . . . If you look back you will certainly find the following of courses you would never have advised and wisely

[40] D. Laing, ed., *The Letters and Journals of Mr. Robert Baillie* (Edinburgh, 1842) III, 458–60. Lauderdale had obtained the principalship of Glasgow University for Baillie, who was a remarkable scholar.

[41] On this point see the important study of W. R. Foster, *Bishop and Presbytery, the Church of Scotland 1661–1688* (London, 1958).

[42] Burnet, *History* I, 369–70.

forbore to curb, hath been far from succeeding well; the errors thereof are now conspicuous enough to the authors."[43]

Lauderdale judged his men correctly. Episcopal incapacity and intolerance, combined with the Dutch war, exceedingly unpopular in Scotland since the United Provinces were Scotland's principal foreign market,[44] produced a revolt in the southwest late in 1666. It was a trifling affair, and easily enough put down, but it seemed to demonstrate to the king that Lauderdale had been right all along about Scotland, and Clarendon, wrong. So, early in 1667, Sharp was temporarily disgraced, to teach him who was master now,[45] and in June Rothes was kicked upstairs into the chancellorship; the treasury was put in commission, as that of England had been a month before. This was the Scottish counterpart of the changes in personnel being made simultaneously in England, preparatory to the removal of Clarendon. In September, after Clarendon's dismissal, Lauderdale sealed his victory by taking over the commissionership from Rothes, and wrote a dithyrambic letter to his friend Tweeddale about the new regime. "Oh, it would do your heart good to see what a new world is here and how bravely all the king's business goes on . . . now the king is the king himself."[46]

Rothes was not pleased at being pushed into the chancellorship. Moray, in discussing it with him, said that the king knew that Rothes would always be "disposed to comply with what he knew to be his Majesty's pleasure," and added that "the king . . . intended the change in the treasury of Scotland to precede that of England (though by the death of E. Southampton it hath fallen out otherwise), as a leading case to the rest, he could say his pleasure is so readily complied with in Scotland that the first notice of it carries always without hesitation."[47] It is hard to believe that Charles and

[43] Sept. 20, 1667, Moray to Lauderdale, Airy, *Lauderdale Papers* II, 69–71.

[44] Rothes's letters to Lauderdale during the war make clear its unpopularity and the economic damage it caused. See, for example, that of June 23, 1666, complaining in Rothes's picturesque orthography of the "strang evill affectednes of our pipill in this countrie, who due rejoays that the duthe ar not overthroun yeay on the contrarie will beliff no neus bot such as say they had the betier of the last ffeght, mor of this dus nou apir than ever over the whole cingdum." *Ibid.* I, 236–37.

[45] He learned. See his bootlicking letter to Lauderdale in July, 1667, and the latter's reply promising forgiveness, *ibid.* II, 28–30, 40–41.

[46] N.L.S. Mss. 3136, f. 23.

[47] June 17, 1667. Moray to Lauderdale, Airy, *Lauderdale Papers* II, 3–4.

Lauderdale ever seriously expected Englishmen to follow a Scottish example. They did imagine, however, that Scotland could always be brought to acquiesce in the royal wishes on account of the malleability of the Scottish Parliament and the blocking of the obvious channel of legitimate religious protest.[48] They would be undeceived in time.

With the fall of Clarendon, which was popular in Scotland,[49] Lauderdale had reached his goal. He was all-powerful there, and English influence had been finally excluded—no more Scottish Councils met at Whitehall after the fall of Middleton.[50] But, although he did not yet know it, Lauderdale had paid a price, and too great a price. His policy of enough rope had discredited not only Archbishop Sharp and his cohorts, but also the whole concept of episcopacy as an institution. The bishops were now so unpopular that compromise and the policy of moderation were no longer possible. The prestige of the crown was hopelessly entangled with episcopacy as a system, however; the bishops as such could not be abandoned. Lauderdale was to struggle with this insoluble dilemma for the next decade and more, and eventually it was to destroy his reputation and his power. The problems of the church loom large in his correspondence in the Cabal period and form a kind of discordant undertone to what was to be the main theme of the next few years: the uses to which Scotland could be put as a base on which to erect the structure of prerogative government and independence of Parliament which it was Charles's intention to achieve.

II

Denis de Repas, a French visitor to Scotland in 1672, described the country and its inhabitants thus:

I did observe the people not to be at all ingenious for any kind of manufacture, for it is certain that there is not any sort of good commodity made in Scotland. . . . I never saw a nation more nasty, lazy . . . than they are. . . . In several places though nature doth afford them all manner of materials to build houses, they are so lazy that they had rather lay [sic] in cabins covered hardly with earth and turfs, and so be exposed to the injury

[48] This channel was the national synod; it was so constituted as to put control absolutely into the hands of the bishops, and partly for this reason it was never summoned. Foster, *Bishop and Presbytery*, pp. 86–87.

[49] Sept. 7, 1667, Rothes to Lauderdale, Airy, *Lauderdale Papers* II, 44.

[50] Burnet, *History* I, 383.

of the weather, than to take the pain to build as they do anywhere else. . . . Except in the great towns they do not do so much as bake bread though they may have plentiful of corn, but make nastily a kind of stuff with oat half grinded which they do call cake which hath no more taste or relish than a piece of wooden trencher. . . . There is good wool enough and plentiful, yet they do not make any sort of cloth, but send it over to Holland [except for plaiding, of which de Repas was very scornful]. They have abundance of goat, bucks, and deer skins, but they do not take the pains to dress them. . . . They do send them to Holland.[51]

Lauderdale was well aware of Scotland's economic backwardness and difficulties, many of which he attributed to the renewal of the Navigation Act, under which Scotland was treated as a foreign country. The act not only prevented Scottish trade with the colonies but also hampered her trade with the Dutch. As early as November, 1661, Lauderdale had attempted to get the act suspended or at least modified to permit five or six Scots ships a year to trade with the English colonies, but in vain. The English argument was that English customs revenues would suffer from Scottish participation in the colonial trade and, worse still, that the Dutch would somehow get a share of it, through their commercial connections with Scotland.[52] Scottish retaliatory levies on English imports annoyed English merchants in the Scottish trade, who petitioned Charles to act. A plan proposed by the Board of Trade to modify the Navigation Act to permit the Scots to participate in everything but the colonial trade, in return for reduction of Scottish tariffs on English goods to 5 per cent and a prohibition of Scottish purchase of foreign ships, foundered on the opposition of the customs farmers.[53] The Dutch war made the economic situation desperate in Scotland; as early as May, 1665, Rothes was writing that it was "as if we were besieged, for in no place in the whole world have we any commerce at this time, and money does grow daily scarcer so as in a short time there will I believe be none." Rothes's gloomy prediction was accurate enough; in 1666 Scottish customs receipts were only one-third of what they had been in 1665.[54]

[51] H.M.C., *Mss. of . . . the Duke of Portland* III (London, 1894), 327–28.

[52] *C.S.P.D.* II, 74, 135–36, 149. T. Keith, *Commercial Relations of England and Scotland 1603–1707* (Cambridge, 1910), pp. 113–14.

[53] *C.S.P.D.* III, 651.

[54] Airy, *Lauderdale Papers* I, 220. Keith, *Commercial Relations,* p. 157.

With the end of the war, Lauderdale and his friends pushed for and obtained a conference between commissioners of the two countries on the question of trade. They expected that Clarendon's fall would improve their chances of success, "most looking on that great man as this country's small friend . . . in the matter of trade."[55] The situation was made more pressing by the prohibitive French tariff of 1667, which further damaged Scottish commerce. Scottish hopes were high that the conference would lead to the grant of the coveted right to trade in the plantations—it was a matter of now or never, wrote Tweeddale—and were reflected in a considerable rise in the selling price of the farm of the Scottish customs.[56]

In view of the difficult state of English domestic politics in the autumn of 1667, Charles, who favored the conference, decided to refer the question to Parliament rather than to appoint commissioners on his own responsibility; it was, he told the houses, "too weighty for himself singly to determine." Lord Keeper Bridgeman, in his speech, hoped that Parliament would find a way to deal with this which would neither damage English trade nor discourage the Scots.[57] The attitude of the Commons was made clear by John Milward's entry in his diary: "It was taken into consideration the trade with Scotland, to prevent the Scots from carrying their commodities to Holland or France."[58] In the debates the foremost advocate of increased trade with Scotland was the new treasury commissioner Sir Thomas Clifford, who pointed out that England had a favorable balance of trade with Scotland, that Scotland supplied raw materials and bought manufactured goods—it was "our Indies." The chief spokesman for caution, embarrassingly enough, was the treasury commission's secretary, Sir George Downing, who was not at all convinced of the value of the Scottish trade and who was determined to do nothing which might damage the interests of the English customs farmers and thus reduce the meager income of the English government. The Scots looked on the pro-

[55] Sept. 7, 1667, Tweeddale to Lauderdale, Airy, *Lauderdale Papers* II, 46.

[56] Sept. 28, 1667, Tweeddale to Lauderdale, B.M. Add. Mss. 23,128, f. 76. Oct. 10, 1667, Moray to Lauderdale, Airy, *Lauderdale Papers* II, 72–75.

[57] P.R.O., S.P. 29/231, f. 64. *His Majesties Most Gracious Speech to Both Houses of Parliament, with the Lord Keepers* (London, 1667).

[58] C. Robbins, ed., *The Diary of John Milward* (Cambridge, 1938), p. 89.

ceedings in Parliament with considerable alarm; they feared, not
the outcome, but delay in the negotiations. The fact that Downing
became a member of the English commission and Clifford did not
might have led them to fear both.[59]

The Scottish commission was dominated by Lauderdale and his
friends Tweeddale and Moray, though it also included two of his
erstwhile opponents, Rothes and Glencairn, who were added to
prevent their caballing at home while Lauderdale and his allies were
busy with the negotiations.[60] The most resplendent member of the
English commission was the duke of Buckingham, but the real
leader was Downing, and the commission was composed mainly of
important members of the House of Commons, "most of whom had
resisted Court policy and were soon to be bought by places."[61] The
personnel of this commission did not augur well for the prospect of
agreement on the points at issue.

When the commissioners first met, on January 13, 1668, Buckingham asked what was wanted by the Scots. Lauderdale replied that
the conditions under which trade was conducted should revert to
what they had been under James I and Charles I, before the Navigation Act. A week later the Scots explained that they wanted to be
treated like the English, Welsh, and Irish under the Navigation Act;
they were prepared to undertake to land all colonial goods in England, except those actually destined for consumption in Scotland.
They also complained of the heavy English import duties on Scottish goods. The English commissioners refused to negotiate on any
issue until the full scope of the Scots' demands was known; so, on
February 3, these were spelled out. The Scots objected to the English
import duties on Scottish cattle, linen cloth, salt, and beer, which
was ten shillings a barrel, "as if Scotsmen were foreigners," to the
duties recently imposed in Cumberland and Northumberland on

---

[59] *Ibid.*, pp. 127, 139–40. A. Grey, *Debates of the House of Commons*
(London, 1763) I, 38–39. Nov. 19, 1667, Moray to Lauderdale, B.M. Add. Mss.
23,128, f. 181. The treasury in fact instructed the governors of the English colonies
to tighten up the enforcement of the Navigation Act, which had been suspended
during the war. W. A. Shaw, ed., *Calendar of Treasury Books* (henceforth *C.T.B.*)
1667–1668 (London, 1905) , pp. 201–2. P.R.O., S.P. 29/231, f. 45. Scotland did not
benefit from the suspension. See, for instance, Mar. 9, 1667, Rothes to Lauderdale,
Airy, *Lauderdale Papers* I, 278–79.

[60] Dec. 25, 1667, Moray to Lauderdale, *ibid.*, pp. 231–32.

[61] E. Hughes, "The Negotiations for a Commercial Union Between
England and Scotland in 1668," *Scottish Historical Review* XXIV (1926–27) , 33.

the export of horses and grain to Scotland, the prohibition of the export of English wool and hides, and the insistence that all English goods destined for Scotland pass through Berwick or Carlisle. But above all the Scots disliked the Navigation Act and insisted that it be dealt with first.[62]

The English commissioners were prepared to discuss the Navigation Act, but before they would do so, they required a list of all Scots ships, so that they would know just how much competition there would be if the Navigation Act were altered to meet Lauderdale's demands. The list was slow in coming, and in the meantime other issues came under discussion, especially salt and coal. The Newcastle coal dealers complained that their business was being hurt because the English export tax on coal was so much higher than the Scottish one; the result was that the Scots were taking over English foreign markets and bringing back manufactured goods which they formerly bought in England, to the detriment of English manufacturing. More important was the fight over salt, which developed into a struggle between the English salt manufacturers and the merchants, who wanted the duty reduced. The argument lasted throughout the summer of 1668 and ended in a victory for the manufacturers: the duty was not lowered.[63]

Even before the list of Scottish ships they requested had been compiled, the English commissioners rejected on principle the Scots' demand for admission to the colonial trade. They were willing, however, to admit the Scots to certain trades—in timber, in the Levant, and, ironically, in foreign salt—for six years. The Scots might have accepted these concessions and used them as a platform from which to bargain further; they did not. They insisted on the full measure of their demands respecting the Navigation Act, and in the end they got nothing. The consequence, as had been freely predicted on both sides, was that Scottish trade continued to be primarily with continental Europe.[64]

---

[62] P.R.O., S.P. 29/253, f. 9. *C.S.P.D.* VIII, 173, 179–80, 187–88, 205. Brown, *Miscellanea Aulica,* pp. 199–202.

[63] Many of the relevant documents are in *ibid.,* pp. 199ff. See the excellent summary by Hughes, "Negotiations," *Sc. Hist. Rev.* XXIV, 37–47.

[64] *C.S.P.D.* VIII, 285–86. Jan. 30, 1668, Tweeddale to Lauderdale, B.M. Add. Mss. 23,128, f. 282. Apr. 21, 1668, Ramsay to Lauderdale, *ibid.* 23,129, f. 75. Oct. 29, 1668, Mein to Williamson, *C.S.P.D.* IX, 40. Hughes, "Negotiations," *Sc. Hist. Rev.* XXIV, 36–37. See also Keith, *Commercial Relations,* pp. 91–93.

If, as most historians have assumed, Lauderdale and his allies had any serious hope or expectation of winning substantial commercial concessions from the English, their tactics were extraordinarily inept. They put forward the one demand which Downing and his friends among the City merchants and the customs farmers would be most likely to resist, and they delayed in meeting the English requests for information. The list of ships was virtually complete by late March, and was completed by April 11, but it was not turned over to the English commissioners, who on June 18 rightly pointed out to the Scots that they were responsible for the resulting delay in the negotiations. Tweeddale thought of the uses of silver to make the English more amenable; "Sir George Downing barks for a bone," he wrote Lauderdale on March 30, "he has been accustomed to get money from Scots men."[65] Lauderdale was not above using bribes to get what he wanted, but he evidently made no effort to fall in with Tweeddale's suggestion that he try Downing's virtue in this case.

The logical conclusion, then, must be that the conference's purpose was not economic in nature at all. And, indeed, Lauderdale virtually said so in his letter to Tweeddale on April 23, 1668. There was no need for protracted negotiation with England over the Navigation Act, he said, because it could be dispensed with by the use of the royal prerogative, as Charles had done during the late war. A public statement to that effect was planned in a couple of weeks; "the old laird is fully of this mind."[66] Charles evidently decided that such a statement would be premature; instead, he set up as a mediator. In May, and again in September, he instructed both sides to prepare statements of their positions; he would study them and make suggestions.[67] Nothing was settled, but not because Charles was doubtful of his prerogative—although the English commissioners, in their September report, made by Downing, were very much opposed to any concessions being made to the Scots by royal authority alone.[68] Only one economic issue was decisively determined in the

[65] B.M. Add. Mss. 23,129, ff. 41, 66. *C.S.P.D.* VIII, 444.

[66] N.L.S. Mss. 3136, f. 39. In January Lauderdale had asked Primrose for copies of the Scottish acts which acknowledged the king's power over foreign trade. B.M. Harl. Mss. 4631, I, 96–97.

[67] P.R.O., S.P. 29/253, ff. 40, 42, 74–76; 104/176, ff. 75–76.

[68] *C.S.P.D.* VIII, 598. P.R.O., S.P. 29/253, ff. 75–76. They "ventured to ask 'how this will relish with your people and with ye Parliament when they shall meete.' " Hughes, "Negotiations," *Sc. Hist. Rev.* XXIV, 34.

Scots' favor in this period, and that was done by prerogative. This was the matter of the English duty on Scots cattle, an issue of obvious importance to the landed classes. Lauderdale had supported the Irish cattle bill in 1666 in the expectation that Scottish cattle raisers would profit from the elimination of Irish competition; Tweeddale felt that, even if the negotiations on commerce broke down on all other points, gaining this one would leave Scotland reasonably well off. Cattle, in Tweeddale's view, was the only major item of Scottish commerce for which no overseas market could be found. In July, 1668, at Lauderdale's instigation, the treasury commission ordered the English customs farmers to explain why they had been charging duty on Scottish cattle; nine months later, in April, 1669, after a great deal of effort and persistence, Lauderdale obtained the king's order to the effect that Scottish cattle were to enter without duty. Charles, he wrote to Kincardine in announcing this triumph, is very favorable to the "Land of Cakes."[69]

It seems, then, that Lauderdale expected the commercial negotiations to fail, indeed, that he pitched on the one issue which most strongly emphasized the conflicting interests of England and Scotland, and which was therefore most likely to invite failure. It is true that he had little to bargain with. About the only thing he might have offered, in return for the many English concessions he asked for, was a reduction in Scottish duties on English goods, and there were powerful Scottish interests opposed to such changes.[70] But no politician as skillful as Lauderdale deliberately courts such a reverse without some purpose. It has usually been assumed that the negotiations for Anglo-Scottish political union which followed on the failure of the commercial negotiations were a consequence of that failure. This was the impression Lauderdale wished to give; in his speech to the Scottish Parliament in October, 1669, in which he formally raised the question of political union, he explained the government's action in just these terms. The commercial negotia-

[69] Lady Burghclere, *The Life of James, First Duke of Ormonde* (London, 1912) II, 123. Apr. 14, Oct. 15, 1668, Tweeddale to Lauderdale, B.M. Add. Mss. 23,129, ff. 71–72; 23,130, f. 70. Apr. 24, 1669, Lauderdale to Kincardine, B.M. Harl. Mss. 4631, I, 107. The course of the struggle can be followed in *C.T.B. 1667–68*, pp. 392ff., and *1669–72* I. The Order in Council, dated May 7, 1669, is on p. 63 of the latter volume.

[70] On January 3, 1668, about a dozen important people, including Kincardine, wrote Lauderdale opposing any reduction in the Scottish duties on imported salt. B.M. Add. Mss. 23,128, f. 242.

tions, he said, "produced no effect, unless it were a conviction of the difficulty, if not impossibility, of settling it in any other way, than by a nearer and more complete union of the two kingdoms."[71] The evidence, however, indicates that political union was what Lauderdale had in mind all the time. The commercial negotiations were intended to demonstrate to the Scots that mere commercial union was unobtainable, that the larger question would have to be broached.

The idea of political union was not a new one to Lauderdale; its achievement had been one of the objectives of the Engagement in 1647. It was being discussed by the earl and his friends before the commercial negotiations even began. On September 21, 1667, Tweeddale, who may have suggested the idea first and who certainly was its most enthusiastic advocate, was hopefully opining that the trade discussions "will fairly introduce the consideration of an union."[72] In October the idea was broached to Lord Keeper Bridgeman by Lauderdale.[73] Throughout the commercial negotiations the idea was never totally out of anybody's mind—Lauderdale wanted extracts of the unprinted act of the Scottish Parliament of 1607 on union sent to him; the English commissioners wanted copies of the articles of union of 1604.[74] Tweeddale referred to union fairly regularly in his letters. At first he expected it to come about as a consequence of success in the commercial negotiations. In June, 1668, when he was expecting Lauderdale to come to Scotland, he hoped the earl would bring with him "a good issue of the business of trade, which will make way for the union proposed, both adding much weight to persuade it."[75] It was only gradually that the drift of Lauderdale's policy became apparent to Tweeddale—Lauderdale was notoriously secretive, and his letters, save those to the king, are not very revealing as to the way in which his mind was working. In September Tweeddale, who was upset by the failure of the commercial negotiations, was more eager for union than ever. "Oh if the

[71] N.L.S. Mss. 597, ff. 214–15. *The Works of His Grace George Villiers, Late Duke of Buckingham* (London, 1715) II, 232.

[72] B.M. Add. Mss. 23,128, f. 56. Burnet, *History* I, 505.

[73] Oct. 14, 1667, Moray to Lauderdale, Airy, *Lauderdale Papers* II, 75.

[74] Jan. 11, 1668, Lauderdale to Primrose, B.M. Harl. Mss. 4631, I, 96–97. Jan. 25, 1668, the English commissioners to the Scottish commissioners, N.L.S. Mss. 2955, f. 22.

[75] B.M. Add. Mss. 23,129, f. 146.

king would mind it," he wrote, "as it is of importance, and all we do or can is but fending over to put off an evil time that must come unless that be done." He soon saw Lauderdale's point, however. "I am glad to hear the union looks so hopeful, for then the trade needs not trouble you much."[76]

Why political union? It has been frequently asserted that Lauderdale was really not in favor of union at all, since his own authority in Scotland would be whittled down by it. The argument was used by Lauderdale's enemies at the time, and has been echoed by historians ever since.[77] This is manifestly mistaken; Lauderdale's authority rested solely on the king's favor, not upon the constitutional relations between England and Scotland. Lauderdale knew his master well enough to know that the surest way to preserve that favor was to further the enhancement of the royal prerogative, and this could be done by means of Scotland. Tweeddale expressed it well when he wrote, in April, 1668, "I am joyed the king and duke have so good an opinion of Scotland and confidence in it, and hope they shall not be disappointed, for it may be formed into a citadel for his majesty's service in time."[78] A citadel for his majesty's service—this was what Lauderdale intended. As early as 1663 he wrote to Moray that if "in any of his dominions [Charles] should require the assistance of Scotland, he may confidently promise to himself a more universal concurrence of the body of this kingdom for maintenance of his authority either within Scotland or in any other of his dominions, where and whensoever he shall command their service, than any of his predecessors could have done."[79] The uprising of 1666 demonstrated that this view was premature, but Lauderdale believed that Scotland could be turned into such a citadel by proper administration and legislation. If it were then politically joined to England, so that the Scottish example, Scottish Parliamentary votes, Scottish soldiers even, could be employed south of the Tweed, Charles would

[76] Sept. 10, Sept. 24, Oct. 15, 1668, Tweeddale to Lauderdale, B.M. Add. Mss. 23,130, ff. 18, 70; Airy, *Lauderdale Papers* II, 119.

[77] Sir George Mackenzie, *Memoirs of the Affairs of Scotland from the Restoration of King Charles II* (ed. T. Thomson, Edinburgh, 1821), p. 140. *Somers Tracts* VIII, 499–508. David Ogg, *England in the Reign of Charles II* (2nd ed., Oxford, 1955) II, 413. Lang, *Mackenzie*, p. 91.

[78] B.M. Add. Mss. 23,129, f. 48. Tweeddale's motives differed from Lauderdale's, according to Burnet (*History* I, 506) : Tweeddale favored union as a bulwark of liberty.

[79] Airy, *Lauderdale Papers* I, 169.

have the untrammeled authority he was seeking. "The king liked it [political union]," commented Burnet, "because he reckoned that, at least for his time, he would be sure of all the members that should be sent up from Scotland." And, far from Scotland being smothered by England, as she had been under Cromwell, it would be by Scotland's means that England was governed—a result bound to appeal to the Covenanter that Lauderdale once had been and the patriot he always was. Burnet saw the truth: Lauderdale, he wrote, "pressed it [union] vehemently."[80] Charles, of course, had no feeling for Lauderdale's patriotic vision; no Stuart was less of a Scot than he. But if the end in view could be achieved, Lauderdale's means were perfectly acceptable to him.

III

There were two sides to Lauderdale's plan. Negotiations for the union had to be brought to a successful conclusion, and Scotland had to be turned into "a citadel for his majesty's service." Serious discussion on the union began in November, 1668, when Lauderdale and Moray had some preliminary talks with Bridgeman and Buckingham, both of whom were enthusiastic for it, and Lauderdale agreed to draw up a preliminary draft.[81] Matters were delayed by Charles's absence in Newmarket and by Lauderdale's own ill health; by the end of the month, a larger meeting had been held—Ashley, Arlington, and Clifford were present this time—and some tentative arrangements were made about tax rates. The question of the precedence of peers, Lauderdale observed, was apt to create difficulties. So was the question whether the combined Parliament should be bicameral or unicameral, as was Scotland's; Lauderdale felt that this made no difference as far as Scotland was concerned.[82] Early in December Lauderdale told Tweeddale that the plan ought to be revealed to a few people in Scotland to gauge the drift of opinion there; an unctuous covering letter was enclosed for Tweeddale to use, which stressed that this was no sudden scheme, but something

[80] Burnet, *History* I, 505.
[81] Nov. 17, 1668, Lauderdale to Tweeddale, N.L.S. Mss. 3136, ff. 49, 50. Tweeddale kept urging his chief forward. "If there be any talk of union with Ireland," he wrote on November 12, "for God's sake make haste with ours." Airy, *Lauderdale Papers* II, 122.
[82] N.L.S. Mss. 3136, f. 138. English peers were very sensitive about the claims of Scottish and Irish peers. See *C.S.P.D.* VIII, 271.

"that a knot of good fellows have been hammering upon some time," and that the king "is much set upon" it.[83] As it happened, the first person with whom Tweeddale discussed the project was Lauderdale's friend the earl of Argyll, and both of them agreed that the weakest spot in Lauderdale's proposed scheme was that it did not provide for a sufficient number of Scots peers in the combined Parliament. "You must either prevail for a greater number or get some assurance of calling more speedily," wrote Tweeddale, if the Scots nobility were to accept the plan. Until this point could be settled, Tweeddale would not discuss the plan with anyone else.[84]

Such a reaction, from the foremost Scottish advocate of union, may have disconcerted Lauderdale; for whatever reason, the project was allowed to slumber for six months. Then, on May 27, 1669, Arlington's secretary Joseph Williamson recorded in his journal, "The old design of uniting England and Scotland . . . they say will be reassumed, his majesty expressing great desire to have all his subjects conspire to one another's happiness under his reign."[85] Four days later Lauderdale presented a detailed plan to the foreign committee of the privy council, which accepted it on June 10. It called for the appointment by the king of commissioners for both kingdoms, who were to have full powers to treat and conclude, subject to the ratification of both Parliaments. There was to be an inseparable union under the king, his heirs and successors, with equal privileges for the subjects of each kingdom in both, and a single bicameral Parliament. There were to be thirty Scottish seats in the Commons, the same number as during the Cromwellian union; the difficulty about peers was got over by stipulating that Charles should summon what Scots peers (and bishops) he wished and determine their precedence. Customs, excise, and poll taxes were to be everywhere equal; other taxes were to be proportional, with England paying 70 per cent, Ireland 18 per cent, and Scotland 12 per cent. The legal systems of the two countries were to remain separate.[86]

[83] *Ibid.*, ff. 56, 58.
[84] Dec. 8, 1668, Tweeddale to Lauderdale, B.M. Add. Mss. 23,131, f. 16.
[85] P.R.O., S.P. 29/271, f. 45.
[86] P.R.O., S.P. 104/176, ff. 155, 157, 161. The peerage question was worrisome still; on May 31 the minutes read that it was "to be chewed over yet further." An alternative plan provided for the election of two bishops and ten temporal lords by their fellows—the germ of the solution of 1707. N.L.S. Mss. 597, ff. 232, 234.

So the great scheme was launched. The king's proclamation in June, summoning both Parliaments to meet at the same time, in October, caused a good many rumors, but the truth got out quickly enough. Opposition began to rise in Scotland; Lauderdale, confident of his grip on Parliament, brushed it aside. "What you say of the cabal which is forming against the union troubles me little," he wrote Tweeddale. "I heard of it last week from E. Kincardine and also who makes himself head of it. I pray you, let him go on, it is a very good means to keep him from being one of the treaty." Kincardine and Tweeddale were not so confident as Lauderdale; there would be many special interests to take into account, and the operation was apt to be costly.[87] Lauderdale was more worried about the method of choosing the commissioners. In a meeting of the foreign committee on June 29 he argued strongly that they must be named by the king, not by Parliament; perhaps with the recent commercial negotiations in mind, he asserted that "if ye Parliaments name them, nothing is like to come of it." The committee was in general agreement on this point, Clifford adding that the king's prerogative would be abridged if he did not have the naming of them.[88] To strengthen his case, Lauderdale asserted, and Clifford agreed, that in the negotiations of James I's time, James had nominated the commissioners. This turned out to be bad history; Bridgeman looked up the records and discovered that in 1604 the Parliaments had named their own commissioners. This was, said Lauderdale, "a stumble";[89] it was one added reason for Lauderdale's conviction that he ought to manage the forthcoming session of the Scottish Parliament in person.

Lauderdale set off for Scotland at the end of September, 1669, having fortified himself for the journey by spending part of the summer drinking the waters.[90] He went armed with a set of instructions from Charles, asking the Scottish Parliament to authorize the

[87] July 13, 1669, Lauderdale to Tweeddale, N.L.S. Mss. 3136, f. 109. Aug. 10, 1669, Tweeddale to Lauderdale, B.M. Add. Mss. 23,132, f. 61. Aug. 12, 1669, Kincardine to Lauderdale, *ibid.*, f. 65. Sir George Mackenzie, who openly opposed the union in Parliament, asserts that Lauderdale smoothed the way by bribery. *Memoirs,* pp. 140–41.

[88] P.R.O., S.P. 104/176, ff. 176–77.

[89] Aug. 31, 1669, Lauderdale to Tweeddale, N.L.S. Mss. 3136, f. 116.

[90] July 27, 1669, Rothes to Lauderdale, B.M. Add. Mss. 23,132, f. 34.

king to appoint a commission with full powers to treat and conclude; the king would determine the size, membership, and quorum
of the commission. The agreement would ultimately be submitted to
Parliament for ratification. Lauderdale duly delivered Charles's
speech to the opening session of Parliament on October 19, complete
with rhetorical flourishes and historical references, to how King
James "meant to have gloried [in the union] as the chiefest action
of his life," but with no details as to the actual form the proposed
union would take.[91] The earl was not worried about effective opposition, in view of the government's control of the Committee of the
Articles. "If they be amiss blame me," he wrote the king, "for I wrote
the lists and not a man was altered."[92] On the very next day the
committee dutifully accepted the king's proposal; it was put to the
full House on October 21. Here, indeed, there were some difficulties:
there was complaint that the whole business was being pushed too
fast, that no one knew what the English Parliament would do, "that
the kingdom was not satisfied with an union, and indeed great pains
have been taken to alarm all sorts of people against it. . . . I knew
it could have been carried clearly," Lauderdale went on, "but I
choosed rather to grant a delay."[93]

Lauderdale's idea of a delay was to put over the final vote for one
day. On October 22 the government's proposal was "without any
alteration unanimously agreed to, without one No excepting one
lawyer."[94] The one lawyer was George Mackenzie of Rosehaugh, a
rising barrister in his early thirties who would soon become a government man and leave an unenviable and partly undeserved reputation as a persecutor: Bluidy Mackenzie. His speech did not directly
attack the principle of union, but it breathed nationalistic suspicion
of England. Mackenzie also urged that Parliament rather than the
king have the nomination of the commissioners, citing the precedent
of 1604 and remarking that Parliament would be more apt than the
king, because better informed, to nominate men who would safeguard Scotland's economic interests. He was interrupted by the
angry Tweeddale, who protested that it was intolerable to have to

[91] *Ibid.*, f. 97. The instructions are in *ibid.*, f. 93.
[92] Oct. 19, 1669, Lauderdale to Charles, Airy, *Lauderdale Papers* II, 142.
[93] Oct. 22, 1669, Lauderdale to Charles, *ibid.*, pp. 143–45.
[94] *Ibid.*

listen to such a long speech, especially when it was directed against the king's wishes, and in the vote Mackenzie found no one who would join him. But he had had his supporters in the debate; Williamson's correspondent Robert Mein reported that the measure passed only "after much dispute."[95]

Having done his job expeditiously if not exactly tactfully, Lauderdale sat back to await action from Westminster. He urged speed on Charles, and "above all get the nomination [of the commissioners] in England, else I shall despair of the success, and they have now a fair example." Charles's ministers were delighted by Lauderdale's work, especially Arlington, who was very anxious that the union succeed, since the alternative method by which Charles was contemplating the strengthening of his prerogative was most distasteful to him. "Your Grace hath played your part well; nothing but the proverb of 'La mariée est trop belle' can be said against it."[96]

Speedy action was not something the Commons was anxious to provide, however. The simultaneous summons of the two Parliaments made some members suspicious, and their first reaction to the proposal, when it was laid before them by the king and Lord Keeper Bridgeman, was "cold"; they were more concerned, apparently, with prosecuting for libel a printer who published a tract vindicating the stand of the House of Lords in the famous case of Skinner *vs.* the East India Company. Sir Robert Moray, whom Lauderdale had left behind in London as his link with Charles and who used to talk politics with the king while they were working in the chemical laboratory together, urged the royal scientist to expedite matters; if pressure were not applied, it would be a month before the Commons took up the measure.[97] On October 28 Moray reported that he had met with the king, Arlington, and Clifford. In view of the delays likely at Westminster, Moray and Clifford proposed, and the king agreed, that the Scottish Parliament could pass an act giving the

[95] *C.S.P.D.* IX, 546. Mackenzie, *Memoirs,* pp. 149–55.

[96] Oct. 22, 1669, Lauderdale to Charles, Airy, *Lauderdale Papers* II, 143–45. Oct. 26, 1669, Arlington to Lauderdale, *ibid.,* p. 147.

[97] June 25/July 5, 1669, Mocenigo to the Doge and Senate of Venice, A. B. Hinds, *et al.,* eds., *Calendar of State Papers, Venetian* (henceforth *C.S.P. Venetian*) (London, 1864–1947) XXXVI, 72–73. Oct. 19, 1669, Arlington to Lauderdale, C. S. Terry, ed., *The Cromwellian Union,* Scottish History Society publication XL (Edinburgh, 1902), pp. 223–24. Oct. 26, 1669, Moray to Lauderdale, Airy, *Lauderdale Papers* II, 147–48.

king the right to issue a commission for the negotiation of the union under the Scottish Great Seal, without waiting for the English Parliament to act; the Scottish Parliament could then adjourn.[98]

This proposal horrified Lauderdale. He had expressly avoided putting the draft of a commission through Parliament in deference to Scottish sensibilities; England was to act first on this point, and whatever passed the English Parliament would then be pushed through in Edinburgh. He now reacted very violently. Mackenzie's may have been the only vote in Parliament against the king's proposal, but his was not the only voice raised in opposition, and he had many supporters in the country. "You cannot imagine what aversion is generally in this kingdom to the union," he wrote Moray on November 2. "The endeavor to have made us slaves by garrisons and the ruin of our trade by severe laws in England frights all ranks of men from having to do with England. What is done is purely in obedience to his majesty. . . . But to press more before England take notice of the matter would render the proposer most odious as the betrayer of his country. For God's sake let his majesty lay any other punishment on me."[99]

A week later Lauderdale was even more outraged to discover that, without waiting for his advice, the king had proceeded to authorize the passage of the act for the commission. The man chiefly responsible for this was the impetuous Clifford, who on October 31 successfully argued for it in the foreign committee, pointing out that the English Parliament was not likely to act on the union until December, and that every day the Scottish Parliament sat cost the government £50, which grieved Clifford in his capacity as treasury commissioner.[100] Lauderdale erupted again. He was amazed to receive such instructions from Charles, he wrote Moray on November 9, and particularly to receive them by an express messenger, which had caused all sorts of rumors. He had consulted with some fifteen members of the Committee of the Articles, and they all agreed, "that it would not pass in the Parliament, and that the propounding it would raise such jealousies as would endanger the . . . whole design." Scottish pride was involved; the country simply could not be

[98] Airy, *Lauderdale Papers* II, 149–50.
[99] *Ibid.*, pp. 154–55.
[100] P.R.O., S.P. 104/176, f. 210. The commission was to be effective on condition that the English Parliament acted similarly.

treated as secondary and subordinate to England. Furthermore there was nothing to be gained by the issue of a blank commission. If the king, when he had considered these objections, still chose to go ahead, Lauderdale would obey him, "but I disclaim all promises of success in this or in the treaty."[101] He wrote on the same day to the king, protesting that he could not "in faithfulness and duty to your service" obey the order until Charles had had the time to digest his objections; he asked the king to read his letter to Moray and then give him his orders. He enclosed this in a waspish covering letter to Moray: "I must say that you have taken much pains to bring me into a great difficulty."[102] It was the beginning of a breach between the two men which was never entirely healed.

On that same day, November 9, Moray wrote from London to his chief. Charles, he said, was much disturbed by Lauderdale's reaction to the plan for the blank commission. The king did not intend to be peremptory, and would not insist. Moray then went into a long explanation of the circumstances of the issuing of the order, which he blamed largely on Clifford, but it was plain that Moray still thought it was a good plan, especially as it was generally agreed, by Clifford and Arlington among others, that nothing could be done to hurry the English Parliament. The king had other bills to get through that body, notably supply, and everything would be jeopardized by too much insistence on the union.[103] Four days later the foreign committee met and came to the same conclusion as the informal gathering on the ninth. The instructions to Lauderdale were canceled, but it was generally agreed that the English Parliament could not be rushed. "Even the aid is slow," Clifford remarked. The committee suggested that Lauderdale might draft a letter to send to Scotland explaining the English Parliament's inaction, but Moray prevented that by pointing out that such a letter could hardly be written without offending somebody. Moray still hankered after the blank commission, and suggested it yet again. "I think I guess how you will relish this. Disappoint me."[104]

Lauderdale did not disappoint him. He was greatly relieved, he wrote Moray, that "I shall not be chid for not obeying the command

101 Airy, *Lauderdale Papers* II, 155–58.
102 B.M. Add. Mss. 23,132, ff. 145, 149.
103 *Ibid.*, ff. 150–51.
104 Airy, *Lauderdale Papers* II, 159–63. P.R.O., S.P. 104/176, ff. 217–18.

you sent me BY THE EXPRESS."[105] He also expressed his gratitude
to the king. "I was afflicted above measure," he wrote, "to have so
great a business miscarry in my hand by precipitation, which will go
well here if we meet with any suitable return." He was less pleased
by the idea that he should draft a letter for Charles to send to him.
"This is a new tormenting hint. Alas, shall I never be trusted." He
was very gloomy now about the prospects for union: "either here or
there I am confident the union is choaked."[106] If nothing was to be
done, he wrote Charles, the business of trade ought to be taken up
again. The king was less pessimistic; the English Parliament's delays
did not mean opposition there. "When the union was to be spoke
of," he told Moray, "there would a hundred be got to bring in the
motion."[107] As November turned into December, however, it became
clear that there would be no action at Westminster before Christmas. In the middle of the month both Parliaments were prorogued;
the king poured as much soothing syrup as he could on Scottish
sensibilities by thanking the Scots for their action on the union,
which he attributed to "your desire of the common welfare of the
Island, and not to any particular benefit you expect to . . . our
ancient kingdom."[108] But there was general disappointment, especially in Whitehall. "The truth is," wrote Arlington, "I had no joy
in thinking, much less writing of the progress of our session in
Parliament, so different from what we promised ourselves it would
be at your Grace's departure from hence."[109] Lauderdale, as he made
his way south, was equally depressed. "I am old and begin to grow
crazy [ill]," he wrote Moray, "so cannot come fast, but I shall come
as I am able and serve truly as long as I live. Though crazy I shall do
as I may, and where the pitcher breaks, there is an end."[110]

The project for union had not advanced very far, therefore, by the

[105] B.M. Add. Mss. 23,132, f. 153. The printed version, Airy, *Lauderdale
Papers* II, 158–59, does not indicate that Lauderdale wrote *by the express* in letters
about twice normal size.

[106] Nov. 16, 1669, Lauderdale to Charles, Airy, *Lauderdale Papers* II,
163–64. Nov. 18, 1669, Lauderdale to Moray, B.M. Add. Mss. 23,132, f. 158.

[107] Nov. 30, 1669, Moray to Lauderdale, Airy, *Lauderdale Papers* II,
165–66.

[108] B.M. Add. Mss. 23,132, f. 180. This statement was composed by
Lauderdale, who, in sending the draft, advised proroguing rather than dissolving
the Scottish Parliament; a dissolution would look like "a quitting the union."
Dec. 2, 1669, Lauderdale to Moray, *ibid.*, f. 167.

[109] Dec. 14, 1669, Arlington to Lauderdale, *ibid.*, f. 183.

[110] *Ibid.*, f. 186.

end of 1669. Lauderdale had much more to show for his effort to make Scotland into a citadel for the king's service. The Parliament of 1669 passed a Militia Act, regulating the pay and dealing with the other details of the organization of the force authorized in 1663, which Lauderdale had paid a good deal of attention to raising and which he had reported on favorably before Parliament met as being "ready to march when and whither you please."[111] The Militia Act caused some murmurings in England, "because," wrote Lauderdale to his master, "it is declared you may command them to any of your dominions, alas that is no new clause in this Act, it was verbatim in the Act six years ago."[112] Another measure, passed just before Parliament rose, when it became apparent that union would be delayed, gave the king the power to regulate Scottish foreign trade in any manner he pleased. The most important act, however, dealt with religion.

By the time of Clarendon's fall the Scottish bishops had sufficiently discredited themselves, in Lauderdale's opinion, and he prepared to improve the position of the nonconformists, as was being planned in England. There were two possible ways of doing this: by toleration or by relaxing the regulations of the established church in order to induce the moderate Presbyterians who still stood outside the Establishment to conform. The latter scheme was advocated by the best of the Scottish bishops, Robert Leighton of Dunblane, who suggested a scheme of accommodation which in effect would have reduced the bishop to the position of *primus inter pares,* of a chief presbyter. Kincardine proposed that this scheme be imposed by legislation; Lauderdale demurred, on the ground that in England it would be regarded as a pulling down of episcopacy and would create political difficulties for the king and the union scheme. Kincardine pressed the point that something must be done, if only on account of the English example: ". . . if there be slackening of the reins there, it will be hard for us to hold them strait here." So a suggestion of Tweeddale's was adopted, whereby deprived Presbyterian ministers who had lived peaceably were to be restored to their parishes or appointed to vacancies under conditions which enabled them to avoid acknowledging the authority of the bishop. Tweeddale be-

[111] Oct. 12, 1669, Lauderdale to Charles, Airy, *Lauderdale Papers* II, 140–41.

[112] *Ibid.,* pp. 163–64.

lieved that this plan would reconcile some moderate nonconformists to the established church and divide the rest. The idea was mooted in 1668 but was put off for a year owing to an attempt on the life of Archbishop Sharp; it was put into effect, by the king's authority, in the summer of 1669.[113]

This plan of restoring the "outed" ministers, called the indulgence, naturally upset the bishops, which bothered Lauderdale not at all. Rather more serious was the fact that it was contrary to the statute of 1662 which had restored episcopacy. This was a simple matter to remedy, in the earl's view; he had the Parliament of 1669 pass a statute which took account of this and of all other contingencies which were likely to arise. This act declared that the king "hath the supreme authority and supremacy over all persons and in all causes ecclesiastical within this his kingdom": in religious matters Charles could do whatever he liked.[114] He did not wait long to exercise his power. Archbishop Burnet and his synod had protested against the policy of indulgence; he was now deprived of his see, which was given to Leighton.

"Never was king so absolute as you are in poor old Scotland," wrote Lauderdale to his master in reporting the passage of this Act of Supremacy.[115] The phrase applies equally well to the whole of Lauderdale's policy in these years. The king's prerogative was to be exalted over all things and all men—as Lauderdale said on another occasion, "the king's edicts were to be considered and obeyed as laws, and more than any other laws."[116] Lauderdale was aware that the Act of Supremacy was an extreme measure; even Sharp had qualms, and Lauderdale was afraid of the reaction of the English bishops. The king, however, expressed only delight with his minister's success in erecting the citadel he sought. With the end of the Parliament, Charles "brags that now Scotland hath the best laws in the world and the completest."[117] Andrew Marvell, no admirer of the king and

[113] Mar. 2, 1669, Kincardine to Lauderdale, *ibid.*, p. 125. Aug. 3, 1669, Tweeddale to Lauderdale, B.M. Add. Mss. 23,132, f. 48. Burnet, *History* I, 496. For religious policy in this period see Mathieson, *Politics and Religion* II, 231–38.

[114] Mathieson, *Politics and Religion* II, 238.

[115] Nov. 16, 1669, Lauderdale to Charles, Airy, *Lauderdale Papers* II, 163–64.

[116] Burnet, *History* I, 603–4.

[117] Nov. 2, 1669, Lauderdale to Moray, B.M. Add. Mss. 23,132, ff. 141–42. Dec. 28, 1669, Moray to Lauderdale, *ibid.*, f. 202.

the men around him, commented rather differently: "many talked that he [Lauderdale] deserved an halter rather than a Garter."[118]

Charles may have been pleased by Lauderdale's erection of the citadel, but he was beginning to have some second thoughts about the union. The project clearly aroused little enthusiasm and was not furthered by the Act of Supremacy. This act alarmed other Englishmen than Andrew Marvell, and in Scotland it aroused opposition on all sides. It was far too Erastian for the taste of the Presbyterians, and the followers of the bishops resented it because it was used to force a most unwelcome religious policy on them. The memories of the Cromwellian union were still strong in Scotland; its political consequences were regarded with hatred, and it had not been in effect long enough for the economic advantages of union to be fully appreciated. The economic disadvantages of the Navigation Act had not yet made themselves widely enough felt for Scotsmen to feel that economic union was an overriding necessity; they tended to attribute their economic distress to the Dutch war.[119] Lauderdale and his master had not been aware of the strength of Scottish feeling on the subject of political union; the widespread opposition to it came as something of a shock to the earl—and, indeed, he may have exaggerated it in his letters to the king and Moray, especially in connection with the proposal for the draft commission. When the Parliamentary session ended in December, Lauderdale had the regalia carried back to Edinburgh castle, and "desired the wives of Edinburgh might take notice, that he had not sold the Crown to the Englishes."[120]

As for the "Englishes," there was no enthusiasm for union outside the king's circle of advisers. All the members of the Cabal favored it,

[118] Mar. 21, 1670, Marvell to his cousin Popple, Margoliouth, *Marvell* II, 300. Yet Marvell was not opposed to union. See "The Loyall Scot" in *ibid.* I, 173–74.

[119] A reading of Louise B. Taylor, ed., *Aberdeen Council Letters* IV (1660–69) (Oxford, 1954) suggests that the chief economic concerns of that community were relief from taxation, the location of the staple port in the Netherlands, and the maintenance of the ancient trade monopoly of the royal burghs.

[120] Mackenzie, *Memoirs*, p. 181. An indication of Scottish sentiment on union is provided by the title of a learned antiquarian tract written in 1670: "The Crown of Scotland not subject to England." It is in B.M. Add. Mss. 32,094, ff. 246–59.

in varying degrees and for widely different reasons: Clifford because it would strengthen the prerogative, Arlington because he feared the alternative, Ashley because it would end commercial disputes. For most English businessmen, however, union with Scotland presaged economic disadvantage. The Venetian ambassador wrote in March, 1670, of "the objection of this country, rich in trade and fertile in climate, to join with the bare, poverty-stricken Scotland."[121] There seemed to be nothing for England to gain from such a union; the dynastic issue which was to loom so large in the reign of Queen Anne did not exist, nor did the large-scale Scottish export of wool which by 1700 had convinced some sections of the English business community that England, too, stood to gain economically from such a union, by being able to end the flow of English raw materials to the Continent.[122] Furthermore, Lauderdale's bypassing of the trade commissioners in his dealings in the matter of the duties on Scottish cattle was bound to raise suspicions as to his *bona fides* in this case. Both Anglicans and dissenters, for different reasons, were alarmed by his religious policy. Those Englishmen who did give some favorable consideration to union thought in terms of Anglicizing Scottish law and institutions,[123] something which Scottish opinion and Lauderdale himself would never have accepted.

In the face of this apathy and opposition, Charles began to cool toward the project of union. At the beginning of 1670 a far more attractive and certain means of procuring his independence from Parliament seemed to be within his grasp. The negotiations with France which were to culminate in the treaty of Dover had been under way for some time, and in January, 1670, Charles, perhaps influenced by the difficulties which had so awkwardly cropped up in the matter of the union, virtually assured the conclusion of the French alliance by giving way to the French on the crucial question of the size of the French subsidy for the projected Dutch war. Scottish union no longer seemed so important. But Charles did not allow the matter to drop. His prestige was involved; he could not allow the English Parliament simply to ignore his wishes in this way.

[121] *C.S.P. Venetian* XXXVI, 167.
[122] On this point see Keith, *Commercial Relations*, pp. 102, 109.
[123] See "A Discourse upon the Union of England and Scotland," written by an Englishman in 1664, in Brown, *Miscellanea Aulica*, pp. 192–98.

Furthermore, if union could be gotten on terms which would guarantee Charles's control of the combined Parliament, a little unpopularity would be a cheap price to pay.

So, with the reassembling of the English Parliament in February, 1670, Charles recommended the union to its consideration once again. Lauderdale was still strongly in favor of union; he told the Venetian ambassador that it was a matter of infinite importance to Scotland. The ambassador was very doubtful of success: England and Scotland were too different in fortune and interests. Charles's supposed enthusiasm for the union, he thought, was a blind, designed to pacify the Scots; the king knew the negotiations were doomed from the beginning.[124] All this pessimism hardly seemed to be justified; when Parliament finally did get around to considering the union question in March, 1670, it gave the king everything he asked. Charles could name the commission, and no attempt was made to tie his hands by special instructions. The Danish ambassador reported that there was some suspicion of the government's purposes and some fear that, in the event of union, Scotsmen would pour into England,[125] but there was no protracted debate. The opponents of union evidently preferred to hold their fire until they could attack the finished treaty. Moray was delighted. Before Parliament met, he wrote Kincardine, there was no reason to believe that it would support union, but "of a sudden all takes to admiration." Charles, too, was pleased; at the end of this session of Parliament he singled out their prompt action for praise.[126]

The Scottish Parliament reconvened in July, 1670. Lauderdale went north once again, armed with a set of royal instructions he had drafted himself, ordering him to get a commission approved like that accepted at Westminster and tax money to pay the commissioners' expenses. The membership of the Scottish commission had already been decided, but Lauderdale was not to reveal it until after

[124] Feb. 11/21, Feb. 20/Mar. 2, Mar. 18/28, 1670, Mocenigo to the Doge and Senate, *C.S.P. Venetian* XXXVI, 160, 162–63, 173. Writing after the event, in May, 1671, Mocenigo expressed the opinion that union would have been beneficial, especially to Scotland. *Ibid.* XXXVII, 55.

[125] Mar. 4, 25, 1670, Lindenov to the Danish Chancery, W. Westergaard, ed., *The First Triple Alliance* (New Haven, 1947), pp. 201, 209–10.

[126] Mar. 26, 1670, Moray to Kincardine, N.L.S. Mss. 4938, f. 163. Margoliouth, *Marvell* II, 105. Kincardine was less optimistic. Mar. 19, 1670, Kincardine to Lauderdale, B.M. Add. Mss. 23,133, f. 56.

the act was passed. There was some grumbling in the Parliament, especially on the matter of the lack of instructions for the commissioners, on the ground that it would be almost impossible for the Parliament to reject a finished settlement, especially if England had already approved it, and that therefore Parliament should take care to secure Scottish interests in advance.[127] But Lauderdale got his way. In fact, he got even more tax money for expenses than he and Charles had originally contemplated.[128] The king and his ministers were pleased, especially those who, like Lauderdale himself, were not in the secret of the recently completed treaty of Dover. Lord Ashley, reported Moray on August 6, "lets no meal pass without remembering you." Even the Venetian ambassador was now convinced that the negotiations would be serious. "The question will not sleep as in the past," he wrote, "since the king prefers to speed it up in order to obtain thereby increased dignity for the crown, profit for his subjects, and prestige for himself."[129]

The passage of the commission for union was not the only action taken by this Parliament in imitation of England. The English Parliament had just renewed, in rather harsher form, the Conventicle Act of 1664; Lauderdale now pushed through what he called a "clanking act"[130] against the field conventicles which had been spreading in Scotland as the extreme Presbyterians fought back against and attempted to discredit Lauderdale's religious policy. Lauderdale's Conventicle Act was a far harsher measure than its English counterpart, since it punished attendance at field conventicles with death. Charles had instructed Lauderdale to take steps against conventicles, but the severity of this law disturbed him. He was "very ill pleased" according to Burnet, but he did not repudiate his commissioner.[131] The timing of the law was a mistake. Even if, as has been suggested,[132] it was intended merely as a threat, its extravagance, taken together with the Act of Supremacy, was bound to give

---

[127] N.L.S. Mss. 597, f. 226. P.R.O., S.P. 104/176, f. 251. Mackenzie, *Memoirs*, pp. 185–87, 190–93.

[128] Five months' cess instead of three. B.M. Add. Mss. 23,134, ff. 53–59. Aug. 2, 1670, Lauderdale to Moray, *ibid.*, f. 81.

[129] *Ibid.*, f. 84. *C.S.P. Venetian* XXXVI, 265.

[130] Aug. 11, 1670, Lauderdale to Moray, Airy, *Lauderdale Papers* II, 200.

[131] *Ibid.*, pp. 185–87. Burnet, *History* I, 523.

[132] By, for example, Robertson, *Moray*, p. 145.

pause to some sections of English opinion respecting the union; it was also an admission that the earl's religious policy was not working well. Furthermore this act provided the first evidence of a tendency which was to grow in Lauderdale in the decade of the 1670's, a tendency toward impatience and violence when he was confronted with opposition. With advancing age and steadily worsening health his methods grew more brutal and less conciliatory, and so did his arrogance toward his personal friends and political allies—witness the extreme irritation he displayed toward Moray over what was no more than an honest mistake in the matter of the draft commission. As Burnet put it, writing of the year 1672, "Lauderdale's way was to govern by fits, and to pass from hot to cold ones always in extremes."[133] Many people, both at the time and since, attributed this change in the earl's character to his second wife, the beautiful and unscrupulous countess of Dysart,[134] who became Lauderdale's mistress after her husband's death and whom he married in 1672, after his own wife had died. Be that as it may, Lauderdale's changed behavior alienated his Scottish friends one after another and made him more unpopular than ever in England, until, at the end, when Charles finally withdrew his support, there was universal pleasure at his fall.

In the late summer of 1670 all this lay in the future, however; Lauderdale's immediate business was to act as the chief Scottish negotiator for union in the conferences which began in September. The other four members of the Cabal were on the English commission. Agreement was reached quickly enough on one article naming the united kingdom *Great Britain* and vesting the crown in the posterity of King James, a concession to the Scots.[135] The question of the civil and ecclesiastical laws of each country was then taken up and, after some discussion, put aside, since the Scots argued that the determination of this question hinged on the settlement of the

[133] Burnet, *History* I, 605.

[134] See, for example, *ibid.*, pp. 438–39.

[135] The original draft had read, "the uniting of the two kingdoms into one monarchy, under his majesty, his heirs and successors, inseparably." The Scots insisted upon and obtained the deletion of the phrase "and successors," since by English law it was possible for a *de facto* king, a usurper, to be a "successor." Sept. 22, 1670, Lauderdale to Tweeddale, N.L.S. Mss. 3136, f. 130. The record of the formal sessions of the commissioners and a private journal containing some information on the private meetings of the English commissioners are in Terry, *Cromwellian Union*, pp. 187–218.

major constitutional point at issue, namely, the composition of the combined Parliament.

The decision to postpone the problem of the laws was made on October 22. On that day the Scottish commissioners, in their separate meeting, began their discussion of the question of Parliamentary membership. If Mackenzie's *Memoirs* are to be trusted—he was not a member of the commission—Lauderdale put forward a plan which would have retained the separate Parliaments in being; they would meet together only in emergencies.[136] This plan would ideally serve Charles's and Lauderdale's purposes. The king, of course, would be the judge of what constituted an emergency, and so, whenever he wished, he could overwhelm the opposition in the Commons with a solid phalanx of Scottish votes. Lauder of Fountainhall, who was to oppose union in 1707 but who in 1670 was a young man just beginning his distinguished career at the bar, believed that the king's object was to overthrow the House of Commons and was sympathetic: "I confess the King has reason to wrest this excessive power out of the commons their hand, it being an unspeakable impairment of his sovereignty."[137]

The plan of occasional joint meetings of the two Parliaments may have been Lauderdale's scheme, but it was not the plan officially presented by the Scottish commissioners. Their plan, adopted on October 25 and presented on November 1, was that the two Parliaments should be combined and that all members of the Scottish Parliament should be joined with that of England. There was no chance that the English would accept this, and it seems likely that Lauderdale put this forward as a bargaining device; he could retreat from it to his real scheme of the occasional meeting. If this was his plan, it failed to work; all the English opposition to the union now made itself felt, and the king, with the treaty of Dover in his pocket, decided to abandon the scheme. The meetings of the commissioners were adjourned on November 12; on the thirteenth a warrant was issued to the Scottish treasury commission to pay their expenses. On the fourteenth Charles called the Scottish commissioners together and told them that he believed the treaty was not feasible now but

---

[136] Mackenzie, *Memoirs,* pp. 206–8.

[137] D. Crawford, ed., *Journals of Sir John Lauder, Lord Fountainhall,* Scottish History Society publication XXXVI (Edinburgh, 1900) , 229–30. The unsympathetic Presbyterian divine James Kirkton shared Fountainhall's view of Charles's purpose. B.M. Harl. Mss. 4631, II, 177–82.

that they would meet again, and before they did so, he would find a way to overcome the obstacles to success. This speech was the death knell of the union project; the commissioners never did meet again. "This was the end of the Court design," wrote the hostile James Kirkton, "a plot as wise as it was just, and as successful as it was wise, and no more of it."[138]

The failure of the negotiations for union involved no diminution in Lauderdale's favor or influence. In the month following their collapse Lauderdale's brother Charles received the lands of the late earl of Dundee, who had left no male heir, and his mistress received confirmation of her patent as countess of Dysart in her own right. Lauderdale continued to be all-powerful in Scotland and to promote Scottish interests; as an Irishman lamented late in 1671, "We want a Lauderdale, etc., at Court for the watching for Ireland as they do for Scotland."[139] And of all the ministers of the Cabal, he alone survived its dissolution with his power and influence unimpaired. He became a duke in 1672. In May, 1674, he "was never more in his Majesty's favor than at present," and a month later he received a signal mark of that favor in being created earl of Guilford in the English peerage, which gave him a seat in the House of Lords.[140] At the same time his government in Scotland became more arbitrary and brutal and grasping, as he wrestled unsuccessfully with the religious animosities which his policy of "enough rope" had helped to create and as he gave way to his natural impatience and short temper with advancing age. His anger was directed especially at his erstwhile Presbyterian friends; he "broke out into the most frantic fits of rage possible," says Burnet, and hoped they would rebel, so that he could import an Irish Catholic army to slit their throats. "Such a fury as this," comments Burnet, "seemed to furnish work for a physician rather than for any other sort of man."[141] As early as December, 1671, Arlington's secretary Joseph Williamson declared that he had dis-

---

[138] *Ibid.*, f. 182. *C.S.P.D.* X, 526. Mackenzie, *Memoirs*, pp. 210–11. There is a very long-winded tract of 1670 in the N.L.S., Mss. 31.7.13, on the whole hostile in tone to the union, which insists that, if it does come about, the entire Scottish Parliament must be incorporated. Lauderdale's proposal may well have been intended to mollify potential Scottish opponents such as the writer of this tract, clearly a lawyer.

[139] *C.S.P.D.* X, 554, 557; XI, 584–85.

[140] *Ibid.* XVI, 238, 272.

[141] Burnet, *History* I, 605.

gusted both nobility and people in Scotland and depended entirely on Charles's favor.[142] One Scottish lord, the earl of Aboyne, even turned his hand to verse to express his feelings:

> The Sceptre and the Crown
> With the gospel and the Gown
> Are now turned all to confusion.
> The Hector of State is the rascall we hate,
> And his plots we will treat in derision.[143]

As for English opinion: in August, 1673, one of Williamson's correspondents noted that Lauderdale was at Ham House and added, "Many wish him hamstringed there, that he never come further."[144]

It was unfortunate for Scotland that the union failed to materialize in 1670; the country might thereby have been spared the troubles of the last decade of the Restoration—the Highland host, the "killing time," and the rest. The chances of the plan's succeeding were never very great, however, and it seems likely that Charles himself never had very much faith in it. He was prepared to allow Lauderdale to try, because he stood to gain a great deal if it worked, and he lost nothing by failure. When the plan ran into difficulties, the king lost interest. The true way to independence of Parliament, a way which would solve all his problems, foreign and domestic, was opening before him: alliance with his cousin of France.

[142] *C.S.P.D.* XII, 45–46.
[143] Quoted in Mackenzie, *Lauderdale,* p. 345, n. 1.
[144] *C.S.P.D.* XV, 475. Ham House belonged to Lauderdale's second wife and was his residence after his liaison with her began.

Chapter 3

The Treaty of Dover

Arlington

First draw an arrant fop, from top to toe,
Whose very looks at first dash shew him so:
Give him a mean, proud Garb, a dapper Face,
A pert, dull Grin, a black patch cross his face,
Two goggle-Eyes, so clear, tho' very dead,
That one may see, thro' them, quite thro' his Head.
Let every nod of his, and subtle wink
Declare the fool would talk, but cannot think.
Let him all other fools so far surpasse
That fools themselves point at him for an ass.

This is the duke of Buckingham's "Advice to a Painter to Draw my L. A----ton, Grand Minster of State."[1] The duke was venting his spleen in his usual extravagant way against a rival whom he detested; yet the tone of the verdict has stuck. Of all the members of the Cabal, Arlington has the meanest reputation. Lauderdale and Shaftesbury have always been given high marks for political skill, however unscrupulous they may have been; Clifford was an honest man; Buckingham was immensely talented. But Arlington has been given credit for none of these things. Burnet, who

[1] *The Works of His Grace George Villiers, Late Duke of Buckingham* (London, 1715) II, 80–82.

did not like him, allows that he was well informed and loyal to his friends but calls him vain, insolent, and extravagant. And, above all, "he had the art of observing the king's temper, and managing it beyond all the men of that time."[2] The verdict of an enemy might be discounted, but Arlington's friends felt the same way. In 1670 his protégé Ralph Montagu, then ambassador in France, wrote to his patron that he had told the French that Arlington's policy was "as you see what is most your master's inclination and interest."[3] The composite picture handed down to posterity is of a dullish and pompous but ingratiating backstairs intriguer, the "Formal Ass" of the doggerel quoted at the beginning of this book, who wormed his way into the confidence of Charles, and thence into high office, and whose tenure of that office led, in the end, to disaster. The view expressed in the most recent general account of the Restoration period is typical. "He had the gift for making the right friends and discarding them at the right moment; but as he lacked courage he never rose to real greatness among the bad men of Charles's Court. . . . Always civil and obliging, his chief talent was that of anticipating and fostering what he thought to be the secret wishes of his royal master."[4]

He had known that royal master for a long time, and this was one of the sources of his influence. He was born in 1618 as plain Henry Bennet, the second son of a country gentleman and the grandson of a Jacobean official and judge who had been convicted of taking bribes. As a second son he was destined for the church; in 1635, at the age of seventeen, he matriculated at Christ Church, Oxford, the family college. He showed no taste for an ecclesiastical career. He did not take orders, as other prospective clerics did; instead, he studied the classics. The atmosphere of Oxford in the late 1630's was heavily Laudian and Royalist, so it is small wonder that young Harry, like the rest of the Bennets, was enthusiastically for the king. Like most undergraduates with literary interests, he tried his hand at poetry, and on the great question of the day, this was the result:

[2] Gilbert Burnet, *The History of My Own Time* (ed. Osmund Airy, Oxford, 1897–1900) I, 180–81. H. C. Foxcroft, ed., *A Supplement to Burnet's History of My Own Time* (London, 1902), pp. 66–67.

[3] H.M.C., *Mss. of the Duke of Buccleuch and Queensberry* (London, 1899) I, 488.

[4] David Ogg, *England in the Reign of Charles II* (2nd ed., Oxford, 1955) I, 327.

> May all our Kings Designes succeed
> And yet no loyall Subject bleed,
> But, in their stead, let Rebels feele
> The sharpest anger of his steele;
> Or, like to Cadmus ofspring bred,
> Their blood by one another shed.[5]

He himself, though anxious to work for the king's cause, had no
mind to bleed for it; he had nothing of the soldier in him, and for
the most part he stayed away from the fighting during the civil war.
He did get involved in one cavalry skirmish in 1644 and received a
saber cut over the bridge of his nose which left a permanent scar. In
later years he always wore a black patch over this scar, as a permanent reminder to Charles II and to everyone else that he had been
wounded in the royal martyr's service.

Bennet's real métier was not soldiering, but politics. In 1643, at
the age of twenty-five, he was taken into the service of the junior
secretary of state, Lord Digby. He spent the next few years chiefly as
a messenger. One of his journeys, in the winter before Naseby, took
him out of England; he was not to return for sixteen years. He did
his job well and tactfully—he was always tactful—and so he earned a
promotion. At the end of 1648 he became secretary to the young
duke of York. This was an important piece of good fortune, because,
while Bennet did not get on well with James, who was only half his
age, the appointment threw him into close association with the
exiled king. He made the most of his opportunity, which came in the
winter of 1651. Charles was in Paris after the disappointments of his
Scottish adventure, which had ended so ruinously at Worcester; in
reaction against the disaster—the king was just twenty-one—he surrounded himself with a group of amusing and frivolous young men.
Bennet was one of them. Not that he was frivolous; he was too coldly
ambitious for that. But he could pretend to be; he was highly
adaptable. With Charles he could be gay; with the older men in
Charles's confidence, like Hyde and Ormonde, he could be both
grave and deferential. Indeed, Hyde thought well of the young man;
he was taken in, he later said: "He [Bennet] practised such a kind of
civility, and had such a mean in making professions that they were

---

[5] Quoted in V. Barbour, *Henry Bennet, Earl of Arlington* (Washington, D.C., 1914), p. 7. My debt to Miss Barbour for the following account of
Arlington's early life will be obvious to all who have read her excellent book.

oftentimes mistaken for friendship, which he never meant, or was guilty of to any man."[6]

Bennet and Hyde became political enemies after the Restoration, but there was never to be a breach between Bennet and the king. The friendship formed in that bitter winter of discontent was occasionally to be strained, but never to be shattered. Temperamentally, they were alike in many ways. Both were affable and easy to get along with when they chose to be; both were patient and intelligent and well informed; both were fertile in immediate expedients but unable to take a long view; both could be tenacious when their minds were made up. The similarity extended so far that they both accepted Roman Catholicism on their deathbeds. Charles genuinely liked Bennet, just as he did Lauderdale. The coarse and brutal Scotsman and the polished and smooth-tongued diplomatist were very different in most ways, but one quality they shared which gave them the longest tenure of office of any of Charles's great ministers of state: they were absolutely dependable. In Bennet's case, this was because his was the perfect courtier's mentality. It accounts for his instinctive and unhesitating royalism in the civil war. It accounts for his continual outward acquiescence in his master's policies, even when he disagreed with them. Charles doubtless never saw the poem Bennet wrote in his Oxford days, but he did not have to see it to discern Bennet's sentiments:

> Y'have liv'd in Court, where wit and language flow,
> Where Iudgements thrive, and where true maners grow;
> Where great and good are seene in ther first springs,
> The breasts of Princes, and the minds of Kings:
> Where beauty shines cloath'd in her brightest rayes,
> To gaine all loves, all wonder, and all praise.[7]

It is this sense of awe in the presence of the great that makes the perfect courtier. The duke of Ormonde once remarked of Arlington that he "expected to be treated as if he had been born with a blue ribbon, forgetting Harry Bennet that was but a very little gentleman."[8] Ormonde was quite wrong. Arlington, though he became an

---

[6] *State Papers Collected by Edward, Earl of Clarendon* (Oxford, 1767–86) III, Supplement, lxxxi.

[7] Quoted in Barbour, *Arlington*, p. 8.

[8] Lady Burghclere, *The Life of James, First Duke of Ormonde* (London, 1912) II, 80.

earl and a Knight of the Garter, though he married into the Orange family, though his only child married one of Charles's bastards, never forgot that he began as a very little gentleman. His pride, which everybody remarked on,[9] was the pride of a man who fears a snub. His extravagant passion for building was that of a man who wants a tangible monument. His periodic fear for his job was not the alarm of the constitutionally timid man, as has often been said; it was the alarm of the *arriviste*. Since he was that sort of man, King Charles, who was as shrewd a reader of character as ever sat on the English throne, knew that, plain Harry Bennet or earl of Arlington, K.G., he was absolutely reliable.

Bennet might be his young master's friend after 1651, but the rewards the exiled court could offer were almost nonexistent. Bennet perforce remained the duke of York's secretary, a task which became more and more awkward as the friction between the brothers increased. The king and Bennet corresponded when they were apart; the tone of the letters shows the easy, bantering intimacy which had developed. "My clothes are come," wrote the king in the summer of 1655, "and I like them very well, all but the sword, which is the worst that I ever saw. I suspect very much that it was you made the choice. Therefore you have no other way to recover your judgment in that particular, but to make choice of a better." And later that summer, "[we] pass our time as well as people can do that have no more money, for we dance, and play as if we had taken the plate-fleet."[10]

At the end of 1656 came the first important turning point in Bennet's career: Charles appointed him as resident to Spain. In October, 1655, Cromwell had struck his bargain with France, so Spain and the exiled court found themselves flung together as partners. The consequence was a treaty signed in April, 1656, by which the Spanish government promised Charles men, money, and supplies to regain his throne, in return for various concessions when that happy event was accomplished. As Bennet was to discover, Spain had no men or money to spare for this purpose, and the treaty was never

[9] See, for example, W. E. Buckley, ed., *Memoirs of Thomas, Earl of Ailesbury, Written by Himself* (Roxburghe Club ed., Westminster, 1890) I, 14. In this passage Ailesbury declares that Bennet's black patch covered a "pretended wound."

[10] Arthur Bryant, ed., *The Letters, Speeches, and Declarations of King Charles II* (London, 1935), p. 39. Thomas Brown, ed., *Miscellanea Aulica* (London, 1702), p. 117.

implemented. So his mission to Spain was a failure, a frustrating failure to one who was so anxious to please and to impress. Bennet nevertheless profited a great deal from his years at the court of the moribund Philip IV. In the first place, he learned the diplomatist's trade: how to be patient, how to read between the lines of politicians' conversation, how to assess a false front, and how to erect one, since both Charles and the Spanish government were in the same position, that of a bankrupt who is hopefully trying to squeeze some advantage out of a fellow unfortunate. Bennet also learned the language—he was good at languages, one of the few men in Charles's entourage who was.

Bennet got more than this invaluable experience out of Spain; he also got the main lines of his future foreign policy. The appalling weakness of the Spanish empire was perfectly apparent to him; so, too, was the ominously growing strength of France. The aggressive designs of France and of her Dutch ally were equally obvious. Out of this situation England could make her profit. Spain was too feeble to protect herself any longer; the Peace of the Pyrenees, at the conclusion of which Bennet was present, showed that. England would protect her from the predatory Franco-Dutch combination and in return would receive trading concessions in the Spanish empire.

With the Restoration Bennet became very eager to return to England to reap his reward. He was not recalled until late January, 1661; it was spring before he got back. By this time pickings were thin; he did get a bedchamber post and a seat in the House of Commons, which Clarendon, at the king's wish, provided for him. He had to decide very quickly whether to become a follower of Clarendon, who was apparently all-powerful in the government, or to join the group of Clarendon's enemies, who clustered around the countess of Castlemaine. He joined the opposition, partly because it was led, for the moment, by his old patron Lord Digby, now earl of Bristol, partly because he disapproved of Clarendon's pro-French foreign policy, which was about to be implemented by the king's marriage to a Portuguese princess. Bennet's first intervention in politics after his return was to join with Bristol in a futile effort to prevent the marriage.[11]

Clarendon, who hated opposition and who also bore grudges, now

[11] May 13/23, 1661, mémoire for d'Estrades, J. J. Jusserand, ed., *Receuil des instructions données aux ambassadeurs de France, Angleterre* (Paris, 1929) I, 270–71.

became Bennet's bitter enemy, but he could not prevent the king's friend's rise. In August, 1661, Bennet got the privy purse, about the only important post previously undistributed, in preference to Clarendon's nominee. Bennet wanted a diplomatic post, however, and early in 1662 he begged the king to appoint him ambassador to France. This prospect was upsetting not only to Clarendon but also to Louis XIV, who rightly regarded Bennet as a partisan of Spain, and the idea was dropped after Louis had indicated that this appointment would not be satisfactory to him.[12] It was fortunate for Bennet that this was the French king's attitude; if he had gone off to Paris as ambassador in the spring of 1662, it is very unlikely that he would have been appointed secretary of state in October.

Samuel Pepys and the other wiseacres who hung about on the fringes of the inner ring at court had an immediate explanation for this startling appointment, startling in that Bennet was the first avowed opponent of Clarendon to get an office on the policy-making level in the English government: petticoat politics. "Here I am told how things go at Court," wrote Pepys when he heard the news, "that the young men get uppermost, and the old, serious lords are out of favour . . . none in Court hath more the King's ear now than Sir Charles Barkeley and Sir H. Bennet, and my Lady Castlemaine."[13] This explanation has been parroted by historians because it seems so typical of the way a man like Charles would operate. The fact of the matter was that an efficient and energetic secretary was badly needed. The man Bennet replaced, Sir Edward Nicholas, a relic of Charles I's official family, was old and tired; the other secretary, Sir William Morice, was a nonentity who owed his position to his relationship to Monck. The secretaries' duties were enormous. Since all correspondence, foreign and domestic, colonial and Irish, flowed through their hands, they were in a position to influence policy in all these areas, and Bennet, during his twelve-year tenure, certainly did so. The Venetian ambassador's assessment of the reasons for his appointment hits closer to the mark than does Pepys's: "a man of wit and ability, affable and courteous, possessing several languages,

[12] *Ibid.*, p. 271 n.

[13] *The Diary of Samuel Pepys* (ed. H. B. Wheatley, London, 1926), Oct. 17, 1662. The question of age is rather misleading. Bennet at the time of his appointment was forty-four, hardly in the first flush of youth. There was less distance in age between him and Clarendon (fifty-three) than between him and Charles (thirty-two).

greatly beloved by the king, and competent for his position from his knowledge of the interests of foreign princes."[14]

Getting into office was one thing; keeping it, which of course meant keeping the king's favor, was quite another. All of Charles's officials had to pay a good deal of attention to the shifting winds of sentiment at court and to the intrigues of their rivals. Bennet was an old hand at this game, and he played it skillfully, though without much real enjoyment. He may have had the courtier's temperament, but the kind of court he preferred was the decorous, indeed pompous, system of the Escorial, rather than the raffish disorderliness of Whitehall. He enjoyed entertaining, and after his marriage in 1666 he and his wife were known for their lavish dinner parties. But he did not enjoy drinking and rowdiness; he was not a woman chaser; he was not even much interested in the theater. He played the game as it had to be played; for example, he was on the notorious committee to get Mistress Stewart for the king.[15] But he would have preferred the game to be other than it was. "We are fallen into a strange age," he wrote to Sir William Temple in 1668, "wherein even the appearance of good morality is become ridiculous."[16]

The chief threat to the new secretary's tenure of office was Lord Chancellor Clarendon himself, who now hated him venomously. He was, writes Clarendon, "very odious generally . . . for his insolent carriage towards all men, and for the manner of his getting into . . . office by dispossessing an old faithful servant."[17] Bennet naturally struck back when he could; one of the most galling of his successes was Charles's order that Clarendon make use of Bennet, William Coventry, Clifford, and a west-country gentleman named Winston Churchill, the father of the future duke of Marlborough, as a committee for the management of Parliament, although Bennet, in Clarendon's opinion, "knew no more of the constitution and laws of England than he did of China."[18] And, indeed, Bennet seems to have paid very little attention to Parliamentary management, especially

[14] A. B. Hinds, *et al.*, eds., *Calendar of State Papers, Venetian* (henceforth *C.S.P. Venetian*) (London 1864–1947) XXXIII, 203.

[15] Pepys, *Diary*, Nov. 9, 1663.

[16] T. Bebington, ed., *The Right Honourable the Earl of Arlington's Letters to Sir William Temple, Bart.* (vol. I) , *and to the Several Ambassadors to Spain* (vol. II) (London, 1701) I, 338.

[17] Edward, Earl of Clarendon, *A Continuation of His History of the Great Rebellion* (Oxford, 1857) II, 486.

[18] *Ibid.* I, 615.

after his elevation to the peerage in 1665. Most of the responsibility was delegated to his protégé Clifford. He was happier when Parliament was not in session. "Although there be safety (as Solomon says) in a multitude of Counsellors," he wrote to Ormonde in 1664, "yet we cannot but think ourselves at ease when we are fairly rid of them."[19]

As secretary, Bennet had a great deal to do with domestic administration; toward domestic problems his attitude was cautious to the point of timidity. This was why he preferred that Parliament not be in session: Parliament was the focus of popular discontent. Bennet had no desire to go on his travels again; like most returned emigrés, he was very nervous about the possibility of insurrection, "which the foolish and discontented people are apt every day to threaten and apprehend," as he wrote Ormonde in November, 1662, about a month after he took office.[20] Bennet always kept his ear close to the ground; the *Calendar of State Papers, Domestic* is full of the letters of his agents, most of them sent to his indefatigable secretary, Joseph Williamson, reporting on the state of public opinion in the countryside. Bennet was concerned not only to sample public opinion but also to mold it; in 1666 Williamson, with his backing, launched the *London Gazette,* which became the official record of the doings of the government. Bennet was so much interested in the *Gazette* that he had one of Williamson's clerks read it to him in the morning as he was getting dressed.[21]

Bennet's fear of popular disturbances led him constantly to search for the popular policy, particularly in domestic affairs. He was always very much alarmed by any move which might lead to difficulties at home; for this reason he opposed concessions to the Catholics, particularly after he had had his fingers burned in the matter of the indulgence in 1663. As Burnet admits, "in the whole course of his ministry he seemed to have made it a maxim, that the king ought to shew no favour to popery, but that all his affairs would be spoiled if ever he turned that way."[22] As with this, so with other matters: caution was the byword.

Bennet was Clarendon's steady enemy, and no man rejoiced more

[19] Brown, *Miscellanea Aulica,* p. 357.
[20] *Ibid.,* p. 280.
[21] M. A. E. Green, *et al.,* eds., *Calendar of State Papers Domestic, Charles II* (henceforth *C.S.P.D.*) (London, 1860ff.) VIII, 550.
[22] Burnet, *History* I, 180.

to see the chancellor fall. Clarendon himself tells the story of looking up at the windows of Whitehall as he was leaving after one of his last interviews with the king and seeing the secretary and Lady Castlemaine laughing at him.[23] The chancellor's dismissal did not make his rival's position secure, however. Buckingham was just as hostile as Clarendon had ever been and with good cause—the secretary had been the moving spirit behind the plan to ruin Buckingham by the trumped-up charge of casting the king's horoscope—and Buckingham was far more dangerous, since he was the king's boon companion and could always get the king's ear. Every proposal made by the secretary in foreign policy was a product of an assessment not only of England's power position abroad, but also of the impact the proposal would have on England's domestic tranquillity and on his personal position vis-à-vis his rivals, actual or potential, for the king's favor. The resulting complexities were frequently staggering.

II

In the third quarter of the seventeenth century English foreign policy was moving toward one of those massive changes of direction which occur at long intervals in the international relations of major states. The last such great change, the one which had set the pattern which still existed in the 1660's, had taken place in the middle years of the reign of Elizabeth, when Spain became clearly identified as the national enemy and when, therefore, France and King Philip II's rebellious subjects in the Netherlands became, potentially, friends and allies. The power position in Europe had substantially altered since Elizabethan times; it had altered, in fact, far more rapidly than had men's minds. The earl of Clarendon, Elizabethan in so many ways, was so in respect to foreign policy too. He believed in and consistently worked for an alliance with France. The chancellor's skill in negotiation was not very great; as Burnet said, he never seemed to understand foreign affairs.[24] His bungling diplomacy in such questions as the sale of Dunkirk in 1662 made it appear that England was a French satellite and effectively concealed from the public the potential advantages of the connection with France.

King Charles, who was not in the least Elizabethan, also favored

[23] Clarendon, *Continuation* II, 451.
[24] Burnet, *History* I, 169. On this point Burnet may have taken his opinion from Lauderdale; see Foxcroft, *Supplement to Burnet's History*, p. 98.

friendship with France, though for utterly different reasons. The key to Charles's approach to foreign affairs lay in his attitude to the Dutch. The Dutch had long since ceased to be the suppliant clients they had been in the days of William the Silent; now they were England's fiercest commercial and colonial rivals. The growing Anglo-Dutch rivalry made an indelible impression on the mind of the king, who was deeply interested in maritime and naval affairs. Charles believed, and the conviction grew on him with the years, that the United Provinces were the permanent and unalterable enemies of England. As the Venetian ambassador put it in 1672, "The king is convinced that the hatred of the Dutch for England is hereditary, that it increased because of trade and became implacable owing to the pretensions of the United Provinces."[25] If permanent Anglo-Dutch hostility is taken as axiomatic, the king's attitude toward France becomes easy enough to understand. It was France which had the choice of allies. As Charles remarked to his council in 1672, "the French will have us or Holland always with them, and if we take them not, Holland will have them."[26]

Bennet's approach to foreign policy was entirely different. It was based on a belief, not in the permanent hostility of the Dutch but rather, in the desirability of alliance with Spain. Given the aggressive designs of Louis XIV on Spain, this policy and that of Charles were incompatible in the long run. Sooner or later war would come between France and Spain, and so, sooner or later, England would have to choose. But in 1662 there was no war, and so, for the moment, a policy of friendliness toward Spain could be followed without disrupting the ties with France which Charles and Clarendon were so anxious to maintain. The one stumbling block was Portugal, whose independence Spain persistently refused to acknowledge. Bennet, in the interests of his pro-Spanish policy, had vainly opposed the Portuguese marriage alliance. In the early years of his tenure as secretary he was encouraged by the king and Clarendon to do what he could with reference to Spain, but always with the proviso that Portuguese interests must be protected. It was a ruinous condition to lay on the negotiations.

Bennet's policy under these circumstances was, somehow or other,

---

[25] *C.S.P. Venetian* XXXVII, 244.

[26] P.R.O., S.P. 104/177, f. 84. For an excellent recent study of Anglo-Dutch relations to 1667 see Charles Wilson, *Profit and Power* (London, 1957).

to patch up an agreement between Spain and Portugal, a line not much favored by Clarendon, who preferred overt support of Portugal in association with France.[27] In January, 1664, Sir Richard Fanshawe, who had been ambassador in Lisbon, was sent to Madrid with instructions to persuade or coerce Philip IV into settling with Portugal and to negotiate a commercial treaty, which would include freedom of trade in the West Indies for English ships and a monopoly of the slave trade to the Spanish colonies for the Royal African Company.[28] This was the price of English friendship: high, but not excessive, in Bennet's view, given Spain's weakness and her perilous diplomatic position.[29] The Spanish government was not convinced. To Bennet's intense exasperation, it would not look facts in the face and stubbornly refused to put itself in his hands.

Across these negotiations and the simultaneous negotiations for a commercial treaty with France there cut the second Dutch war. Bennet's attitude toward this war is not entirely clear. Cautious as he was, his inclination was always to favor peace. On the other hand, the war party was led by his friends, foremost among whom was Clifford, and his enemy Clarendon was openly opposed to war. Bennet at this stage leaned to the anti-Dutch side. The idea of trying conclusions with the Dutch once again was a popular notion with the country at large, and Bennet believed always in the importance of public support to the success of any line in foreign policy. He was particularly concerned with the opinions of the people who counted, the Parliamentary classes: landed gentry, lawyers, businessmen. It was the merchant community which was most eager to renew the attack on the Dutch. The first Dutch war had been highly profitable to English businessmen; they were hopeful that a second one would be still more so. In November, 1664, the normally tightfisted House of Commons voted the enormous sum of £2,500,000 to equip the fleet. Clarendon had proposed asking

[27] See the letters to Sir Richard Fanshawe written by Bennet and Clarendon in April and May, 1663, in H.M.C., *Mss. of J. M. Heathcote* (London, 1899), pp. 75–77, 87–90.

[28] Bebington, *Arlington's Letters* II, 4–9. Bennet, along with most other prominent courtiers, was a shareholder in the African Company. For the significance of this company in connection with the English attitude toward Spain see A. P. Thornton, *West-India Policy Under the Restoration* (Oxford, 1956), pp. 79–80.

[29] See Oct. 6, 1664, Bennet to Fanshawe, Bebington, *Arlington's Letters* II, 51–53.

for this huge amount, over the protests of Bennet and Coventry, in order to dampen the popular enthusiasm for war, and his plan had backfired. Clifford reported that "there was not one person but freely declared for the war, whatever else his motion tended unto"— something of an exaggeration.[30] This vote was ample proof for Bennet, if any more was needed, of the popularity of the war policy, a popularity which he had helped to foster by authorizing the publication of Thomas Mun's famous treatise, *England's Treasure by Foreign Trade*, in 1664, as the crisis with the Dutch approached.[31] Yet it is possible that he hoped to avoid war after all. Sir George Downing, currently ambassador at The Hague and generally regarded at the time as the best-informed Englishman on Dutch affairs, kept assuring his government that at the last minute the Dutch would back down. It may well be that Bennet believed him.[32]

The war brought the aspiring secretary one thing he had always wanted: a peerage. At the end of 1665 he became Baron Arlington, after the town of Harlington in Sussex, where he had spent his childhood. He had thought of calling himself Lord Bennet but decided that this did not have a very aristocratic ring, and besides, according to the Oxford antiquary Anthony Wood, "there was an old bawd at Westminster called 'lady Benet.'"[33] The war also saw the secretary take a wife, a step he may well have postponed until his elevation to the peerage allowed him to aim high. The lady he won was a wealthy Netherlander, Isabella van Beverwaert, the daughter of a bastard son of Prince Maurice; her sister was married to Arlington's good friend the earl of Ossory, Ormonde's eldest son. She turned out to be an ideal wife for the somewhat elderly bridegroom—he was forty-eight—not only because of her financial and social standing, but also because she loved to entertain. Their friend John Evelyn wrote of them in 1677, after a visit to their great house at Euston, "They love fine things and to live easily, pompously, but very hospitable; but with so vast expense as plunges

[30] Nov. 25, 1664, Clifford to Henry Coventry, B.M. Add. Mss. 32,094, ff. 24–27.

[31] Wilson, *Profit and Power*, p. 125.

[32] My interpretation of Bennet's attitude to the war in general follows that of Miss Barbour, *Arlington*, pp. 76ff.

[33] Andrew Clark, ed., *The Life and Times of Anthony Wood* (Oxford, 1892) II, 7.

my Lord into debt exceedingly"—one reason why Arlington, who was not born to wealth, found it necessary to cling to office, for, as Evelyn went on to say, "he knows not how to retrench."[34] The only child of the marriage was a daughter, Isabella, who eventually became the wife of one of Charles's bastards, the duke of Grafton, a marriage which delighted Arlington's parvenu heart.

In retrospect, Arlington's Dutch wife seemed to be the only English gain from the war, at least according to Andrew Marvell, who wrote in 1666:

> Our sum amounts yet only to have won
> A Bastard Orange for pimp Arlington.[35]

And, indeed, the war was a failure in almost every way, and for no one more than for Arlington. The diplomatic problem presented by the war was that posed by most wars: to find allies for oneself and to deny them to the enemy. On both counts Arlington failed. The only active ally England found was the bellicose but useless bishop of Münster, who had to be subsidized and whose vaunted incendiary projectiles struck no terror into the hearts of the Dutch.[36] There is a decidedly Offenbachian flavor about the Münster affair; far less entertaining was Arlington's inability either to win the alliance of Spain or to prevent the intervention of France on the side of the Dutch. He failed because he was overreached by Louis XIV.

The French king was not pleased by the outbreak of the Anglo-Dutch war; it threatened to complicate his plans. He was eagerly awaiting the death of his father-in-law, King Philip IV of Spain; all the diplomatists of Europe knew that this would be the occasion for some sort of French claim on Spain. It was therefore very much to Louis' advantage to see to it that when the moment came Spain was diplomatically isolated. Hitherto he had done well; he was allied with Holland, on good terms with his cousin of England, and he was unofficially encouraging the Portuguese. The emperor was too weak and too far away to throw his weight effectively against France without the aid of one of the two maritime powers. Then came the

---

[34] E. S. DeBeer, ed., *The Diary of John Evelyn* (Oxford, 1958) IV, 118–19.

[35] George deF. Lord, ed., *Poems on Affairs of State* (New Haven, 1963) I (1660–78), 51.

[36] For the bishop of Münster see the article by C. Brinkmann "Charles II and the Bishop of Münster in the Anglo-Dutch War of 1665–1666," *English Historical Review* XXI (1906), 686–98.

Anglo-Dutch war, which virtually guaranteed the end of Spain's isolation, since, if the war were still going on when Louis struck at Spain, one of the two belligerents would be available to her.

Under these circumstances Louis' policy, from the end of 1664 on, was either to prevent the war if he could, or failing this, to bring it to a quick end. For this purpose he sent a distinguished mission to England, the *célèbre ambassade*. It got nowhere. Arlington was prepared to spin out negotiations with the French, in order to give them an excuse for not joining the Dutch, but he opposed any concessions to them. He did not favor accepting their offer of mediation, on the ground that the London merchants, who were spoiling for a fight, might be angered and refuse further loans to the government.[37] The French, he felt, were bluffing in threatening to side with the Dutch. Their real purpose was to attack the Spanish Netherlands; therefore they would not complicate their problems by attacking England as well.[38] This was clear to Arlington; it would soon be clear enough to Spain, too, and Spain would be driven to accept the English alliance on English terms. Arlington's real attitude toward the French can be seen from the action of the prize commission, of which he was a member. It adopted a set of rules on the carrying of enemy goods by neutral ships which, if strictly enforced, would seriously hamper French commerce. The cautious secretary would hardly have permitted this if he had believed that there was any substance to the French warnings and threats.[39]

Arlington completely failed to fathom the French tactics, which were far more subtle than he imagined. With the failure of the *célèbre ambassade* Louis XIV decided to alter his course somewhat. He formally declared war on England at the beginning of 1666, but he had no intention of doing any serious fighting. This move was a

[37] Barbour, *Arlington*, p. 84, n. 39. See also Aug. 9, 1665, William Coventry to Arlington, *C.S.P.D.* IV, 510. In 1664 the Common Council of the City of London, in its anti-Dutch enthusiasm, had lent the government £100,000. C. H. Hartmann, *Clifford of the Cabal* (London, 1937), p. 35.

[38] On December 27, 1665, Fanshawe wrote that it was believed in Madrid that France had laid claim to Brabant and Hainault. Bebington, *Arlington's Letters* II, 161–63.

[39] Arlington may have been misled to some extent by the English ambassador in Paris, Lord Holles, who reported widespread division and discontent in France. See, for instance, his letters of October 11/21 and 18/28, 1665, in T. H. Lister, *Life and Administration of Edward, First Earl of Clarendon* (London, 1838) III, 409–10, 413–14.

perfect example of Clausewitz' aphorism about war and diplomacy. It would put the Dutch under obligation to Louis and bring them to the peace table when he so wished. It would dishearten the English and make them less eager for further fighting, but it would not alienate them completely. Above all, it would disrupt English diplomatic strategy in Spain.

Spain was the crucial diplomatic battleground of this war, and the French success there was decisive. Only if Spain were won could Arlington's broader scheme of a coalition including the empire, various German princes, and the Scandinavian countries be realized. At the beginning of the war Arlington's plan was to win the Spanish by a combination of promises and threats, the promise being to help Spain resist French pressure and patch up an agreement with Portugal, with the threat that, if Spain was recalcitrant, it would be a simple matter for England to strike a bargain with France at Spanish expense. Arlington remained hopeful throughout the summer and fall of 1665; his optimism reached its peak after the death of Philip IV in September, which, he thought, would certainly frighten Spain into compliance.[40] He failed to realize that the divided and incompetent regency for the boy-king Charles II of Spain was motivated chiefly by its paralyzing fear of a French attack. The Spanish were therefore much relieved by Louis XIV's declaration of war on England and took at face value the smooth assurances of his ambassador in Madrid that France had no aggressive designs on them. Their attitude toward England hardened, and in negotiation with the earl of Sandwich, a friend of Arlington's who replaced Fanshawe as ambassador in 1666, they began to talk of English surrender of Tangier and Jamaica and English abandonment of Portugal as the indispensable conditions of a treaty.

Arlington's optimism was rather slow to vanish. In March, 1666, he was still hopeful, but by April he had become discouraged; it was impossible to find friends anywhere, he wrote to Fanshawe, when France thwarted him at every turn. By August he was ready to throw in his hand. He was afraid that France might stir up a revolt in Ireland, and as for Spain, he was utterly exasperated. He told Sandwich that if Spain continued to be unreasonable, he should confine himself to the commercial treaty; to Sir William Temple, the Eng-

[40] See his letter of November 4, 1665, to Fanshawe, Bebington, *Arlington's Letters* II, 96–100.

lish resident at Brussels, he complained that Spanish fatuity would make England pro-French, "contrary to our intentions." Spanish blindness and her desperate hope that the French promises were genuine had baffled Arlington's schemes.[41]

Several months later, in May, 1667, England got from Spain everything Arlington had originally wanted: a commercial treaty, a promise to accept English mediation to arrange a long-term truce with Portugal, and a reciprocal promise not to aid the other power's enemies. This reversal of Spanish policy was owing to their forcible awakening to the true nature of French designs: in the spring of 1667 Louis XIV, perhaps no longer much caring whether England and Holland made peace or not, launched what he hoped would be a military promenade into the Spanish Netherlands which, he said, were the rightful property of his wife. Spain's *volte-face* came too late to alter the result of the Dutch war. June was to see the naval disaster in the Medway, and in July peace was made at Breda. A month or so later the earl of Clarendon was dismissed, the scapegoat of a war he never wanted, and Arlington, in spite of his conspicuous lack of diplomatic success during the war, emerged as the king's chief adviser in foreign policy.

III

The prospect which lay before the secretary in the late summer of 1667 was anything but bright. The war had been a disaster and had ended with a resounding national humiliation. The government's financial condition was precarious in the extreme, and its prestige at home and abroad was at a low ebb. It had no firm friend among the powers of western and northern Europe; the commercial treaty with Spain, although of great potential value, had been born of Spanish desperation rather than a conviction of mutual interest. Furthermore, England's hands were nominally tied; she was pledged to both Spain *and* France not to aid the enemies of the other. In April, 1667, Charles had privately assured Louis XIV that his negotiations with

[41] Mar. 13, Aug. 25, 1666, Arlington to Ormonde, Brown, *Miscellanea Aulica*, pp. 387–88, 414–15. Apr. 26, 1666, Arlington to Fanshawe, Bebington, *Arlington's Letters* II, 173–75. Aug. 23, 1666, Arlington to Sandwich, *ibid.*, pp. 190–91. Aug. 27, 1666, Arlington to Temple, *ibid.* I, 94. For a concise account of Anglo-Spanish relations during the Dutch war, see Thornton, *West-India Policy*, pp. 89–100. See also K. Feiling, *British Foreign Policy 1660–1672* (London, 1930), pp. 167–83.

Spain were purely commercial, that he would make no agreement directed against France for a year, and that during that year he would negotiate an alliance with France.[42]

Arlington was not in the mood for an adventurous policy after the war. On August 8, 1667, he wrote to Sandwich that the uncertain domestic situation precluded any new foreign commitments; he felt the same way on October 31, two months after that situation had been clarified by Clarendon's fall. English opinion was hostile to France, he reported, but an actively anti-French policy was impossible without a Parliamentary subsidy, which was not likely to be forthcoming.[43] Part of Arlington's uncertainty was personal; his campaign against his rival Buckingham based on the astrology charge had just fallen through, and he was himself under attack for his part in the division of the fleet which had allowed the Dutch to maul Monck's squadron in the Four Days' Battle in June, 1666. Caution was the watchword, then, but not necessarily neutrality. England could scarcely remain indifferent to the outcome of any contest involving the Low Countries. Some sort of policy must be formulated toward the Franco-Spanish war, and very soon, if France was not to be allowed to win by default.

Charles and Arlington and everyone else agreed that England's position could never be improved until the Franco-Dutch connection was shattered. The alliance between the strongest commercial state in Europe and the state with the greatest land army was irresistible as long as it held together, and it was acutely dangerous for England. As Arlington put it in a letter to Temple in August, "if France and Holland remain as united after the peace, as they were during the treaty of it, we are not secure that they may not, taking advantage of our distempers at home, break out again upon us."[44] The alliance could be broken only if the interests of the partners diverged sufficiently to make a connection with England seem more attractive than continuation of the *status quo*. In the French invasion of Flanders Arlington, prompted by Temple and by Baron

[42] F. A. M. Mignet, ed., *Négociations relatives à la succession d'Espagne sous Louis XIV* (Paris, 1835–42) II, 43. The concessions were not all on one side; Louis made a reciprocal pledge and agreed to make peace on the basis of the *status quo ante*, which meant returning the island of St. Christopher to England. *Ibid.*, pp. 44–45.

[43] Bebington, *Arlington's Letters* II, 232, 264–65.

[44] *Ibid.* I, 179–80.

Lisola, the anti-French agent of the emperor, thought he saw the lever to pry the alliance apart.

During the war Arlington had tried intermittently to make a separate peace with the Dutch; his efforts had got nowhere. Then, in May, 1667, Temple, from Brussels, sent to Arlington what purported to be a Spanish analysis of English policy but which may simply have reflected Temple's own wishes. England, wrote Temple, was playing a deep game; her plan, after peace was made with Holland and France, was to offer to mediate in the war between France and Spain and, on receiving the expected French refusal, to side with Spain, in alliance with the Dutch, and defeat France. In August Lisola assured the secretary that Holland was ready to break with France to keep Flanders out of French hands.[45]

The policy of breaking the Franco-Dutch alliance by means of an agreement with the Dutch appealed very strongly to Arlington. The threat to Spain and the Spanish empire, that potential commercial gold mine, came from France, rather than the Dutch. So, too, did the threat to the balance of power; the French ambassador in London reported a general fear that France was aiming at universal monarchy, a fear certainly shared by Arlington and admitted even by Buckingham, who was now pro-French because Arlington was not.[46] Popular opinion was very anti-French, a factor which always counted heavily with Arlington. When the French invaded Flanders in May, 1667, the Spanish ambassador began to raise volunteers. "It is not credible" wrote Arlington to Temple, "how willingly men, of all qualities, run into the Spanish service, and openly protest against the French."[47] Arlington made no secret of the fact that he, too, was against the French. The Spanish ambassador Molina rejoiced at Clarendon's fall and offered Arlington the support of the Parliamentary votes he had bought. The marquis de Ruvigny, Louis XIV's envoy, was correspondingly gloomy. Arlington, he wrote, "would join with the devil to ruin an enemy." To Charles he complained that some of the English council were partisans of Spain; the king

[45] May 17/27, 1667, Temple to Arlington, *The Works of Sir William Temple* (London, 1814) I, 273–74. Aug. 2, 1667, Arlington to Temple, Bebington, *Arlington's Letters* I, 179–80.

[46] Sept. 9/19, 1667, Ruvigny to Lionne, Mignet, *Négociations* II, 513–14. See also L. von Ranke, *History of England Principally in the Seventeenth Century* (Oxford, 1875) III, 523.

[47] Bebington, *Arlington's Letters* I, 165–66.

rejoined that "Lord Arlington was not as black as people made him out to be." The French did not agree, and Ruvigny, who in October, 1667, described Arlington as "Espagnol par lui-même et Hollandais par sa femme," actually thought at one time of asking Charles to exclude Arlington from all discussions dealing with foreign affairs.[48]

In his conversation with Ruvigny, King Charles remarked that while most of his advisers and Parliament feared the French, he personally favored a close alliance with King Louis.[49] This was not mere politeness on Charles's part. He agreed with Arlington that the Franco-Dutch alliance had to be broken. But he also believed that no satisfactory permanent agreement could be made with the Dutch. He did not give the same weight to the preservation of the decaying Spanish monarchy as Arlington did, because he did not feel that French aggrandizement on the European continent was a danger to England. French naval and commercial aggrandizement was another matter. As he wrote to his sister Henrietta, the wife of Louis XIV's brother, in September, 1668, the principal obstacle to Anglo-French friendship was "the great application there is at this time in France to establish trade and to be very considerable at sea, which is so jealous a point to us here who can be only considerable by our trade and power by sea, as any steps that France makes that way must . . . be a great hinderance to an entire friendship . . . it must be dangerous to me at home to make an entire league till first the great and principal interest of this nation be secured which is trade."[50]

Arlington would have found no fault with these sentiments. Where they differed was over the question of means. Charles wanted an alliance with France, provided that England's commercial and naval interests could be safeguarded and provided it could be given an anti-Dutch edge. These two provisos complemented each other in the king's mind: if Holland were thoroughly pulverized and her commercial preeminence destroyed, England would acquire the lion's share of the carrying trade the Dutch relinquished.

So the king himself, with his pro-French proclivities, was the chief

[48] Sept. 12/22, 1667, Ruvigny to Lionne, Mignet, *Négociations* II, 514–16. Ranke, *History* III, 163. L. André, *Louis XIV et l'Europe* (Paris, 1950), p. 109. Barbour, *Arlington*, p. 128. Feiling, *British Foreign Policy*, p. 79.

[49] Mignet, *Négociations* II, 514–15.

[50] C. H. Hartmann, *Charles II and Madame* (London, 1934), pp. 223–24. The recent increases in French naval construction had been carefully noted in England. June 23, 1668, Williamson's Journal, P.R.O., S.P. 29/253, f. 50.

obstacle to the policy of protecting Spain by alliance with the Dutch. Arlington would have to move very cautiously, especially since the majority of the Council's subcommittee on foreign affairs did not sympathize with him; only the lord keeper, Sir Orlando Bridgeman, an honest and unimaginative Cavalier of the old school, was pronouncedly anti-French. And the leader of the pro-French faction was the duke of Buckingham, who had no convictions himself but who hoped to exploit the difference of opinion between Charles and Arlington to ruin the secretary, his enemy, and in his view, the only obstacle to his own unquestioned preeminence in Charles's councils. The odds appeared to favor Buckingham—or so insiders like Samuel Pepys believed.[51] Under these circumstances Arlington had to play a complicated double game. There would have to be serious negotiations with France. Arlington expected that nothing would come of these, and in the meantime the possibility of an agreement with the United Provinces could be kept alive by means of the pro-Dutch Sir William Temple at Brussels, so that when the French negotiations failed, as they surely would, the king could be confronted with an alternative which he would have to accept.

Negotiations between France and England had been decided upon by the two kings before the war had even ended; they began in earnest with the signing of the treaty of Breda. Louis chose as his ambassador an honest but rather obtuse Huguenot, the marquis de Ruvigny, no doubt in order to humor English religious prejudice. Ruvigny was instructed to sound the English out, to try to get them to make the first concrete proposal, and to point out how easy it would be for France to settle affairs on the Continent without England. A political agreement was to come first; the commercial treaty which had been under discussion before the war would then follow as a matter of course. As a test of English good faith, Ruvigny was to ask Charles to put a stop to Spanish recruiting in England; it was a violation of the king's pledge to engage in no hostile action for a year.[52]

So the fencing began. It emerged soon enough that the original French hope was that England would join her in fighting Spain in Flanders and take her profit in conquests in the West Indies.

[51] See, for example, Pepys, *Diary*, Nov. 15, Dec. 30, 1667.
[52] Aug. 1/11, 1667, instructions for Ruvigny, Mignet, *Négociations* II, 505–12. Jusserand, *Receuil* II, 10–28.

Arlington had little trouble blocking this; having just emerged from one disastrous war, no English statesman wanted to plunge into another. The French were prepared, rather grudgingly, to accept this; they were aware of Charles's domestic problems. The question now was what terms the French would offer for England's neutrality. So tense was the situation and so acute the mutual suspicions of Arlington and Buckingham that they took to visiting Ruvigny together. The crucial interview took place on December 12, 1667. Arlington formulated the English position very clearly: any Anglo-French alliance must be directed against Holland. There must be no partition of the Spanish Netherlands which would profit the Dutch. The Anglo-French commercial treaty must be completed in two months. Buckingham added that France should conquer and hand over Ostend and Nieuport to England, so that Parliament could be shown the tangible advantages of alliance with France.

Louis XIV was appalled by this proposal; the only clause he found reasonable was that dealing with the commercial treaty. He refused to break with the Dutch or to consider war with them unless they first broke the Franco-Dutch treaty of 1662 by helping Spain. He would not conquer seaports for a neutral England. If England joined the European war against Spain, he would conquer a port for her, but he did not say which one. If England wished to make conquests in the West Indies, France would provide some naval assistance or, if Charles preferred, a subsidy of 200,000 crowns—£50,000. In any event, Charles must promise to make no agreement with the Dutch for the duration of the Franco-Spanish war.[53]

Arlington was overjoyed at the French counter-offer, which was just as unacceptable to England as the English proposals had been to France. Each side had staked out its extreme position; under normal circumstances there would now be a round of bargaining. But the times were not normal; Arlington believed that France and Spain would soon end their war and that English neutrality would have no further market value.[54] There was no time to chaffer with France; instead, a bargain must be struck with the Dutch, and quickly.

---

[53] The course of the Anglo-French negotiations can be followed in Mignet, *Négociations* II, 514–46. See also Barbour, *Arlington*, pp. 120–29.

[54] Arlington's reasoning was based on Spain's failure to offer England any inducement to help them in the war. See his letter of November 11, 1667, to Temple, Bebington, *Arlington's Letters* I, 189.

Throughout the negotiation with France Arlington had kept in touch with the Dutch, trying to determine their attitude to the Franco-Spanish conflict, whether they preferred a speedy end to the war in the interest of the balance of power or a policy of cooperation with France to partition the Spanish Netherlands. In dealing with the Dutch Arlington had a few cards in his hand. One was placed there by Louis XIV: in September, 1667, the French king had made known the terms on which he would make peace. They provided for substantial French gains and for a virtual repudiation of his wife's renunciation of her claim to the Spanish crown, but they did not involve French absorption of all of the Spanish Netherlands. A second card had been handed to Arlington by Ruvigny, who agreed to a memorandum summarizing one of their conversations in which the possibility of an Anglo-French alliance against the Dutch had been discussed; this could be shown to the Dutch at the proper time. Finally, Arlington could hold out to the Dutch the promise of immediate implementation of the commercial clauses of the treaty of Breda, which modified the Navigation Act to the extent of permitting the Dutch to bring German-made goods to England.

Arlington's negotiations with the Dutch envoys in England got nowhere, but Temple's letters convinced him that Jan De Witt, the grand pensionary of Holland and the leading politician of the Dutch Republic, was anxious to put an end to the war, if only to demonstrate to the French that Dutch interests in the Spanish Netherlands must be taken into account. In any case, the Dutch had to be smoked out, and soon. On November 25, 1667, the day of the first of his and Buckingham's interviews with Ruvigny, Arlington drew up a set of instructions for Temple: he was to find out from De Witt if the Dutch would enter into an alliance to preserve the Spanish Netherlands, even if it were directed against France. Then, characteristically, the secretary had a fit of caution—this was the time of the impeachment of Clarendon, and Buckingham's star was rising. The instructions were not sent off for a couple of weeks. When they finally were, Temple moved rapidly, and got De Witt to agree to joint mediation on the basis of the "alternatives," as Louis XIV's terms were called. Temple arrived in England with this news at just the right moment: Louis XIV's proposals had just been communicated. In their irritation the king and the rest of the pro-French group allowed Arlington and Temple to go ahead, especially since the proposal was not, on the face of it, anti-French; Louis XIV could hardly object if his ally and his royal cousin got for him what he said he wanted. And so, very rapidly, the treaty was made. Temple returned to The Hague on January 8, 1668, and by the thirteenth had concluded, with Holland and Sweden, an agreement to force a peace on the basis of the "alternatives." De Witt's acceptance may well have been speeded up by a look at Ruvigny's memorandum on an Anglo-French alliance. Nor was this all. The treaty also comprised a defensive alliance among the signatories; De Witt agreed to this in return for the implementation of the commercial clauses of the treaty of Breda. For once secrecy was maintained in that maelstrom of gossip which was the English court; Ruvigny was caught completely by surprise.[55]

The Triple Alliance was a great triumph for Arlington, and he was overwhelmed with joy and relief. "God be thanked it is done," he wrote, "and that both the world abroad and at home understand it to be both honourable and safe for his majesty, and foretell we shall find the Parliament much better complexioned for it."[56] And, indeed, the treaty was very popular in England. "The great applause which this new league first received has so tickled my Lord Arlington that he could not refrain from making known to his friends that he is the sole author of it," wrote Ruvigny sourly, "but perhaps he will repent of it soon."[57] For the moment, however, the secretary's cup seemed to be running over. For in this same month of January Buckingham disgraced himself by fighting a duel with his mistress' husband, the earl of Shrewsbury, and mortally wounding him. Charles was not the man to sympathize with cuckolds, and he was fond of the duke, but he could hardly help comparing the January activities of the two rivals for his ear in a way favorable to the secretary. One consequence was the reorganization of the committee on foreign affairs of the privy council, which now became Arlington's committee, and which itself became known as the "Cabal"; it

---

[55] This summary of the Anglo-Dutch negotiations follows the standard accounts in Barbour, *Arlington*, pp. 131–35, and Feiling, *British Foreign Policy*, pp. 245–56. Temple's account of his negotiations is in *Works of Sir William Temple* I, 295–307.

[56] Feiling, *British Foreign Policy*, p. 256.

[57] Jusserand, *Receuil* II, 44. Ruvigny himself believed in Arlington's responsibility. Jan. 20/30, 1668, Ruvigny to Louis XIV, Mignet, *Négociations* II, 562–63.

was to meet every Monday at his lodgings in Whitehall, and his secretary, Joseph Williamson, became its secretary.[58] His control of the personnel of the diplomatic service became more complete, and in the fall of 1668 he was able to force the replacement of Sir William Morice, his colleague as secretary of state, by his own nominee Sir John Trevor. As one courtier put it in February, 1668, "though Lord Arlington labors with all art imaginable not to be thought a premier minister, yet he is either so, or a favorite, for he is the sole guide that the king relies upon."[59]

No one knew better than the secretary that his resounding diplomatic triumph would fall to pieces in his hands unless it was consolidated. Alliance with the Dutch was far more popular in the nation at large than at court. Buckingham's influence was checked but not ruined, and Arlington's effort to build up Parliamentary and territorial influence in north England, Buckingham's bailiwick, by getting Williamson elected as M.P. for Appleby, failed.[60] His closest political ally, Sir Thomas Clifford, was violently anti-Dutch. Clifford believed that another war with the Dutch was both inevitable and desirable, and he tried to use his position on the treasury commission to prevent the sending of Temple to The Hague as ambassador by slashing ambassadorial salaries: Temple was not a rich man.[61] This was the first rift between Clifford and Arlington; it was ultimately to lead to a complete break between them which had much to do with the dissolution of the Cabal.

Clifford might grumble and Buckingham jeer, but the only opinion that really counted was the king's. And Arlington knew perfectly well that Charles had not changed his mind. As soon as the Triple Alliance was signed, Charles hastened to explain himself to his sister and through her to Louis XIV. Henrietta might be "a little sur-

[58] *C.S.P.D.* VIII, 261. Jan. 31, 1668, Williamson's Journal, P.R.O., S.P. 29/253, f. 14. Pepys, *Diary*, Feb. 8, 1669. See also F. M. G. Evans, *The Principal Secretary of State* (Manchester, 1923), p. 236.

[59] *C.S.P.D.* VIII, 258–59.

[60] *Ibid.*, pp. xxix–xxxi, 187, 219. Andrew Browning, "Parties and Party Organization in the Reign of Charles II," *Transactions of the Royal Historical Society* 4th ser. XXX (1948), 31.

[61] Hartmann, *Clifford*, pp. 132–33. July 22, 1668, Temple to Sir John Temple, *Works of Sir William Temple* I, 436–39. In this letter Temple quotes Clifford as saying of the Triple Alliance, "Well, for all this noise, we must yet have another war with the Dutch before it be long."

prised" by the treaty, wrote Charles, but she should not be. Its purpose was to get peace on France's terms, and there was really nothing else Charles could do, "finding my propositions to France receive so cold an answer, which in effect was as good as a refusal."[62] The implication was clear: Charles did not regard the Triple Alliance as in any way impairing his relations with France. To him, it was to serve as a demonstration to Louis that the English alliance was valuable and must be bought at a decent price.

There was only one policy for Arlington to follow under these circumstances: the Triple Alliance must be made so useful and effective that France would not be able to induce Charles to break it. The king was not insensitive to public opinion; Arlington tried to keep it in its present state by encouraging the publication of pro-Dutch tracts.[63] After a long and difficult negotiation Arlington got a firm pledge from Sweden to adhere to the alliance on condition that a subsidy be paid. The subsidy was to come ultimately from Spain, which shows clearly enough that, for all the polite language used to Louis XIV, Spain was the real beneficiary of the alliance. It was not easy to convince the Spaniards of this. They did agree, at long last, in February, 1668, under the prodding of the earl of Sandwich, to come to terms with Portugal—another substantial victory for Arlington's diplomacy—but in Flanders they felt that their alleged friends were compelling them first to pay for French aggression and then to subsidize those friends to guarantee an unsatisfactory treaty. Their tergiversations were infuriating to Arlington, who had raised the question of alliance with Spain in the foreign committee; he wrote to Temple in May that the behavior of the viceroy in Brussels was "all so enigmatical that it makes me mad to think of it."[64] The Spaniards really had no choice, however; if England, Holland, and France were agreed on the peace terms, they would have to acquiesce. The decision for peace or war would be taken, not in Madrid, but in Paris.

Louis XIV was not pleased by the Triple Alliance. He showed his annoyance by the friendly treatment he accorded to the exiled Clarendon, with whom he had dealt harshly before. He ultimately decided to make peace with Spain on the basis of the "alternatives,"

---

[62] Hartmann, *Charles II and Madame,* p. 200.
[63] See, for example, Pepys, *Diary,* Feb. 10, 1668.
[64] Bebington, *Arlington's Letters* I, 336. P.R.O., S.P. 104/176, f. 13.

not because he was intimidated by the Triple Alliance but because continuing the war was no longer necessary. In January, 1668, Louis and the emperor had secretly come to terms over the Spanish inheritance. The Hapsburgs would get Spain, Milan, and the West Indies when the sickly king of Spain finally went to his reward; France would get Flanders, Franche-Comté, and the Two Sicilies. This treaty was a crucial and frequently overlooked factor in the determination of French foreign policy in the next few years. It meant that, no matter what happened to the Spanish throne itself, France would be able to acquire the Spanish Netherlands when Charles II died. Now Louis' problem was to prevent anyone else from disputing his claim to them—and that meant the Dutch. Louis' attack on the Dutch in 1672 was not in pursuit of "a secondary and subsidiary object,"[65] as so many historians have assumed; it was a precautionary move—preventive aggression. The Dutch interest in Flanders and their peril from possible French annexation were far greater than that of England, as Arlington had recognized.[66] The Triple Alliance had demonstrated to Louis the Dutch awareness of their danger. The Triple Alliance must be dissolved, and the first step must be peace with Spain. So, in April, 1668, peace was made, at Aix-la-Chapelle. Louis acquired part of Flanders and, more important for the future, virtual recognition by Spain that his wife's claims were still valid.

The shift in Louis' policy and the peace of Aix laid the foundation for the Anglo-French alliance so much desired by Charles; the two countries could now unite against their common enemy. Charles, if he gave any thought to the possible long-term danger to England of French domination of the Low Countries, discounted it; English naval supremacy, which he would take care to safeguard and foster, would obviate that. In any event, Charles's foreign policy was always determined by the exigencies of his position at home. To achieve his domestic political goals only an alliance with France would serve, not because Louis XIV was absolutist and Catholic, as has often been thought, but because France was the strongest power in Europe. Only by alliance with France could success in foreign policy be had on the cheap. If Louis XIV had learned from the

---

[65] The phrase in Ogg's, *England in the Reign of Charles II* I, 349.
[66] See his letter of October 4, 1667, to Temple, Bebington, *Arlington's Letters* I, 183.

Triple Alliance, Charles had learned from the second Dutch war. England alone could not defeat the Dutch, but England and France together could easily do so. Such a victory would reconcile the English public to the French alliance, which Charles knew would be unpopular in the beginning. The Dutch defeat would also, by enormously expanding English trade, swell the king's revenues so greatly that his financial problems would be solved and a long stride taken toward independence of Parliament. The alternative policy, urged by Arlington, would have none of these advantages. The European balance might be preserved but only at considerable cost; no one could pretend that the defense of the moribund Spanish empire by the Triple Alliance would not involve considerable immediate expense,[67] however profitable it might prove to be for the merchants in the long run. These costs meant, not independence of Parliament, but reliance upon it. If the king's policy meant subservience to France abroad, Arlington's meant postponing the strengthening of the crown at home.

The secretary saw the situation very clearly, and this explains why he was so infuriated by Spain's myopic refusal to subsidize the Triple Alliance. He was also disappointed by Parliament's failure to vote more than £300,000 by way of supply to set out the fleet in February, 1668.[68] He did his best to demonstrate the advantages of the alliance to his master, but the difficulties were considerable. Spain continued to procrastinate and dodge in the matter of subsidy payments, and the Dutch would do nothing to make Arlington's job easier. They would not agree to a favorable commercial treaty, and the old points of contention, such as the claims of the East India Company, continued to be agitated. It was not at all clear that in signing the Triple Alliance Jan De Witt did not have the same design as Charles: to enhance his value in the eyes of Louis XIV. Charles believed this was at least a strong possibility.[69] Arlington finally turned to the plan, first mentioned just after the signing of the alliance, of enhancing its value by increasing its size, by in-

---

[67] The discussions of the foreign committee of the council, which were taken up during much of 1668 and 1669 with the problem of the Swedish subsidy, make this clear. P.R.O., S.P. 104/176, ff. 17ff.

[68] See his letter of February 28 to Temple, Bebington, *Arlington's Letters* I, 237.

[69] June 28/July 8, 1668, Ruvigny's mémoire, Mignet, *Négociations* III, 16. Cf. Feiling, *British Foreign Policy*, p. 282.

cluding Denmark, the Empire, and various German states such as
Saxony and Brandenburg. If the alliance were large enough, Louis
XIV might hesitate to renew his aggressions, peace would be pre-
served, and the potential costs of an anti-French policy minimized.[70]

Charles was perfectly content to allow Arlington to see what he
could do with the Dutch, but he proposed to resume negotiations
with France. He told Ruvigny in April, 1668, that he wanted an
alliance with France; a month later he suggested that he and Louis
should negotiate "de gentilhomme à gentilhomme."[71] Each side
wanted the other to make the first proposal; each side feared that the
other would use a concrete proposal to bargain with the Dutch.
Arlington, to Ruvigny's annoyance, used France's unwillingness to
make the first move as evidence of French duplicity; if France really
wanted the alliance, he said, Louis would have no hesitation in
making his terms known.[72]

This argument had some effect with Charles, but it could serve
only until the first move was made. Arlington's real device for
stalling the negotiations was to insist that a commercial treaty precede any political agreement with France; to do anything else, he
said, would be like building a house roof first.[73] There was much
sense in the advice, and Charles would have done well to heed it.
The English business community was very anti-French, owing to its
belief that the current balance of Anglo-French trade was very
unfavorable to England; its attitude was hardened by Colbert's
prohibitive tariff of 1667, which raised duties on foreign manufactured goods about 100 per cent. The textile industry was particularly affected; France was the only major European market in
which the value of English woolen exports declined in the 1660's.
This had considerable impact on business opinion, even though the
cloth trade was becoming less important in many men's eyes.[74] The
English reaction to the French tariff of 1667 was a motion in Parlia-

[70] Anglo-Dutch negotiations can be followed in Bebington, *Arlington's
Letters* I, 352ff., and *Works of Sir William Temple* I, 427ff. There is also an
occasional illuminating remark in the correspondence of Lindenov, the Danish
resident in London, printed in W. Westergaard, ed., *The First Triple Alliance*
(New Haven, 1947).

[71] Mignet, *Négociations* III, 9–11.

[72] See Ruvigny's memorandum of June 28/July 8, 1668, *ibid.*, pp.
14–18.

[73] *Ibid.*, p. 12.

[74] On this point see Wilson, *Profit and Power*, p. 155.

ment to raise the duties on French imports,[75] and in 1668 the £300,000 supply was to be raised by increased levies on wine, brandy, and linen, all French commodities. Equally important, perhaps, was the changing attitude toward the Dutch. The second Dutch war, which the merchant class as a whole had supported in the hope that it would be as profitable as the first, had been a disappointment. There had been no economic expansion; there was no reason to believe that a third war would differ from the second. Londoners in particular had reasons for a softening of attitude: the timber necessary for the repair of the devastation caused by the great fire of 1666 had to be largely imported from Scandinavia; most of it was brought by Dutch ships. The City of London was instrumental in supporting requests for exemption from the Navigation Act for these ships.[76]

Arlington was well aware of the shifting currents of mercantile opinion, and he was convinced that these groups would have to be won over if an alliance with France was to have any chance of success. Hence his insistence on a commercial treaty, which would have the additional advantage of testing French good faith. If Louis were sincere in his desire for an alliance, he should have no objection to relaxing the new tariff in England's favor. Arlington's judgment on this point was borne out by the event. Shortly before the great storm broke around Charles's head in 1678, one of the most venomous haters of France, Andrew Marvell, in his brilliant pamphlet *An Account of the Growth of Popery and Arbitrary Government in England* pointed to France's refusal to negotiate a commercial treaty as proof of her perfidy.[77]

Charles knew that Arlington's position had some merit; he told his sister so in the letter quoted above,[78] and in mid-September, 1668,

[75] C. Robbins, ed., *The Diary of John Milward* (Cambridge, 1938) , p. 109.

[76] Nov. 12, 1668, Lindenov to the Danish Chancery, Westergaard, *First Triple Alliance*, pp. 35–36. The government was usually hostile to such requests. *Ibid.*, pp. 91–92, 100–101.

[77] The pamphlet is in A. B. Grosart, ed., *The Complete Prose Works of Andrew Marvell, M.P.*, Fuller Worthies Library (London, 1872–75) . For the attitudes of the English merchants see D. G. E. Hall, "Anglo-French Trade Relations Under Charles II," *History* n.s. VII (1922–23) , 17–30; M. Priestley, "Anglo-French Trade and the 'Unfavourable Balance' Controversy 1660–1685," *Economic History Review* 2nd ser. IV (1951) , 37–52; Wilson, *Profit and Power*, chap. X, esp. pp. 151, 156; P. de Ségur-Dupeyron, *Histoire des négociations commerciales et maritimes du règne de Louis XIV* (Paris, 1863) I, 175ff.

[78] See above, p. 89.

he went so far as to adopt his secretary's views momentarily. "The reason why I begin with the treaty of commerce," he wrote Henrietta, "is because I must enter first upon those matters which will render the rest more plausible here, for you know that the thing which is nearest the heart of this nation is trade and all that belongs to it."[79] Louis XIV, struck by English insistence on the point, had rather irritably instructed his new ambassador to discuss a commercial treaty but to spin the negotiations out and await a favorable moment for reopening the question of the political alliance.[80]

The new French ambassador was no less a person than Charles Colbert de Croissy, brother of the great Colbert; he replaced Ruvigny in August, 1668. In Croissy's instructions the new turn in French policy was made explicit for the first time: France was prepared to align herself with England against the Dutch. The great obstacle to the achievement of French designs was Arlington; ". . . if the affairs of England were today in other hands than those of the said lord . . . the close alliance between their majesties . . . would be very easy to arrange, and would almost conclude itself." But, unhappily, affairs *were* in Arlington's hands, and he was pro-Spanish and pro-Dutch and took advice from De Witt. Louis was prepared to go to any lengths to smash the Triple Alliance: Croissy was instructed to try the effect on Arlington of a lump sum of £25,000 and a pension of £2,500 a year. English ministers "have scarcely ever felt scruples about taking French money," Louis observed, but Arlington's "aversion for this crown and his commitments to Spain and Holland" may make him unbribable. Croissy was nevertheless to try; if Arlington turned out to be incorruptible, further instructions would be sent.[81]

Croissy's first reports confirmed the solidity of Arlington's position. Louis deplored the fact that he should be powerful enough to conduct affairs "according to his whims, rather than in the real interest of his master," but, such being the case, Croissy was instructed to mark time and talk to the secretary about commerce.[82] There might be other ways of winning—using Buckingham, per-

[79] Hartmann, *Charles II and Madame,* p. 225.
[80] Mignet, *Négociations* III, 44–46.
[81] The instructions, dated July 23/Aug. 2, 1668, are in Jusserand, *Receuil* II, 54–92.
[82] Aug. 17/27, 1668, Louis to Croissy, Mignet, *Négociations* III, 44–46.

haps, or trying to frighten Arlington with the bogey of the restoration of Clarendon. Louis rather fancied this last idea, but he had no idea of how to go about making it seem plausible. Buckingham turned out to be a broken reed; by the end of the year it became evident that he could not deliver on his gaudy promises, and Louis washed his hands of him, partly because one of the duke's suggestions was that France should suspend all naval building. Arlington, Louis wrote in December, 1668, is "the absolute master of English affairs."[83]

IV

Louis XIV was wrong. King Charles was master in England, and it was in this month of December that he seems to have decided to overrule his secretary and to go ahead with the French alliance. His affairs were apparently at a standstill. The Scottish union scheme was temporarily stalled, the financial disorder was worse than ever, and the religious problem was no nearer solution. The Triple Alliance had shown gain, but not gain enough; it might increase the government's popularity at home, but it did not enhance the royal power. Only the French alliance would give the king what he wanted. So his decision was made, not only as to policy but also as to method. He would negotiate by means of his sister, with whom he had always corresponded; this would insure secrecy and minimize the possibilities of betrayal. He informed her, on December 19, that he was about to send her a cipher, something he had never found necessary before. This and his decision on December 11 to prorogue Parliament from March to October, 1669, because, as he said, he was not in need of money, are the earliest indications that Charles had definitely made up his mind.[84]

Charles now faced perhaps his most serious difficulty. Somehow or other Arlington must be persuaded to cooperate. Charles knew that the alliance must be constructed secretly; English opinion was so anti-French that premature disclosure of the negotiations would be utterly disastrous. Arlington, since he was in charge of the day-to-day operation of foreign policy, could not be kept out of the

[83] *Ibid.*, pp. 62–63. See also Louis' letter of Oct. 28/Nov. 7, 1668, *ibid.*, pp. 52–54.

[84] Hartmann, *Charles II and Madame*, p. 227. P.R.O., S.P. 29/253, f. 98.

secret; sooner or later a leak would develop in Paris or London. The
king may have thought of kicking Arlington upstairs to the office of
lord treasurer—rumors to this effect circulated in the autumn of
1668[85]—but this was hardly feasible. Arlington's opposition to
France was too well known; his replacement by a pro-French secretary would make the king's new direction in foreign policy immediately apparent. Arlington was, in fact, the one man in England
whose acquiescence in the French alliance was absolutely indispensable.

Charles found the solution to his difficulty, a solution which, he
anticipated, could be put to use in several directions. On January 25,
1669, a meeting allegedly took place attended by Charles, his brother
James, Arlington, Clifford, and Lord Arundell of Wardour. At this
meeting the king announced his conversion to Catholicism and his
intention of seeking French help in making a public declaration to
this effect. Whether this meeting ever really occurred is open to
serious doubt. It is mentioned in only one source,[86] which is notoriously inaccurate in other respects, and Charles's letter to Henrietta
on March 22 implies that James had just been let into the secret.
"Before this comes to your hands you will clearly see upon what
score 363 [that is, James] is come into the business," wrote Charles,
the context making it clear that "the business" is that of the French
alliance and the king's declaration of Catholicism.[87] Whether or not
the meeting took place is unimportant; the king certainly adopted
the policy of Catholicity, as it was called. It is impossible to believe
that Charles was sincere, and there has been endless speculation as to
his motives. Three explanations have been put forward, either singly
or in combination: Charles did this to please his sister, who, he told
Croissy, was the only woman who had any influence over him,[88] or he
admired the Catholic absolutism of Louis XIV, or he wanted money
from France. None of these explanations is adequate, because they

---

[85] See, for example, Pepys, *Diary*, Sept. 28, 1668.
     [86] J. S. Clarke, ed., *The Life of James II . . . Collected Out of
Memoirs Writ of His Own Hand* (London, 1816) I, 441–43.
     [87] Hartmann, *Charles II and Madame*, pp. 241–42. On the other hand,
on January 24, the day before the alleged meeting, Pepys was summoned to state
how soon the fleet could put to sea. Pepys's biographer regards this as the first
concrete intimation of a new Dutch war. Arthur Bryant, *Samuel Pepys* (new ed.,
London, 1947) I, 380.
     [88] Jusserand, *Receuil* II, 98.

ignore the uses to which this supposed conversion was actually put. True, Louis XIV did pay Charles something, but very little, only £166,000, nowhere near enough to justify the political dangers involved. It seems more likely that the Catholicity scheme was used, in the first instance, to persuade the indispensable Arlington to acquiesce in the policy of the French alliance. Charles knew that it would have this effect, because it immediately changed the whole nature of the argument. As long as decisions in foreign policy were taken solely on the basis of the national welfare, Arlington could and did oppose his master with an untroubled mind. But now, Charles had involved his personal position as king and the royal conscience; when that happened, Arlington, Royalist and courtier that he was, would bow and acquiesce.

Arlington was appalled by Charles's proposal to declare himself a Catholic. This ran counter to all his notions of prudent politics; concessions to the Catholics were the quickest possible way to bring about a political explosion. He told Croissy some years later that he accepted it only "pour éviter sa perte."[89] This we may take leave to doubt; what would have meant his ruin was a refusal to go along with the French alliance rather than the Catholicity scheme. Fortunately for himself, Arlington had a little time to readjust his thinking, because the French themselves had not yet given Charles a formal written statement of their intention to fight the Dutch, either because they did not trust the English or because Louis was himself still hopeful of Dutch concessions which would make the war unnecessary. If the French were indeed wavering, they had ceased to do so in June, 1669, when they gave Charles the written statement for which he had been clamoring.[90] Serious negotiations could now begin.

By this time Arlington had made up his mind as to his course. He was reassured to learn that the king had not become a religious enthusiast. Some illumination on this point was no doubt provided

---

[89] Nov. 10/20, 1673, Croissy to Louis XIV, Mignet, *Négociations* IV, 236.

[90] Hartmann, *Charles II and Madame*, pp. 263–67. As late as June 7 Charles had written his sister, "I would fain know . . . how ready 323 [France] is to break with 299 [Holland]." *Ibid.*, p. 258. For the view that the final decision was not taken until May, 1669, see H. H. Rowen, *The Ambassador Prepares for War: The Dutch Embassy of Arnauld de Pomponne 1669–1671* (The Hague, 1957), pp. 36–37, 70–74.

by Charles's attitude to the astrologer-abbé Pregnani, who was sent to England by Louis in the spring of 1669 to play upon Charles's alleged superstition and who discredited himself by his inability to pick the winners at the Newmarket races. A more serious worry to Arlington was the apparent resurgence of Buckingham's influence. The spring of 1669 saw the duke's ridicule bring down William Coventry; Arlington's friend, the duke of Ormonde, was dismissed from his position as lord lieutenant of Ireland, again thanks to Buckingham. These were signs and portents; it looked as if Arlington was slipping, and politicians like Trevor began to make approaches to the giddy duke.[91] Arlington became nervous and frightened for his job, which was really much more secure than he thought it was. What may finally have precipitated his decision were the letters he began to receive from his friend Ralph Montagu, who had gone to France as ambassador in April, 1669. Montagu reported that France was determined to have an alliance and would grant such favorable terms that Charles would be unable to refuse and that "whatever is done, I would have your Lordship have the doing it." Henrietta, he pointed out, was the key figure, and Arlington had better ingratiate himself with her; she was suspicious of him, as were all the French court, but it could be done.[92]

So Arlington decided that he would "have the doing it." He had not changed his opinion; he was still opposed to the French alliance. But now he must appear to acquiesce. It might be possible to prevent the alliance still, by making such excessive demands that the French would back away. Failing that, the secretary saw a splendid use for the Catholicity scheme. One of the objections to the French alliance was the fact that France, as the stronger partner, would determine, not so much the immediate goals of the alliance—they would be set down in the treaty—but rather, the way in which those goals were to be achieved. The timing of the partners' moves would be decided by Louis XIV. The Catholicity scheme might be used to prevent this, to give control of the alliance to Charles, if it were

[91] On this point see Andrew Browning, *Thomas Osborne, Earl of Danby and Duke of Leeds* (Glasgow, 1951) I, 70. Apr. 28/May 8, 1669, Montagu to Arlington, H.M.C., *Buccleuch and Queensberry Mss.* I, 423–24. Apr. 29, 1669, Arlington to Williamson, *C.S.P.D.* IX, 300–301.

[92] Montagu's letters are printed in H.M.C., *Buccleuch and Queensberry Mss.* I, 421ff. The quoted phrase is in the letter of Apr. 23/May 3, 1669, p. 423.

written into the treaty that the public announcement of Charles's conversion was to be the first step and if the timing of that announcement were left entirely up to Charles. It was an ingenious scheme—in fact, too clever by half. Neither Charles nor Arlington saw the long-range dangers inherent in it.

Clearly the first essential step for the secretary in his new role of apparent convert was to neutralize Charles's sister. This he did in a letter written in June. It was a skillful letter. Arlington did not overdo it; he allowed his reluctance to show. And he wrote one sentence which must have come from the heart. "I have been all my life a good servant of the King, my master, and such I will die, by the grace of God, and I would not, for all the wealth of the world, act any other part than that of a good Englishman."[93] The letter did some good; it helped to convince Henrietta that her brother had been right in his constant assurances to her that Arlington would do as he was told. Even more effective, perhaps, was a ploy devised by Montagu, who suggested that Arlington take the initiative in and thus get the credit for persuading Charles to make Henrietta a small gift of money.[94] In any event, Charles had made it clear that the French would have to deal with Arlington. So, for whatever reason, French complaints about Arlington, which had been numerous and noisy since the summer of 1667, ceased in the summer of 1669, as both sides got down to work.

The secretary's first plan was to revive the commercial treaty. Throughout the summer there were discussions in the council and with the French ambassador. Finally, at the end of August, after some delay caused by Arlington's poor health,[95] a draft was presented to Croissy. The English terms were pitched very high. Among other things, they asked that English merchants in France be treated like Frenchmen, while the disabilities on Frenchmen in England remained; there was to be a mutual reduction of freight rates, which would benefit English shipping more than French, because there was more of it; neither side was obliged to adhere to the manufacturing specifications of the other, which would raise havoc with Colbert's regulatory system; and, above all, the French tariff of 1667 was to be

---

93 The letter is given in Barbour, *Arlington,* pp. 160–61.

94 H.M.C., *Buccleuch and Queensberry Mss.* I, 430–31, 433, 435.

95 Aug. 19, 1669, J. Dodington to Lord Fauconberg, H.M.C., *Mss. in Various Collections* (London, 1903) II, 129.

eliminated, with no corresponding reduction in English tariffs.[96] The French were appalled by this; there was a new outburst of hostility to Arlington at the French court, and they caught eagerly at the story that the king at one of his convivial suppers had had Arlington imitated by Buckingham and Bab May, thinking that it meant his fall. They hoped in vain; it merely meant that the secretary's solemn Spanish gravity lent itself to ridicule and that he and Buckingham had quarreled again. As Montagu sarcastically put it to his chief on hearing of the quarrel, "I can only comfort you as the divines use to do for the loss of the good things of the world, which, whilst we did enjoy, were so uncertain, that we ought never to have set our hearts much upon them."[97]

The English commercial proposals were admirably designed to prevent any Anglo-French treaty, but they did not do so, owing chiefly to Henrietta, who now made her one effective intervention in the negotiations. In a long and skillful letter to her brother she put the French government's case. The real way to expand English commerce was to pulverize the Dutch: "Indeed what is there more glorious and more profitable than to extend the confines of your kingdom beyond the sea and to become supreme in commerce, which is what your people most passionately desire, and what will probably never occur so long as the Republic of Holland exists?" Charles, with his powerful anti-Dutch prejudices, was easily convinced. The commercial treaty was allowed to drop.[98]

So Arlington, having failed to wreck the proposed alliance in this rather indirect way, was faced with the more dangerous alternative of having to ruin it on political grounds. The negotiations moved slowly, possibly owing to the elaborate precautions which were taken

[96] Ségur-Dupeyron, *Histoire des négociations commerciales* I, 246–52.

[97] Sept. 18/28, Oct. 9/19, 1669, Montagu to Arlington, H.M.C., *Buccleuch and Queensberry Mss.* I, 441, 442–43. One of the results of this new quarrel, it seems likely, was a libel circulated at the beginning of the Parliamentary session in October which has the Buckingham touch: "This poor man is but the sign of a secretary, and can do nothing that belongs to his place but receive the profits of it. . . . Were he freed from the fear of Parliament [he] would be as insolent as he is ignorant." Evans, *Principal Secretary of State*, p. 127. Hartmann, *Clifford*, pp. 145–46.

[98] Hartmann, *Charles II and Madame*, pp. 277–81. The French did make some small commercial concessions to England, however. In March, 1670, it was reported that the French government had instructed its merchants in Genoa to stop using Dutch ships and to use those of England or of other nations instead. Westergaard, *First Triple Alliance*, p. 206.

to prevent leaks. Charles's first proposals were clearly unacceptable: he wanted Louis never to build any more warships and to agree that Charles should not be asked to do anything contrary to the Triple Alliance! Louis would have no part of this, although he did agree to build no warships for a year; he also made clear his dislike of the Catholicity scheme, which, he feared, might delay the attack on Holland. Charles's reply was oblique; he agreed to uphold Louis' rights to various Spanish possessions, if and when these should accrue, but he had financial troubles and Parliament could not be counted on to help. Unless Louis could supply him with £1,000,000, France had better start the war by herself; England would join in later on.[99]

These exchanges took place between June and September, 1669; it seems likely that Arlington was unaware of them, or else Charles would not have made the pledge respecting Spain so readily.[100] With the dropping of the commercial negotiations, however, Arlington was brought into the political discussions, as was Croissy, who now learned of the whole affair for the first time. The secretary's first concern was to retrieve Charles's slip respecting Spain; he did this indirectly by suggesting that, to cover the real negotiations, it be declared that Charles was discussing with France the possibility of English mediation of the dispute which had arisen over the treaty of Aix. Louis, who had no intention of attacking Spain just now, was willing to accept this. He also accepted the Catholicity scheme after Charles had made it clear, in his oblique way, that otherwise Louis would have to launch his attack on the Dutch all by himself.[101] Then the secretary settled down to draw up a draft, which was finally presented to Croissy in mid-December. It rendered the ambassador speechless with astonishment and his master thoroughly indignant. This was Arlington's major effort to sabotage the negotiations.

France was to pay for the Catholicity scheme to the tune of £200,000 in six months and to provide more money and troops if Charles got into trouble with his subjects when the time came. France was to promise to abide by the treaty of Aix and not to attack Spain; in the event that France did inherit claims to Spanish terri-

99 Hartmann, *Charles II and Madame*, pp. 264–71.

100 This apparently troubled even Henrietta; see her letter of September, 1669, to Arlington, *ibid.*, pp. 275–77.

101 Ségur-Dupeyron, *Histoire des négociations commerciales* I, 259–60.

tory in the future, England would supply troops and ships to make good those claims at French expense. France was to conquer Minorca and Ostend for England and to help England conquer all of Spanish America. As for the Dutch war, there would be one, but France must pay an annual subsidy of £800,000 while it lasted, and England's territorial share was to be Walcheren, Sluys, and Cadzand. France might decide when the war was to begin, but it could not start until after the Catholicity scheme had been put into effect and all domestic troubles resulting from it pacified. The timing of the declaration of Catholicity was, of course, left to Charles.[102]

Some of these demands were clearly and obviously outrageous—that on Spanish America, for instance—and after a certain amount of palaver were allowed to drop. The items on which the secretary was counting to break up the negotiations were the enormous subsidy and possibly the Catholicity scheme, to which the French could not openly object but which they obviously disliked. The subsidy was the really crucial matter; Louis told Croissy that it was utterly impossible to pay so much and that there was no point in even discussing anything else until the English saw reason on this. Arlington, when Croissy protested, said that £800,000 a year was what it cost to activate the fleet.[103] Croissy suggested that it was not necessary to set out the whole fleet, but Arlington said that it was. In stressing this so heavily, the secretary was relying on the deep concern for English naval and commercial expansion which was felt not only by Charles, but by all the men around him—one of the few things on which the Cabal were all agreed—to keep the king from giving way. Charles held firm for quite a while. On January 14 the king told Croissy that he knew that Louis was scandalized and so was his sister; he was ashamed to ask for so much, he said, but he needed it. Some time in the next four days, however, the king changed his mind. On January 18 Charles saw Croissy again and told him that each country should arm forty-three ships, and that England would accept a

[102] Mignet, *Négociations* III, 117–23. In the first draft, in Clifford's hand, the subsidy figure was £600,000. J. J. S. Shaw, "A Biography of Thomas Clifford" (unpublished Ph.D. thesis, University of Glasgow, n.d.), appendix, pp. 214–21.

[103] Arlington was right about this. See his memorandum of February 15, 1670, in *C.S.P.D.* X, 68–69; cf. also *ibid.*, pp. 205–6. This was the amount asked of Parliament for the fleet in October, 1670. H. M. Margoliouth, ed., *The Poems and Letters of Andrew Marvell* (Oxford, 1952) II, 107–8.

subsidy of £300,000. This, said the king, was less than he needed, but he was so anxious for the alliance that he was willing to make concessions.[104] This was the real turning point in the negotiations. Arlington had lost his gamble; now there was nothing to do but make the treaty as advantageous as possible and cling to the Catholicity clause like a limpet. The timing of events would still be in English hands; the war might still be avoided after all.

The complications of English policy necessitated very careful handling of the Dutch, whose suspicions were beginning to take shape early in 1669. The change in policy must be kept from them, and so the Triple Alliance must be maintained. Discussions as to strengthening it must go on, but it must not be really strengthened. As to the commercial and colonial disputes between England and Holland, they should not be settled, but English willingness to settle must not be questioned. Arlington took care that the French understood all this very clearly.[105] There was a further complication, provided by the French, who leaked information about England's new course in order to alienate the Dutch and deprive England of the alternative to alliance with France. Faced with all this, Arlington acted with enormous skill. The Triple Alliance was, indeed, strengthened in form just as the substance was leaking out of it. Temple was deceived and, being so, helped, all unintentionally, to deceive his friend De Witt. Arlington avoided unnecessary complications, such as the proposal of Lady Castlemaine's fatuous husband to publish a history of the last Dutch war. In the foreign committee the secretary still spoke of the value of the Triple Alliance—speeches which were intended primarily for Charles and only secondarily as a cover for the negotiations with France.[106] Not until May, 1670, did the Dutch become suspicious enough to send an important representative to England to find out what was afoot. The astonishing thing about Arlington's performance was that it really did preserve the possibility of an Anglo-Dutch agreement, if the secretary could

[104] Both interviews are reported in Croissy's dispatch of January 19/29, 1670, Mignet, *Négociations* III, 138–46. The Anglo-French negotiations can be followed in *ibid.*, pp. 100ff.; cf. also Hartmann, *Charles II and Madame*, pp. 264ff.

[105] Nov. 25/Dec. 5, 1669, Croissy to Louis XIV, Mignet, *Négociations* III, 113.

[106] Sept. 11/21, 1669, Castlemaine to Arlington, *C.S.P.D.* IX, 488. P.R.O., S.P. 104/176, ff. 201–3.

prevent the French treaty or, failing that, avoid the war it contemplated.

Arlington's rearguard action on the French treaty from January, 1670, until it was finally signed on Henrietta's visit to Dover in late May was not particularly effective, however. His first suggestion after the king's surrender on the subsidy, that the treaty omit the war altogether and deal only with Catholicity and the Spanish inheritance, was quickly rejected by the French.[107] Louis did promise to abide by the treaty of Aix and to make no treaties respecting the Spanish inheritance without English consent, an easy promise to make in view of his existing treaty with the emperor. The clauses respecting the disposition of Spanish territory were necessarily vague; England could not simultaneously pose as Spain's defender and particularize on her share of the loot. Control of naval operations was kept in English hands; the subsidy was set at £250,000. The Catholicity clause was retained, though in somewhat weakened form; the reference to Charles's having restored peace at home was deleted on French insistence. Had it not been removed, any minor riot could be used as an excuse to delay the war. The retention of the Catholicity clause was an absolutely disastrous English victory; sometime in April Louis XIV began to appreciate that fact and to see what an exceedingly useful weapon his cousin of England was thrusting into his hands. He ordered Croissy to do what he could on a number of minor points still remaining but to give way rather than hold up the treaty any longer.[108]

Louis' shift of attitude was brought on by his sudden awareness that Charles's Catholicity scheme was entirely insincere. What may have opened his eyes was the amusing and scandalous Roos divorce case, which came before the House of Lords in March, 1670. John Manners, Lord Roos, the heir to the earldom of Rutland, was saddled with an incompatible and promiscuous wife, who had named her son Ignotus, after his father. Roos had long since ceased to live with her or to acknowledge her children, but she was still his wife. He now asked the Lords to dissolve the marriage, so that he

[107] Feb. 6/16, 1670, Louis XIV to Croissy, Mignet, *Négociations* III, 147–51.

[108] See his letters to Croissy of April 6/16 and May 11/21, 1670, *ibid.*, pp. 168–69, 172–76. When the treaty was finally concluded, Pomponne was of the opinion that, with respect to territory, Louis had given away too much. Rowen, *Pomponne*, pp. 179–80.

might rewed and get a legitimate heir. There was no precedent for this bill; it caused an extended debate, enlivened by a speech from Buckingham in support of a general law permitting either partner to get a divorce for adultery; this, he said, would impose moral restraints on men as well as women. The political implications of this affair were apparent to everyone. The inner ring at court was pushing it: Buckingham, Ashley, Arlington, Lauderdale, Anglesey. The duke of York and his friends were resisting it for obvious reasons. "It is my opinion," wrote Andrew Marvell, "that Lauderdale at one ear talks to the king of Monmouth, and Buckingham at the other of a new queen. It is also my opinion," he went on, "that the king was never since his coming in, nay, all things considered, no king since the Conquest, so absolutely powerful at home as he is at present."[109] If anyone's eyes were still closed, Charles opened them by himself attending the House of Lords, incognito, to listen to the debate. The king continued to make a practice of this, even after the Roos case was over, standing by the fireplace and making jokes with his friends; it was better, he said, than going to a play. Charles may indeed have thought so, but even if the peers were less entertaining than Nelly and her colleagues, some such remark was necessary to mask the king's increasing interest and participation in the day-to-day business of government as the alliance which represented the culmination of his planning and on which his hopes of true independence of Parliament rested took shape.[110]

If King Charles was going to emulate Henry VIII and put away his wife because she gave him no heirs, if, as it turned out, he was merely toying with the plan and eventually decided against it, it was obvious that he had no intention of declaring himself a Catholic. Louis saw that he did not have to worry about the Catholicity clause, and he made no objection to its retention. As a political weapon it might be useful in the future, so he did not even mind paying for it. If, as seemed likely, English opinion remained anti-Catholic, the clause would afford Louis infinite opportunities to blackmail Charles. A calculated indiscretion would raise a dreadful political storm; to avoid this, Charles would have to renounce all thought of

109 Margoliouth, *Marvell* II, 301–2.
110 *Ibid.*, p. 303. Louise F. Brown, *The First Earl of Shaftesbury* (New York, 1933), pp. 188–89. There is an entertaining account of the Roos case in John H. Wilson, *A Rake and His Times* (New York, 1954), pp. 159–62.

an anti-French foreign policy. Charles and Arlington were so infatuated with their own cleverness, so convinced that the clause gave
them control of the alliance, that they completely failed to see the
dangers involved. It was an appalling mistake.

V

It was not long after the signing of the treaty and its tragic
aftermath of Henrietta's death that Arlington awoke to the extent of
his miscalculation. The treaty of Dover as it stood was a completely
unusable document. It could not be communicated to Parliament or
even to the other members of Charles's inner ring. Ashley was an
ex-Cromwellian; Buckingham was the patron of Independency.
Even Lauderdale, who after all had signed the Covenant in his
youth, was not entirely trustworthy in such a matter as this; how
much less so were good Protestants like Bridgeman and Prince
Rupert and Ormonde. So, within six weeks of the signing of the
treaty there arose the idea of a second, false treaty which would be
like the first, except that the Catholicity clause would not be mentioned.[111] The French alliance and the war would be sold to the
Protestants on the grounds of commercial advantage, and, as Buckingham put it in a propaganda pamphlet of 1672, "If ever Holland
should be in danger of a conquest, by the conjunction of the French
and us, the Dutch would rather choose to become part of our
government, than submit themselves to the power of France."[112]
The negotiation of this treaty was to be entrusted to Buckingham in
order to lull his suspicions and flatter his vanity. Arlington was
delighted by this; he must have gotten a great deal of malicious
enjoyment out of his solemn consultations with the duke over terms
and Buckingham's accounts of his triumphs over every diplomatic
obstacle—including Arlington's own feigned reluctance and objections. All this playacting concealed one hard political fact, however:
a treaty without the Catholicity clause was a treaty without a timing
device. A date for the beginning of the war had to be set; the spring
of 1672 was finally decided upon. Both sides knew, and knew that the
other knew, that Charles's declaration of his conversion was not

[111] July 4/14, 1670, Croissy to Louis XIV, Mignet, *Négociations* III,
215–19.
[112] *A Letter to Sir Thomas Osborn . . . Upon the Reading of a Book,
Called, The Present Interest of England Stated* (London, 1672) , p. 16.

going to take place. Arlington vehemently insisted that Louis pay the money stipulated in the Catholicity clause, in the hope of breaking up the alliance if Louis refused. Louis gave way, however; [113] in the simulated treaty these payments were disguised as part of an enlarged war subsidy. To compensate for the shattering of the timing device, France agreed that England should have, in addition to the Dutch territory already promised, the islands of Goree and Woorne, which would give England control of the mouth of the Meuse, as Walcheren, Sluys, and Cadzand did of the Scheldt. But at the same time Louis exacted his first dividend on the Catholicity clause: Charles reluctantly agreed to a written declaration that the simulated treaty in no way invalidated the royal promise to declare himself Catholic at a suitable time.[114]

This *traité simulé* was signed in December, 1670; by that time the drift of English policy was becoming more and more obvious. In September, 1670, came the rude awakening of Sir William Temple: he was recalled, ostensibly to consult about the French occupation of Lorraine and the question of the emperor's adherence to the Triple Alliance but really because his continued presence at The Hague was creating difficulties. Arlington was very embarrassed when his trusting and once trusted friend appeared in his anteroom. He kept Temple waiting a long time, and then, when he finally admitted the ambassador, he refused to discuss anything important and finally called in his little daughter to cut short the interview. Shortly thereafter Temple saw Clifford, to whom he supported the policy of the Dutch alliance until the irascible Sir Thomas lost his temper and told Temple that instead of defending the Dutch he should tell the world what rascals they were.[115] Clifford and Arlington were in fact putting John Evelyn to work on this very task; in January, 1671, the diarist submitted a partial draft of a history of the last Dutch war for comments.[116] The work was never published, which was just as well; Evelyn's prose style was hardly suited to effective propaganda.

The secretary continued fitfully to resist the policy to which his master had committed the country, but his activity was curtailed

[113] Nov. 7/17, 9/19, 1670, Croissy to Louis XIV, Mignet, *Négociations* III, 242–44, 245–46. Nov. 15/25, 1670, Louis to Croissy, *ibid.*, pp. 250–52.

[114] *Ibid.*, pp. 265–67. The simulated treaty is given on pp. 256–65.

[115] *Works of Sir William Temple* II, 173–75.

[116] DeBeer, *Diary of John Evelyn* III, 522–23, 558. *C.S.P.D.* X, 490; XI, 54–56.

partly by bad health and partly by a sense of its futility. He refused
to take money from Louis XIV, although he suggested that a pension to Buckingham's mistress would be helpful to France. He tried
to cause trouble by leaking the secret of the war to Rupert and
Ormonde. He suggested in a roundabout way to De Witt that he try
to propitiate Charles by some spectacular concession to young William of Orange, the king's nephew; the betterment of William's
political position was one of the objectives of the proposed war. His
schemes were not forwarded by the denseness and gullibility of the
representative sent by the Dutch to London early in 1671, who
concluded that the Anglo-French design went no further than a plan
to exhaust the Dutch financially by pursuing a sort of cold-war
policy.[117] Arlington even tried to reopen the question of the fleet,
proposing that France provide an extra million livres instead of the
ships stipulated in the treaty. Louis XIV was "extremely perplexed
and startled" by this suggestion but not startled enough to fail to
reject it out of hand.[118] This plan was mooted in December, 1671,
but by then it was really too late. The late summer and early fall of
1671 had seen the final decisions: Temple was replaced as ambassador to The Hague by the anti-Dutch Sir George Downing, a clear
portent of war, and Parliament was prorogued till October, 1672,
by which time, it was hoped, the Dutch would be utterly defeated
and the triumph of the king's policy assured.

One of the major reasons for Arlington's original acquiescence in
the French alliance was the fact that it entailed no alteration of
English policy toward Spain. Friendship with Spain was still the
basic tenet of Arlington's policy, and throughout the negotiations
with France he had steadily pursued it; his proposal that England
mediate between the two powers was perfectly sincere. From the
beginning it had been understood that Spanish neutrality in the
forthcoming war was what was wanted. This was the easy way out;
the alternative, making Spain an active partner in the alliance,
would have complicated the negotiations and made impossible that
vague French acquiescence in English commercial expansion in the

[117] Feiling, *British Foreign Policy*, pp. 315, 319–20. B.M. Add. Mss.
35,852, ff. 54–56.

[118] Dec. 3/15–6/16, 14/24, 1671, Montagu to Arlington, H.M.C., *Buccleuch and Queensberry Mss.* I, 507–10.

Spanish empire which Arlington regarded as one of the few advantages of a distasteful policy. It was, nevertheless, a blunder on Arlington's part, another example of his shortsightedness. He had no assurance that Spain would remain neutral and be as satisfied as he was with the sincerity of the French pledge to stand by the treaty of Aix.

Throughout 1669 Arlington had been prodding Spain in three directions: first, to subsidize the Triple Alliance so that King Charles might at the last minute be induced to change his mind; second, to give France no excuse for denouncing the treaty of Aix; and third, to clarify the commercial treaty of 1667. The Spanish government was either too blind or too poor to do the first until it was too late; her conduct toward France was stupid enough to drive Arlington to exasperation;[119] but the third was accomplished. Sir William Godolphin, a man with a good deal more skill and finesse than Fanshawe or Sandwich, was sent to Madrid in the autumn of 1669, and by July, 1670, he had brought the Spaniards to terms. England got recognition of her title to Jamaica and her other West Indian possessions; the subjects of the two crowns were forbidden to trade with each other there, but the treaty contemplated the possibility of licensing exceptions to this prohibition in the future. In return, England agreed to put a stop to the privateering, to call it by no worse a name, which had been going on, and the truculent governor of Jamaica, William Modyford, was recalled. Arlington was delighted by the news of the treaty, and congratulated Godolphin warmly.[120] This success took some of the sting out of the defeat he had suffered over the French treaty; it might be possible to combine his Spanish policy and the king's French policy after all.

In less than a year Arlington's hopes were blown to pieces by the activities of Modyford and the piratical Henry Morgan. Taking advantage of careless draftsmanship in a letter of instructions and of Arlington's neglect to communicate the text of the treaty to him

[119] See Arlington's letters of February 7 and May 9, 1670, to Godolphin, Bebington, *Arlington's Letters* II, 291–92, 296–97.

[120] Aug. 19, 1670, Arlington to Godolphin, Bebington, *Arlington's Letters* II, 300–302. In 1670 Arlington helped revive the Council of Foreign Plantations, of which his friend Sandwich became president, in order to tighten the government's grip on colonial administration. Thornton, *West-India Policy*, pp. 116–18, 157–58. Brown, *Shaftesbury*, pp. 144–45.

promptly, Modyford gave Morgan his head, and the celebrated raid on Portobello and Panama was the result.[121] The Spaniards were furious. They had made the treaty chiefly in order to put an end to English raids on their possessions and shipping. Now they were confronted with this blatant example of bad faith, which had apparently been abetted by the English government, which waited until the last possible moment to proclaim the treaty in the Indies. Spain did not denounce the treaty, but Morgan's exploit dissipated whatever goodwill might have accrued. Worse was to follow. On August 25, 1671, Montagu reported a conversation he had with a former ambassador to England, d'Estrades, who believed that when the war came Spain would join the Dutch and that France would not be sorry: they could then gobble up the rest of Flanders. A week later the Spanish ambassador told Arlington that France was planning to attack Spain.[122] Arlington suddenly awoke to the fact that Spain was slipping from his grasp. The young earl of Sunderland, who was to have a long and dubious political career, was appointed as envoy extraordinary to Madrid, his first important mission; he was to assure Spain that the English guarantee of the treaty of Aix still stood and that France had promised not to attack Spain during the minority of Charles II if Spain would decline the Dutch alliance. It was all far too late. In December Spain came down on the Dutch side. Pious Catholic though she was, the Spanish queen regent could not be moved even by the Catholicity scheme.[123]

So, on the eve of the final decisions which ushered in the war, Arlington's diplomacy was in ruins. All that he had striven for since his accession to power had broken in his hands. Spain, whom he had tried so hard to conciliate, was hostile. The alliance with France, which could not be concealed much longer, would evoke widespread

[121] In June, 1670, Arlington wrote Modyford telling him to keep the privateers in the state in which they were when the letter was received—that is, in the state of peace which had been previously ordered. By the time the letter was received, the endemic private warfare had broken out again, so Modyford followed the letter of the instructions, though he knew perfectly well what Arlington meant. For the whole question of the treaty and its aftermath see Thornton, *West-India Policy*, pp. 111–23.

[122] H.M.C., *Buccleuch and Queensberry Mss.* I, 500–501. Sept. 1/11, 1671, Alberti to the Doge and Senate, *C.S.P. Venetian* XXXVII, 105.

[123] Oct. 9, 1671, Arlington to Godolphin, Bebington, *Arlington's Letters* II, 334–39. Feiling, *British Foreign Policy*, pp. 327–28, 334–37. See also P.R.O., S.P. 104/176, ff. 297, 300.

public indignation. The secretary knew very well how hated the French were by all classes of people. One of Joseph Williamson's correspondents in Coventry reported a rumor that children were being kidnapped by French agents "for their blood, to cure the French king of a leprosy." The business class, whose support Arlington valued so highly, wanted no alliance with France and no war for both religious and economic reasons.[124] Even the rulers of the East India Company, of all English merchants the most anti-Dutch, were not anxious to see hostilities renewed; their proposals for a settlement with the Dutch were "eminently reasonable and on the whole moderate."[125] French economic policy made things worse; it was regarded as being directed against England. "You cannot imagine," wrote William Perwich, an agent of Arlington's in France, in September, 1669, "how Mr. Colbert does turn and wind in this matter of trade, and makes no difficulty to do anything, though manifestly against all treaties, to break the neck of our English sale of drapery here."[126] In 1670 there was some sentiment in Parliament for the complete prohibition of French imports, and even the pro-French Buckingham was constrained to complain to Louis XIV about the ill treatment of English merchants in France while he was negotiating the *traité simulé*. In 1671 matters were no better. Perwich complained that France granted greater privileges to the bishop of Liège than to England. "I wonder how they can pretend to court his majesty's friendship at home," he wrote, "when his subjects are so manifestly insulted . . . abroad." French harassment continued; Arlington despairingly remarked in the foreign committee of the council on March 18, 1672, the day after war was declared, that "this matter of trade, if not adjusted, will be so oppressive and ruinous to our merchants that it will turn the spirits of the people against France to a degree that will break the king's alliance."[127] As for the politicians, Andrew Marvell, an opponent of the government wrote in August, 1671, "We truckle to France in all things, to the prejudice

[124] *C.S.P.D.* XI, 452. Williamson's notes, *ibid.*, pp. 496–97, 562–63.

[125] Shafaat Ahmad Khan, *The East India Trade in the XVIIth Century* (Oxford, 1923), pp. 125–26. Cf. their attitude prior to the second Dutch war, *ibid.*, pp. 105–9.

[126] M. B. Curran, ed., *The Despatches of William Perwich*, Camden Society 3rd ser. V (London, 1903), 33.

[127] *Ibid.*, pp. 152–53, 158–59. H.M.C., *Buccleuch and Queensberry Mss.* I, 482–83.

of our alliance and honour." Samuel Pepys, when he heard the rumor that France was about to bribe Charles to break the Dutch alliance, commented in his diary that this "will make the Parliament and kingdom mad, and turn to our ruin." The Venetian ambassador summed it up in October, 1671: ". . . although the king may join France, his subjects will not follow him."[128] There was only one hope for the salvation of any part of Arlington's policy: the war must be short and overwhelmingly successful. Victory would prevent the public explosion; if it were won speedily, Spain, slow to move at the best of times, might not intervene.

Paradoxically, Arlington's personal position never stood higher in men's eyes than in late 1671 and early 1672, as the war he so dreaded was about to be launched. It was at his mansion at Euston, in October, 1671, that Charles at last bedded down Louise de Quérouaille, during a house party of the most lavish sort. Nine months later, in June, 1672, Croissy assured his government that Arlington was all-powerful: "You have in his person the law and the prophets of England."[129] Croissy, and the world in general, were mistaken. Charles had not abandoned his old friend, but the king knew—none better—that the secretary had no enthusiasm for the policy he had been required to adopt. There was a man in the inner ring who was enthusiastic for it, however, and who was experienced in the most immediate problem confronting Charles, that of finance. Once the new course in foreign policy had been set and the war decided upon, some way of paying for it had to be found. The man of the moment was Thomas Clifford.

[128] Margoliouth, *Marvell* II, 311. Pepys, *Diary*, Apr. 28, 1669. *C.S.P. Venetian* XXXVII, 116.

[129] Jusserand, *Receuil* II, 166, n. In April, 1672, Arlington was made an earl.

Chapter 4

The Financial Reef

Clifford

Now, Painter, shew us in the blackest dye
The Counsellors of all this villany.
Clifford, who first appeared in humble guise,
Was thought soe meeke, soe prudent, and soe wise;
But when he came to act upon the stage,
He proved the mad Cethegus of his age.
He and his Duke had both to great a minde
To be by justice and by laws confin'd:
Their boyling heads can hear no other sounds
Than fleets and Armyes, battles, blood and wounds;
And to destroy our libertyes they hope
By Irish fools and by a doting Pope.[1]

Neither Andrew Marvell nor Henry Savile are exactly trustworthy witnesses where the members of the Cabal are concerned, but anyone who could be described as "the mad Cethegus of his age," even by a bitter enemy, is not the sort of man one would expect to find high in the favor of Charles II. Thomas Clifford was really very unlike the other politicians to whom

[1] "Advice to a Painter to Draw the Duke by," H. M. Margoliouth, ed., *The Poems and Letters of Andrew Marvell* (Oxford, 1952) I, 199. The poem has been attributed to both Marvell and Henry Savile.

Charles gave his confidence after 1667; he was in many ways the type of the Cavalier country gentleman. John Evelyn, who was his friend, describes him as "a valiant, uncorrupt gentleman, ambitious, not covetous, generous, passionate, and a most constant, sincere friend to me."[2] He might have added, though he doubtless thought it unnecessary because everybody knew it, that Clifford was absolutely loyal to his king; his was the loyalty of the mastiff dog of the quatrain of Chapter 1. In two respects, however, Clifford did not resemble the typical Royalist gentleman. One was his enormous energy before his health began to give way—he died at the age of forty-three—the quality which first brought him to the attention of the aspiring Sir Henry Bennet and, through him, of the king. The second, and in the end the more significant, was his acceptance of Roman Catholicism.

Clifford needed to be remarkable in some way to make an important political career for himself. Unlike the other members of the Cabal, he was a nobody in 1660; he was merely a Devonshire squire with a seat for Totnes in Parliament. He was born in 1630, the eldest son of the cadet branch of an old family. He was too young to take part in the civil war, in which his family were on the king's side and suffered for it; toward the end of the war he matriculated at Exeter College, Oxford, like many another Devonshire man. At college, according to Anthony Wood, his contemporaries regarded him as "a young man of a very unsettled head, or of a roving, shattered brain,"[3] a description which, given Wood's spiteful nature, may well be *ex post facto*. Clifford did not take a degree at Oxford. He put in some time at the Inns of Court; then, in 1650, he married a Devonshire girl, who was to present him with a great many children, and settled down on his small estates to await better times. The marriage was a happy one; Clifford resembled his patron Arlington in not being a womanizer. The rumor which circulated after his death linking him with the countess of Falmouth seems to be quite without foundation.[4]

In 1660 Thomas Clifford, M.P., was just another Royalist squire. He was presented to the king in August of that year, along with his fellow member for Totnes and the two aldermen of the town, to

---

[2] E. S. DeBeer, ed., *The Diary of John Evelyn* (Oxford, 1958) IV, 20.

[3] Anthony Wood, *Athenae Oxonienses* (London, 1721) II, 93.

[4] Nov. 10, 1674, Dr. Prideaux to Mrs. Coffin, H.M.C., 5th Report, pt. I (London, 1876), p. 374.

present Charles with a gift of money; he remarked that it would have been greater save for the decay of trade. The king must have heard hundreds of such speeches, and this one doubtless made no more impression than any other. What was impressive, especially to Sir Henry Bennet, was Clifford's considerable activity in Commons in these years—he spoke a great deal and averaged fifty committees a year—and the fact that Clifford was clearly unhappy with the policies of Clarendon. He was one of those who felt that the Act of Indemnity and Oblivion was indeed indemnity for the king's enemies and oblivion for his friends, and he favored an unsuccessful motion for an inquiry into the purchase of offices after the Restoration. This energetic backwoods Cavalier could be useful. By the middle of 1662 Bennet had enlisted Clifford in his faction. We find him writing a letter to Ormonde on Clifford's behalf, describing him as a man of "virtue and good parts," and as his particular friend.[5] In September of that year Clifford obtained a share of the farm of the customs duties on logwood, which he retained until 1668, and early in 1663, a reversion of the first tellership of the exchequer to fall vacant.[6] Bennet was always as generous to his friends as it was possible for him to be, and, indeed, the only fault with which Evelyn charged Clifford was his ingratitude to his patron.

It was in Parliament that Clifford was expected to earn his rewards. He fought, though vainly, for the abortive indulgence scheme of 1662, and in 1663 he, along with his fellow west-country man, Winston Churchill, was forced upon Clarendon by Bennet and Sir William Coventry; henceforth these four were to be consulted by the chancellor in regard to the management of Parliament. Clifford was included in this small group because he was Bennet's friend and because he was believed to have influence in the House, an influence which Clarendon discounted in a vain effort to avoid having this unpalatable committee imposed upon him.[7] The future lord treasurer's rise to power had begun.

[5] Quoted in J. J. S. Shaw, "A Biography of Thomas Clifford" (unpublished Ph.D. thesis, University of Glasgow, n.d.), p. 19.

[6] W. A. Shaw, ed., *Calendar of Treasury Books* (henceforth *C.T.B.*) *1667–1668*, p. 402. M. A. E. Green, *et. al.*, eds., *Calendar of State Papers Domestic, Charles II* (henceforth *C.S.P.D.*) (London, 1860ff.) III, 50.

[7] Clarendon says that he was not much impressed by Clifford's ability or his influence, but he granted that Clifford was honest. Edward, Earl of Clarendon, *A Continuation of His History of the Great Rebellion* (Oxford, 1857) I, 617, 619.

On the whole, Clarendon was right. Clifford's influence in the
House was an illusion, which had been created by his espousal of
popular causes at the beginning of his career and by his constant,
hurrying activity. People nevertheless believed that he had influence,[8] and this belief certainly furthered his career. There is some
irony in this, since Clifford was anything but a Commons man.
Parliament, in his view, ought to serve as the handmaiden of the
prerogative. The clearest expression of his opinion came in February, 1668, when Sir Richard Temple introduced a bill which would
have revived the principle of the Triennial Act of 1641, and one of
his supporters spoke of "compelling the king by law." Clifford
violently opposed this "bill of ill consequence," as he called it, as
being contrary to the monarchical principle. The bill got very little
support, and Clifford had the satisfaction of not only seeing it
withdrawn but also of having the House order that in future no bill
of this nature was to be introduced without the House's leave.[9]

As a Parliamentary manager Clifford was not very successful,
though this was not entirely his fault. After Clarendon's fall he and
Joseph Williamson took over the old, loose Clarendonian organization and attempted to manipulate it, employing some of the tech-
niques of bribery and patronage which Danby was to use so successfully in the days of his greatness. Clifford labored under two serious
handicaps, however, which Danby did not have, quite apart from his
lack of Danby's inventiveness and imagination in exploiting the
opportunities available to him. In the first place, Clifford and Arlington never controlled all the sources of patronage as Danby did;
there were other, hostile channels to the king's ear and the king's
favor, notably through Buckingham, and this immensely complicated the problem of building up a body of Parliamentary supporters and then holding it in line. Even more serious was the lack of
a coherent and consistent public policy for which Clifford could be
the spokesman. Charles's real policy during these years had to be
carried out behind the scenes. It was a policy of which Clifford
wholeheartedly approved, but he knew very well that it would be
ruined by disclosure. So he was compelled to operate in a vacuum, to

---

[8] Roger North, *Examen* (London, 1740), p. 38, describes Clifford in
1672 as one "who had once a mighty sway in the House of Commons."

[9] A. Grey, *Debates of the House of Commons* (London, 1763) I, 82–84.
C. Robbins, ed., *The Diary of John Milward* (Cambridge, 1938), pp. 189–90.
W. Cobbett, *Parliamentary History of England* (London, 1808) IV, 410–12.

try to build up a body of support for the king and for the prerogative without being able to explain what it was that the king was seeking, and by the late 1660's, with the failure of the Dutch war, the possibility of building a party on the basis of blind loyalty to the monarchy had long since passed, if, indeed, it ever existed. The consequence was that Clifford was open to the charge of bribing for bribery's sake, of employing corruption either to destroy the independence of Parliament and ruin the country or for the nefarious purpose of his own personal aggrandizement.

Buckingham and his friends were occasionally able to take devastating advantage of this anomalous state of affairs. In October, 1669, an anonymous pamphlet called *The Alarum* was distributed in Westminster Hall, which accused Arlington, Clifford, and Ashley of corruption in the duke's usual hyperbolic style. Arlington is the chief villain, of course, but Clifford is not far behind:

Here is one who hath a great mind to be a minister. . . . He playeth at no small game, nor catcheth at small profits, by which he would seem to neglect his fortune, but it is that he may make it all at once. He sets up to be generous, by being free of the king's wine at his table and of his money in the treasury; but do not mistake the man, he hath too much ambition and too little money to be content. He would be at the top, and thinketh of it at this very hour; and if things succeed as he hath laid them you will see him throw off my Lord Arlington's livery and set up for himself. But in order to this the great work of cheating the Parliament must be carried on, in which he neither spareth his own pains nor the king's money.

And to what end?

To persuade a good king to be a tyrant, and to endeavor to make a free people slaves. . . . When this is to be done Sir Thomas Clifford will be no small man; a great part of the military model of government will be left to him. In his nature he loveth absolute power, and therefore whispereth it to the king, a plausible text to princes; and to make it more so he pretendeth it is easy to be compassed. By this he recommends himself to favour and insinuateth himself into power, gets to be trusted with the secret and the contrivance. In short he is one that needeth a civil war, and therefore sure to promote a standing army.[10]

This was the most extravagant of the attacks on Clifford, but it was not unique. A year or so later, for example, he was accused of being

[10] *C.S.P.D.* IX, 541–42. I have quoted from the excerpt in Andrew Browning, ed., *English Historical Documents 1660–1714* (New York, 1953), pp. 235–36.

the "chief commissioner for the managing the bribe money where-with to buy votes in the Parliament House."[11]

These attacks were very difficult for Clifford to answer, partly because, with respect to public affairs at least, they hit close to the truth. Arlington was in a less difficult position; he had negotiated the Triple Alliance and could declare, with perfect sincerity, that he supported it wholeheartedly. And the Triple Alliance was the public policy of the Cabal period, the screen behind which Charles was playing his deep and complicated game. But it was a screen which could not shield Thomas Clifford; all the world knew that he was violently anti-Dutch, and the paradox of his rise to favor at a time when English policy had ostensibly become pro-Dutch was bound to excite comment—and suspicion.

Clifford had been hostile to the Hollanders from the beginning. The economic interests of his Devonshire constituents were suffering from Dutch competition. Before the Dutch war he was chairman of a Commons committee which was empowered to consider an anti-Dutch petition presented by the City merchants and to look into the question of the growth of English trade. In April, 1664, he gave the committee's report, a long catalogue of the wrongs suffered by English traders at Dutch hands. The House concluded that the Dutch were the greatest obstacle to English commercial expansion and asked Charles to do something about it. What Clifford wanted was war, to redress these economic grievances; he was "the acknowledged leader of the war party."[12]

Clifford got his wish, and it was the war that made his reputation. He was appointed to the commission to care for wounded men and prisoners and to the much more important prize commission, which was headed by Ashley and Arlington, and in March, 1665, he joined the fleet as the representative of both commissions. His job was to see to it that sick, wounded, and prisoners were distributed among the towns of the various coastal districts and that embezzlement of prizes

---

[11] Andrew Browning, "Parties and Party Organization in the Reign of Charles II," *Transactions of the Royal Historical Society* 4th ser. XXX (1948), 23.

[12] Charles Wilson, *Profit and Power* (London, 1957), p. 123. Shafaat Ahmad Khan, *The East India Trade in the XVIIth Century* (Oxford, 1923), p. 103. A letter of Sir William Temple's, dated September 30/October 10, 1667, states that some people in Holland believed Clifford to have been motivated by religious considerations. *The Works of Sir William Temple* (London, 1814) I, 290. There is no corroborating evidence for this.

by individual captains was kept to a minimum. He did a diligent, honest job, especially with the accounts, so much so that in June, 1665, he was rewarded with a gift of a ship taken as prize, the *Patriarch Isaac,* which he could dispose of for his own profit.[13] In July and August of that year he accompanied the earl of Sandwich to Bergen in the attempt to lay hands on the Dutch East India convoy there with the connivance of the Danish authorities, an attempt which ended in failure. The fault was not Clifford's; in fact, Sandwich used Clifford as his apologist to the government in Whitehall for the fiasco. No sooner had Clifford returned from Scandinavia than he was sent back again, with a commission as envoy extraordinary, to collaborate with the resident ambassadors in Copenhagen and Stockholm in an attempt to negotiate a triple alliance against the Dutch. This was an ill conceived and rather desperate plan of Arlington's, and it failed, as it was bound to do. Still, Clifford did not acquit himself particularly well. He allowed himself to be over-reached by the Danes, and he quarreled with Henry Coventry, the ambassador in Sweden. He was recalled rather abruptly at the end of the year; Arlington had evidently concluded, and rightly, that his favorite protégé's talents were not suited to diplomacy. Clifford was too straightforward and too quick tempered for the subtleties of diplomatic negotiation. No blame was attached to him for his failure, but it is significant that he was never used for this sort of work again.[14]

The summer of 1666 saw Clifford back with the fleet. He was present at the Four Days' Battle, having hurried to get there, and was very critical of the behavior of some of the ships' captains: if there was any characteristic Clifford disliked in a man, it was lack of courage. "If the king do not cause some of the captains to be hanged he will never be well served," he wrote to Arlington after the battle.[15] Throughout the summer he continued to report at length from the fleet to Arlington, and he became the secretary's chief

[13] *C.S.P.D.* IV, 452. C. H. Hartmann, *Clifford of the Cabal* (London, 1937), p. 41.

[14] It is true, as C. H. Hartmann has pointed out in *Charles II and Madame* (London, 1934), that Clifford had much to do with the working out of the provisions of the treaty of Dover. But he played no part in the negotiations with France, which were conducted by Charles and Arlington. There is a long account in Hartmann, *Clifford,* pp. 46–102, of Clifford's doings at Bergen and at the Danish and Swedish courts.

[15] *C.S.P.D.* V, xix–xxiv, 430–32.

source of information from there. His name began to be mentioned as that of a rising man. Samuel Pepys, who knew everybody, did not know Clifford in October, 1664, but in September, 1666, he wrote that Clifford "appears a very fine gentleman, and much set by at Court for his activity in going to sea, and stoutness every where, and stirring up and down."[16] Clearly such a man could expect to be rewarded for his services.

During the war certain minor plums had come his way, such as a share in the Irish wine licenses, and a knighthood; at the end of November, 1666, he got his first major political appointment, as comptroller of the household, in succession to the chancellor's deceased friend Sir Hugh Pollard; within ten days he was made a privy councillor as well. His appointment as comptroller caused surprise, according to Evelyn, since Clifford was accounted "a valiant and daring person, but by no means fit for a supple and flattering courtier."[17] No doubt his honesty and efficiency as a prize commissioner recommended him to Charles; more important, this was part of the process of replacement of Clarendonians by new men which preceded the chancellor's fall. The major appointment, however, the one which was to determine Clifford's future career, was made in May, 1667, when he became one of the five commissioners of the treasury, along with Monck, Ashley, Sir William Coventry, and Sir John Duncombe. "The choice [of the commission] is observed to have been of the king's own making," wrote Joseph Williamson in his journal, "much different from the forward judgements of the town."[18] One reason for the employment of a commission was to provide greater governmental influence in the House of Commons, influence which Clifford was expected to supply. Clifford could hardly be regarded as a financial expert, although by now he knew a good deal about the problems of the household, but he was willing to work hard, and he clearly believed in the necessity of new taxes, a position which must have appealed to Charles—at least, he made a proposal in Commons in October, 1666, for a general excise on all inland goods, a motion which horrified the House and was quickly dropped.[19] But, more than anything else, Clifford owed his position

[16] *The Diary of Samuel Pepys* (ed. H. B. Wheatley, London, 1926), Oct. 11, 1664, Sept. 17, 1666.
[17] DeBeer, *Diary of John Evelyn* III, 469–70.
[18] P.R.O., S.P. 29/231, f. 22.
[19] Robbins, *Diary of John Milward*, p. 35.

in what might be called the second circle of the king's advisers to the fact that he was Arlington's man. Pepys, who always wanted to know everything about everybody, gossiped about the new man in April, 1667, with Evelyn. Pepys had believed that Clifford was a member of the senior branch of the family and was rich and learned; Evelyn disabused him of all these misconceptions. Clifford, he said, was poor: he had no more than £140 a year and was only learned enough to be a J.P. The king's favor did not stop with the appointment to the treasury commission. In September, 1667, Clifford and his family took up residence at court, and the king attended his housewarming. In June, 1668, he became treasurer of the household. A month earlier Sir William Coventry had described him to Pepys as a man with enemies, because he was "suddenly rising and a creature of my Lord Arlington's."[20]

Arlington was not simply being altruistic in urging Clifford's claims to preferment. The reputation Clifford had gained during the war was to stand the secretary in good stead when the Commons launched its investigation of the miscarriages of the war in the fall of 1667. All the officials who were responsible for its conduct were in jeopardy. As Pepys put it, "I see everybody is upon his own defense, and spares not to blame another to defend himself, and the same course I shall take."[21] Clarendon was scapegoat-in-chief, and Arlington reluctantly supported the impeachment of the chancellor in order to avoid a similar fate for himself, a fate which he knew Buckingham would be only too happy to mete out to him. Clifford took very little part in the proceedings against Clarendon, though his one recorded intervention in the debate, a statement that "it will make an end of all impeachments here, to have witnesses examined," was certainly hostile to the chancellor.[22] It was Clifford's task to defend the secretary against the charge that he was to blame for the failure of intelligence which led to the division of the fleet in 1666, and he did so successfully, partly by finding other scapegoats,[23] chiefly by getting himself and Colonel Kirkby, who was not un-

[20] Pepys, *Diary*, Apr. 26, June 24, 1667, May 19, 1668. P.R.O., S.P. 29/231, f. 59.

[21] Pepys, *Diary*, Oct. 20, 1667.

[22] Cobbett, *Parliamentary History* IV, 377.

[23] Commissioner Pett, for instance, an ex-Cromwellian who was blamed for the lamentable state of the defenses at Chatham and who, so Clifford said, had hired men at his own expense to pursue Charles after Worcester. Pepys, *Diary*, Nov. 13, 1667.

friendly to Arlington, designated by the House to look into Arlington's papers and report back. The report, delivered in February, 1668, was a whitewash. "The intelligence was so far from being defective," said Clifford, "that it was very good."[24] This was hardly true, but by that time the danger to the secretary, now basking in popularity thanks to the Triple Alliance, was past.

II

The new treasury commission set briskly to work in the summer of 1667. It needed all the energy and optimism it could muster because the government's financial condition was appallingly bad at the end of the war; the debt, as calculated by Clifford in September of that year, stood at about £2,500,000,[25] and it was clear that Parliament would renew its demand for its own commission of inquiry when it reassembled. Rumors of bankruptcy were rife; so, too, were rumors that the new commissioners were unfriendly to the goldsmiths who were the government's principal creditors. A run started on them, which was considerably accelerated when Monck withdrew £12,000 he had deposited with them; on June 18, to quiet people's "vain and groundless fears," Charles had to issue a proclamation promising that the exchequer would continue to meet its obligations.[26] The government's financial distress was such that it was reduced to borrowing small sums from its own officials; the rates of interest at which it had to borrow on the money market were so high that Pepys remarked that "some think that the Dutch themselves will send over money."[27]

In these circumstances the commissioners' problem was threefold: expenditures had to be cut, the ordinary sources of revenue had to be made to yield more, and Parliament must be sufficiently convinced of the government's probity and its necessities to vote additional taxes. All of these lines of approach were diligently followed in the next four years, and, to a greater or lesser degree, they all failed. Because they failed, Clifford was led to advise, and Charles to

---

[24] Grey, *Debates* I, 74–79.

[25] Shaw, "Clifford," p. 110.

[26] *C.S.P.D.* VII, xxxix, 204. Dorothy K. Clark, "A Restoration Goldsmith-Banking House," in *Essays in Modern English History in Honor of Wilbur Cortez Abbott* (Cambridge, Mass., 1941), pp. 33–34. The quoted phrase is in Williamson's Journal, P.R.O., S.P. 29/231, f. 29.

[27] Pepys, *Diary,* Aug. 23–24, 1667.

adopt, the gamble of the Stop of the Exchequer, a partial and qualified declaration of bankruptcy. The gamble failed, not because it was a piece of financial folly, but because the political calculations on which it was based turned out to be mistaken.

Before any attempt at financial improvement could be made by the commissioners, they had to know where they stood. So a spate of orders followed their appointment, orders in which it is not difficult to see the hand of the secretary of the commission, Sir George Downing. A register was to be kept of all tallies struck on any branch of the revenue, "that they may be paid orderly," and exchequer officials were ordered to work longer hours. On May 31, 1667, the farmers of the customs were ordered to present their accounts of receipts and payments for London every Monday "and the like quarterly for the outports"; similar instructions were issued and reissued to the whole host of officials and farmers of various kinds who had to do with the gathering up of the king's monies. The intention was that there should be available each week a statement of the government's cash position for each branch of the revenue and also that the "great inconvenience and prejudice which happen to his majesty" from delays in paying and accounting be ended.[28] All through the *Calendar of Treasury Books* for these years run items like this:

Write Mr. Izaakson, receiver of the duty on logwood, for an account of that farm from the beginning.

Mr. Lawrence [solicitor to the excise] to give an account at the end of every term of what he has done on all processes to get the king's money. [August 12, 1667]

Write all officers of [any of] his majesty's receipts to prepare their account of receipts and debts of their offices to Sept. 29, and to be brought in to the treasury by Oct. 2. [September 17, 1667][29]

Getting a complete and accurate budgetary statement was not easy for Downing. As late as October, 1669, after two-and-a-half-years' work, we find this: "A book to be kept in which is to be entered the total [issues or assignments] charged each year on each branch of the revenue and on the exchequer in general, as also what part of

[28] *C.T.B. 1667–68*, pp. 3, 5–6, 42–43, 256–57; *1669–72* I, 167–68. On September 9, 1665, Pepys noted in his *Diary* that it was the general opinion that officers of state were both lazy and greedy in financial matters.

[29] *C.T.B. 1667–68*, pp. 59, 84.

what is so charged remains unpaid."[30] Owing to the skillful editing
of the treasury books by Dr. Shaw, we have a clearer picture of the
state of King Charles's finances than he ever had, but Downing's
accounts were sufficient to demonstrate what all the commissioners
knew: that the government could not even meet its current bills,
save by the contraction of loans from the goldsmiths or from the
farmers of the various branches of the revenue at very high rates of
interest.[31] Also scattered through the *Calendar* with depressing regu-
larity are items such as these:

My Lords to represent to the king the impossibility of finding money to
disband the army and to take care of paying the seamen, and carrying on
the present expenses. [August 7, 1667]

My Lords say that unless the Parliament do help the king they cannot
pay these debts. [January 17, 1668]

Nothing to be done in it, the king being so much in debt. [July 1, 1668]

Upon the order of the council about the remain of the king's subscrip-
tion to the Royal [Africa] Company, report to be made that there is no
money. [January 21, 1670][32]

Retrenchment was the obvious first step, and it was duly tried.
The king promised not to authorize additional charges on the revenue without consulting the treasury commissioners. In July, 1667, a
ten-man committee was appointed which included all the commissioners and the two secretaries of state to deal with the problem, one
of several fact-finding commissions employed by the new rulers of
the treasury. The king was asked to sign nothing for secret service
except what really was so expended, in order to eliminate concealed
pensions and to grant no more places for life. Clifford, in writing to
Ormonde about the new committee, said that as far as household
expenses, Clifford's particular province, were concerned, current
expenditures were to be compared with those of the sixth year of the
late king. Clifford was not optimistic about the result: the two years
seemed to be about the same. A preliminary report by the committee
in November was found not to be drastic enough, and Charles

[30] *C.T.B. 1669–72* I, 144.

[31] Usually 10 per cent, occasionally more; on November 18, 1667, the
commissioners resolved to ask the privy council to authorize them to borrow at
that figure "because can't get money cheaper." *C.T.B. 1667–68*, p. 121. Clark,
"Restoration Banking House," *Essays . . . in Honor of Wilbur Cortez Abbott*,
pp. 17–18.

[32] *C.T.B. 1667–68*, pp. 56, 231, 369; *1669–72* I, 347.

ordered them to try again and to make further cuts. They did so, and in January, 1668, instructions were issued to various departments respecting their expenditures: Arlington and Morice, for example, were ordered to spend no more than £4,000 a year for intelligence. One useful by-product of this was an Order in Council on January 31 that all major expenditures, save for secret service, pass through the treasury commission.[33] The retrenchments proved inadequate; in May, 1668, the committee was ordered to set to work again, and in July it produced yet another scheme, which calculated the king's annual income at £1,030,000 and which proposed to cut expenditures to £996,475 15s. 10d. Whatever was left over was to go in pensions for those who had helped the king escape from England after the disaster at Worcester.[34] The plan simply did not work; expenses could not be kept so low in view of the mountain of debt and the anticipatory mortgaging of all the major branches of the revenue in return for loans.[35] In December, 1668, the navy commissioners wrote despairingly to the treasury lords, saying that they simply could not get along on £200,000 a year, in view of the navy's debt and the past two years of neglect, which had to be repaired. Their credit was exhausted, they said, and they asked either for more money or for instructions as to how they should spend the money they had, since it was clearly insufficient for all their needs.[36]

The navy was always the treasury commission's principal headache. When the commissioners took over the treasury the navy's debt stood at £951,000; it increased by the end of the war. The amount still owed to the seamen in March, 1668, was enough to cause

[33] P.R.O., S.P. 29/231, ff. 42, 75. *C.S.P.D.* VII, 338; VIII, 197–98, 202. *C.T.B. 1667–68*, pp. 2–3, 46–47, 61. Louise F. Brown, *The First Earl of Shaftesbury* (New York, 1933), p. 181. Shaw, "Clifford," appendix, pp. 159–60. See also S. B. Baxter, *The Development of the Treasury 1660–1702* (Cambridge, Mass., 1957), pp. 12–15, and John Beresford, *The Godfather of Downing Street, Sir George Downing 1623–1684* (London, 1925), pp. 218–19.

[34] P.R.O., S.P. 29/253, ff. 42, 58. *C.S.P.D.* VIII, 499. *C.T.B. 1667–68*, p. 325.

[35] This worked roughly as follows: A. would lend the government £10,000 and receive a promise of repayment with interest on, let us say, the excise revenues of a specific month. In this way all the important branches of the revenue were tied up months, even years, in advance. On September 14, 1668, the commissioners were told that the excise was committed for two years in advance, and was, in fact, overcommitted to the extent of £70,000 a year. *C.T.B. 1667–68*, p. 136. A month earlier the estimate of overcommittedness had been £80,000 a year. *Ibid.*, p. 413.

[36] *C.S.P.D.* IX 119–20. See also *C.T.B. 1667–68*, p. 502.

expressions of surprise on the part of the treasury commission; in December Downing told Pepys that there was no hope of paying the debt unless Parliament acted. All that could be done out of the king's ordinary revenue, he said, was to try to meet current expenses and keep the interest rates from going any higher. Clifford believed the navy office inefficiently run and argued with both the duke of York and Sir William Coventry about it, so he was doubtless pleased at Coventry's removal from the treasury commission early in 1669 as a consequence of the latter's quarrel with Buckingham. Coventry was resentful, and Pepys reported that he talked of Clifford's "folly, ambition, and desire of popularity . . . the rudeness of his tongue and passions when angry." He might have added, though he did not, that Clifford was honest enough to admit his mistakes. In March, 1669, Pepys had an interview with Clifford and was able to convince him that inefficiency was not the navy's basic problem, as, indeed, it was not. The retrenchment was seriously undertaken, some graft was eliminated, but expenditures simply could not be kept to £200,000 a year. At the end of 1670 the deficit for the previous year was £138,000, and the estimated charges for the following year were set at £660,000, for which, by May 24, 1671, the navy had received £110,000.[37]

Under such circumstances retrenchment was a palliative, no more. Money could be, and was, saved: pensions were cut or stopped; attempts were occasionally made to eliminate unnecessary posts in the financial bureaucracy; ambassadors were required to return or purchase the plate they took with them to grace their tables overseas; accounts were scrutinized with care—in July, 1667, the earl of Sandwich's request for £5,000 for the expenses of his embassy to Spain was rejected because it was insufficiently specific.[38] The administration of the city of Bombay, which Charles had acquired along with Catherine of Braganza in 1662, produced an annual deficit of £5,000, so Charles sold his rights there to the East India Company for a nominal rent. Even the yeomen of the guard were reduced in

[37] *C.T.B. 1667–68*, pp. 53, 269. Pepys, *Diary*, Sept. 25, Dec. 27, 1668, Mar. 6, 29, 1669. J. R. Tanner, ed., *A Descriptive Catalogue of the Naval Manuscripts in the Pepysian Library at Magdalene College, Cambridge* (London, 1903) I, 98–107. See also Arthur Bryant, *Samuel Pepys* (new ed., London, 1947) I, 363–64, 381–82.
[38] Brown, *Shaftesbury*, pp. 182–83. *C.T.B. 1667–68*, pp. 45–46, 335–36, 476. *The Collection of Autograph Letters and Historical Documents Formed by Alfred Morrison: The Bulstrode Papers* (privately printed, 1897) I, 44.

strength, from 200 to 100. All these measures helped, but sufficient savings proved impossible to make. For example, on July 7, 1669, Clifford and Duncombe discussed the matter of retrenchment in the Irish establishments with Ormonde, Arlington, and Trevor, among others. "If the whole retrenchments go on," the treasury minute book reads, "yet the king will have but £15,887 in his purse at the end of four years, because the retrenchments will not begin till Xmas next, and so this year will be a greater debt than was accounted upon."[39] Plainly, the only solution was to increase the government's income.

The most obvious source of greater revenue was to increase the take from the tax farmers—virtually all the important branches of the revenue were farmed—and, of course, to be sure that arrears were paid up, not only by farmers, but by all others who owed the king money, such as those ecclesiastics who owed first-fruits and tenths.[40] This was not easy to do, however. The farmers, far from being willing to pay more, clamored for deductions from what they already owed on the ground that the war and various natural calamities, such as the fire and the plague, had cut into their anticipated take. Even Arlington made such requests with respect to his farm of the post office.[41] There were long and complicated discussions between the commissioners and the farmers, particularly of the customs and the excise, over these deductions.[42] Many of them had to be allowed, and occasionally tax exemptions had to be granted, such as the exemption to the City of London from the hearth tax after the fire. Usually some sort of compromise was reached. The government could not afford to be exigent with the farmers—just the reverse, in fact—because it was dependent on them for loans to tide over the emergencies that were constantly arising.[43]

[39] Khan, *East India Trade*, pp. 137–38. P.R.O., S.P. 29/271, f. 9. *C.T.B. 1669–72* I, 102. The Irish debt as of September, 1670, stood at about £245,000. *C.S.P.D.* XI, 54.

[40] *C.T.B. 1667–68*, pp. 426–27. Sept. 23, 1668, Downing to Williamson, *C.S.P.D.* VIII, 603.

[41] *C.S.P.D.* VIII, 52, 109. *C.T.B. 1667–68*, pp. 39, 49.

[42] See, for example, that of July 22, 1669, with the customs farmers and that of October 25, 1669, with the farmers of the London excise, *C.T.B. 1669–72* I, 114–16, 150–51.

[43] *Bulstrode Papers* I, 90. For example, on September 6, 1667, Clifford moved that a letter be written to the London excise farmers promising them a new lease, so that they would lend him money in his capacity as comptroller of the household. *C.T.B. 1667–68*, p. 77. See D. M. Gill, "The Relationship Between

Farming was a pernicious and inefficient system of collecting revenues for many reasons besides the obvious one that the government was not getting everything to which it was entitled. It was disliked by both the merchants and the landed class and by many officials; Sir William Coventry wrote in 1665 of the "dismal necessity" of farming the hearth money.[44] From the beginning the system had not worked as expected. When the excise was farmed at the beginning of Charles's reign, the plan was to use local gentlemen as the farmers in the various counties, to reward them for their loyalty, and, perhaps, to make the tax more palatable. This scheme had fallen through because the moneyed men of the City could offer better terms, and so the country gentlemen were gradually squeezed out and often given a pension on the excise by way of compensation for their loss as the excise contracts were periodically renewed and new ones made as a consequence of such things as the grant of additional duties by Parliament in 1670. The upshot was that control over the excise farm for the whole country was concentrated in the hands of the London group. Clifford, shortly before his resignation as lord treasurer in the summer of 1673, let the whole of the excise for three years to one group—at a substantially increased annual rent, to be sure. But there was considerable danger in allowing the farm to be so concentrated; it made the government too dependent on a small group of financiers who could exercise a form of political blackmail by refusing to make the loans the government required or, alternatively, gouge the government by raising the interest rates.[45]

Fear of the possibility that the excise farmers might also get control of the customs farm and thus completely monopolize the two major branches of the revenue was one of the factors which led to what was to be a very significant action by the treasury commission in September, 1671: the decision to end the farming of the customs altogether and to replace the farmers by a board headed by the

the Treasury and the Excise and Customs Commissioners (1660–1714) ," *Cambridge Historical Journal* IV (1932) , 96–98, for a discussion of how these loans further complicated the treasury's bookkeeping problems.

[44] *C.S.P.D.* V, 125. E. Hughes, *Studies in Administration and Finance, 1558–1825* (Manchester, 1934) , p. 156.

[45] Gill, "Relationship," *Cam. Hist. J.* IV, 94–96. Andrew Browning, *Thomas Osborne, Earl of Danby and Duke of Leeds* (Glasgow, 1951) I, 130–31, 168–69.

indefatigable Downing. The immediate cause of the decision was the greed of the farmers, who, after they had struck their bargain with the government, attempted to alter it to their own advantage. Charles was made very angry by this and refused; the farmers surrendered their lease, perhaps with the expectation of getting it back again when the government found it could get no better terms elsewhere. Ashley and Clifford proposed that a commission be appointed to supervise the collection, and so it was decided, to the satisfaction of the merchant community, who felt that salaried commissioners would be less rapacious than the farmers had been.[46] The decision was an indication of the hardening of the government's attitude toward the city financiers which was to be revealed again, in much more dramatic fashion, in a few months.

The end of customs farming did not appear to be a revolutionary decision at the time. The customs had been collected directly before, and the hearth tax,[47] the most unpopular of all Restoration levies and the most difficult to collect, had ceased to be farmed in 1667, though the farm was to be renewed by Danby in 1674. But the customs were never to be farmed again, and farming of the excise and the hearth tax was to cease in the 1680's. The decision of September, 1671, meant the beginning of the end of tax farming in England.

Clifford's part in these various transactions was not very striking. He did his work conscientiously; his record of attendance at the meetings of the treasury commission was good; but his mind was neither original nor acute in financial questions. He was good at the routine administrative chores: drawing up working papers or decid-

---

[46] Sept. 9, 1671, Martyn Ryder to George Treby, H.M.C., 13th Report, appendix, pt. VI (London, 1893), p. 6. Sept. 12, 22, 1671, Lindenov to Christian V, W. Westergaard, ed., *The First Triple Alliance* (New Haven, 1947), pp. 448–49, 458. Clifford's friend Alderman Bucknall, who was an excise farmer and involved in the negotiations for the customs farm in 1671, was also instrumental in a bid to gain control of the Irish revenue structure in 1669. *C.T.B. 1669–72* I, 107. There had been a proposal by a banking triumvirate to farm the entire revenue in 1663. Clark, "Restoration Banking House," *Essays . . . in Honor of Wilbur Cortez Abbott*, p. 18. For a discussion of the significance of the end of customs farming, see Hughes, *Studies*, pp. 138–43. Another subsidiary difficulty with tax farming was that some of the farmers were M.P.s who could not be prosecuted for debt. See, for example, *C.T.B. 1667–68*, pp. 353–54.

[47] For the hearth tax see L. M. Marshall, "The Levying of the Hearth Tax, 1662–1689," *English Historical Review* LI (1936), 628–46.

ing where to assign this warrant or that.[48] He had an occasional useful suggestion, such as that brewers ought not to be allowed to share in the excise farm because of the possibilities of fraud. He saw the danger of allowing all the revenue farms to be concentrated in one group of men.[49] An indication of the way his mind ran can perhaps be seen in his recording the suggestion that a new order be created, the *Royal Oak,* which could be profitably sold, and the even more extreme proposal that the hearth tax and the excise be abolished and purveyance and tenure by knight service revived.[50] It was not that Clifford had ideas that were shunted aside; during his tenure as lord treasurer he initiated no new policies. His one significant contribution was the Stop of the Exchequer.

The commissioners' attempt to increase the hereditary revenue did bear some fruit; they were, indeed, "turning every stone to advance and improve the king's revenue." The excise, for instance, according to Shaw, produced approximately £250,000 in the year 1668–69 (Michelmas to Michelmas); in 1670–71 it produced £380,000. The total hereditary revenue over the same period rose from £650,000 to £800,000.[51] This was something; it was hardly enough. Only a very considerable expansion of trade could swell these revenues to the point where they would enable the king to meet his current expenses without further borrowing and, if he could, to begin to cut down on his debt. Such an expansion was not taking place.

The government's financial difficulties were compounded throughout the whole of the Restoration period by the lack of an adequate collecting machinery and by the general lack of willingness to pay taxes anyway, which was in large measure a reflection of and a reaction to the political upheavals and financial exactions of the civil war period, when the country was heavily overtaxed. The nation had not yet accustomed itself to the realization that the king could not live of his own at all any more and that the ordinary expenses of government must be met by taxation. A standing army

[48] See, for example, *C.T.B. 1667–68,* p. 460; *1669–72* I, 117–19, 153, 407, 491.

[49] See his speech in the Commons on November 10, 1670, Grey, *Debates* I, 282.

[50] Shaw, "Clifford," pp. 118–19.

[51] *C.T.B. 1669–72* I, viii–xi. The quotation is from a newsletter of November 21, 1667. *Bulstrode Papers* I, 9.

would have been extremely useful in connection with tax collection; it did not exist. The prerogative courts would also have been useful; they did not exist either. The system of tax farming inhibited, indeed, prevented, the growth of an efficient financial bureaucracy, and the lack of such a bureaucracy made tax farming all the more necessary—it was a vicious circle. Collectors were inefficient or dishonest, especially in connection with the hated hearth money. In July, 1667, for instance, the treasury commission found it "strange" that the collector in Northamptonshire should have discovered 8,000 chimneys and collected only £300. In February, 1668, "My lords find their accounts very lame."[52] The situation of the hearth money was not unique, and conscientious officials like Pepys shook their heads over it. On November 9, 1663, he recorded in his *Diary* the view of one of his friends that "half of what money the Parliament gives the king is not so much as gathered."

The local authorities were not helpful to the government. "Perhaps it would be an exaggeration to say that no justice of the peace let a day pass without defrauding the crown, but as a group they were apathetic and often hostile to the collectors of the direct revenues, and they were certainly less than sympathetic to the needs of the central administration."[53] The king could get justice at Westminster, but even here unsuspected difficulties sometimes arose. In January, 1670, the chief baron of the exchequer, on being asked why he did not assist the subfarmers of the hearth money against delinquents, replied that prosecution for such small debts was too troublesome and expensive. Ashley reminded him that the government's revenue was largely made up of shillings and sixpences; the chief baron continued to hedge in the face of this obvious truth.[54] "We do not usually think of the English as the most delinquent taxpayers in Europe, but this was probably the case in the second half of the seventeenth century."[55]

There was another difficulty: sheer administrative inefficiency at the center. The Clarendonian regime had not been notably efficient, but it had possessed a recognized head who could be, and was, held

---

[52] *C.T.B. 1667–68*, pp. 27, 245. The rate was two shillings a chimney, save for the very poor. The government never did realize much from the hearth money until Danby's time. See Browning, *Danby* II, 29–30.

[53] Baxter, *Treasury*, p. 80.

[54] *C.T.B. 1669–72* I, 351–52.

[55] Baxter, *Treasury*, p. 79.

responsible, whether justly or not, for its shortcomings. After 1667, however, there was no administrative head. Arlington came closest to occupying this position, but his preeminence was never acknowledged, and he had no control over the activity of the treasury commission. Clarendon's conciliar system of government had provided a focus in the privy council, where policy questions could be thrashed out and a certain amount of consistency in the activity of the various branches of government obtained. No such focus existed after 1667, not even in the foreign committee of the council. The king contributed to this situation, since he prevented anyone from acting as chief of the administration. He was himself its policy-making head, but his attention to detail was intermittent at best, and the secrecy with which his real policy had to be pursued made consistency and efficient administrative supervision impossible. If an administration is to be cohesive, either it must be headed by an efficient administrator or its purposes and principles must be widely known and publicly accepted by those in responsible positions. Since neither condition obtained, confusion and inefficiency was frequently the result. To cite but one example among many: on May 12, 1669, the question of an abatement in the Irish revenue claimed by the farmers was discussed at length. At the end of the record comes this note: "All the debate here came upon an order of council brought hither for £15,000 abatement, but how that [order] came my lords know not."[56] Lack of coordination was not the only difficulty; there was inefficiency inside the treasury commission's own organization. As late as April, 1670, almost three years after they had set out to do this, we find that "Sir G. Downing to make a certificate how every branch of the revenue was charged at Xmas and how since. And thenceforward every Monday a weekly certificate to be made to my Lords what warrants are charged the week before and on what branch of the revenue each warrant is charged."[57]

Administrative efficiency would have helped, but it was not the solution to the king's financial problems. Even an efficient administration could not have done more than provide a modicum of relief. There remained Parliament. Only Parliament could provide enough money for the king to pay off all his debts, and everybody

[56] *C.T.B. 1669–72* I, 68.
[57] *Ibid.*, p. 420.

knew it.[58] Here Clifford, with his experience and supposed influence in the House, might have been expected to produce results. Clifford was a politician rather than a financier; it is a measure of his lack of political skill and insight that no such results were forthcoming. His opponents suspected Clifford of all sorts of sinister machinations. He was the "bribe master general";[59] here, once more, is his enemy Andrew Marvell:

> And place me by the Barr on the left hand
> Circean Clifford with his charming Wand,
> Our Pig-eyed Duncomb in his Dover Fashion
> Sate by the worst Attorney of the Nacion,
> This great triumvirate that can devide
> The spoyls of England; and along that side
> Place Falstaffs Regement of Thread-bare Coates
> All looking this way how to give their votes,
> Their new made band of Pentioners
> That give their votes more by their eyes than ears.[60]

King Charles's plans might have gone better if Clifford had possessed some of the Machiavellian skill attributed to him. But he did not. Consider, for instance, the situation in the excise. When Clifford, as lord treasurer, let the whole excise to a single group in 1673, there was some £20,000 a year owing in pensions, chiefly to country gentlemen who had at one time held part of the excise farm and who were being compensated for having been squeezed out by the City financiers. Clifford did not see, as Danby did, that this pension money, taken over and paid out by himself, could be used to build political support in Parliament; he allowed the farmers to go on paying the pensions.[61]

Unhappily for Clifford's and the government's hopes for financial help from Parliament, the habitually delinquent attitude of Englishmen of the Restoration period toward the payment of taxes, only occasionally in abeyance in the first seven years of Charles's reign, as

[58] For example, on July 6, 1669, the treasury minute book reads, "Sir William Bolton called in. He shall be amongst the first to be settled with when the Parliament provides money to pay the king's debts." *Ibid.*, p. 101.

[59] Hughes, *Studies*, p. 152, n. 618. See also Browning, *Danby* I, 82–83.

[60] "Further Advice to a Painter," written late in 1670 or early in 1671. Margoliouth, *Marvell* I, 168.

[61] Browning, *Danby* I, 168–69. By the fall of 1675 some thirty-odd M.P.s were receiving excise pensions from Danby. *Ibid.*, pp. 170–71.

for instance in the flush of enthusiasm which marked the opening of
the Dutch war, had returned in full force. Indeed, it was aggravated
by the failures of that war. Parliament met in the autumn of 1667 in
a very uncharitable mood. The king realized that, in addition to
allowing them to make a scapegoat of Clarendon—no great hardship—he would have to permit the investigation of his expenditures
which he had so vigorously resisted before. The treasury commissioners wanted funds, but no tax money was asked for; Charles
realized that the first wave of anger over the miscarriages of the war
would have to subside. So, Lord Keeper Bridgeman, at the opening
of the session, told the Commons, "His majesty formerly promised
that you should have an account of the moneys given towards the
war: which his majesty hath commanded his officers to make ready:
and since that way of Commission wherein he had put the examina-
tion of them hath been ineffectual he is willing that you should
follow your own method. Examine them in what way and as strictly
as you please."[62]

This was a humiliating step for the king to have to take, and he
bitterly resented it. The personnel of the commission named to look
into the accounts was not objectionable from Charles's point of
view. Excepting possibly Buckingham's man Colonel Thompson,
who was a millenarian in religion and an ex-official of the Cromwellian regime, it contained no outright opponent of the court, a fact
which underlines very sharply the unintentionally disastrous nature
of its report. Charles's officials accounted for approximately
£5,813,000; the commission declared that it could not be sure of
£1,378,000 of this but that the balance, £4,335,000, had been spent
on the war. Dr. Shaw states that the commission's arithmetic was at
fault here; Charles spent on the war what he said he had. Furthermore, Charles voluntarily accounted for £1,458,000 of money which
had not been voted for the war, but which he had spent on it
anyway. Some of this, like the money realized from the sale of prizes,
perhaps ought to have been so spent, but some of it, such as hearth
money, was supposed to be used for the normal expenses of government.[63] Because of the commissioners' faulty arithmetic and igno-

[62] Quoted in *C.T.B. 1667–68*, p. 1. In September orders had been issued
to the relevant officials to prepare their accounts in anticipation of this inquiry.
C.S.P.D. VII, 470–71. P.R.O., S.P. 29/231, f. 57.

[63] This account is based on Shaw's introduction to *C.T.B. 1667–68*, pp.
1–lxxxv.

rance of treasury procedures, because of the Commons' failure to realize that the king had in fact dipped into his regular income to pay for the war, the report was treated in Parliament, when it was finally considered there in 1669, as simply one more example of governmental waste, inefficiency, mismanagement, and corruption.

Charles regarded the matter very differently. He and his treasury commissioners did not misread the report: the nature of their financial dilemma was now made painfully clear to them—and at a moment when the negotiations for the treaty of Dover, and its consequence, a new war with the Dutch, were moving toward their conclusion. Charles put it this way in his speech to Parliament in February, 1670:

> When we last met I asked you for a supply, and I ask it now again with greater instance. The uneasiness and straightness of my affairs cannot continue without very ill effects to the whole kingdom. Consider this seriously and speedily. It is yours and the kingdom's interest as well as mine, and the ill consequences of a want of an effectual supply must not lie at my door. And that no misapprehensions or mistakes touching the expenses of the late war may remain with you, I . . . do affirm to you that no part of those moneys that you gave to me for that war have been diverted to other uses, but on the contrary, besides all those supplies a very great sum hath been raised out of my standing revenue and credit, and a very great debt contracted, and all for the war.[64]

All this was true enough, but Parliament paid no heed. In February, 1668, before the report was completed, Charles asked for a supply. He had some reason to hope for success. Clarendon, the principal scapegoat for the late troubles, was now in exile, and the Triple Alliance had just been signed; the money was to be used to set out a fleet in consequence of that agreement.[65] There was trouble from the beginning. Some members wanted an inquiry into the king's debts; others wanted to be informed of the exact terms of the treaty before any supply was voted. This last suggestion was scotched by Solicitor-General Finch on the ground that it constituted an invasion of the prerogative. But the mood of the members was shown by the fact that, when the House went into Grand Committee on supply, one of those who had demanded this information was voted into the chair.

[64] *Ibid.*, p. lxxxvi. According to a memorandum dated February 15, 1670, drawn up by Arlington, the cost of the war exceeded the sums voted for it by Parliament by £1,620,000. *C.S.P.D.* X, 68–69.

[65] P.R.O., S.P. 29/253, f. 16.

Some even argued that there should be no supply at all, on the ground that the king had enough money from previous grants to set out the fleet. Finally it was decided that £300,000 should be raised over a two-year period, but not by means of a land tax or a home excise.[66] After a good deal of debate it was voted, partly, at least, out of anti-French feeling, that the money should be raised by an increased levy on imported wines and spirits. A poll tax was considered and rejected. The usual fanciful suggestions cropped up in the debates, notably the proposal of that aging firebrand William Prynne that the government might usefully confiscate the estates of duelists, that is, Buckingham's; the duke had just fought his engagement with the earl of Shrewsbury. Clifford seems to have sat silent throughout most of these discussions. There is no evidence of leadership on his part, and only once did he intervene to any effect, toward the end, when he successfully opposed an effort to appropriate part of the new levy specifically to the navy.[67]

The results of this session could hardly be called encouraging to the government. Pepys, who knew how desperate the navy's financial straits were and who was convinced that £300,000 was not nearly enough for the fleet,[68] concluded a gloomy passage in his *Diary* on April 30, 1668, with the phrase, "So we are all poor, and in pieces—God help us!" The measure of the government's difficulties can be seen in the decision taken in the autumn of 1668 to look into the question of the sale of crown property—that is, the rents of the fee farms, which were expensive to collect and which might realize some four or five hundred thousand pounds, which would be used to clear off some of the anticipations currently charged on the customs and the excise.[69]

The session of 1669–70 was not much better. This time £400,000 was to be raised on virtually the same items, but the debate was sharper in tone, with accusations of mismanagement and, significantly enough, attacks on the moneyed men of the City who were profiting from the government's financial straits. Clifford tried to get

[66] Grey, *Debates* I, 84–85, 89–90. Robbins, *Diary of John Milward*, pp. 191–92, 198.

[67] Grey, *Debates* I, 118–20, 148. The relevant debates are in *ibid.*, pp. 94ff., and in Robbins, *Diary of John Milward*, pp. 202ff. See also Margoliouth, *Marvell* II, 65–75.

[68] Pepys, *Diary*, Feb. 26, 1668.

[69] P.R.O., S.P. 29/253, f. 76.

a larger sum voted, asking, "If you know of a debt upon one office of £500,000, will four do it?" This was all in vain. The opposition persisted in its view that the king's revenues were greater than ever; comparisons with the high taxes levied by the Dutch to pay off their war debt failed to make any impression.[70] Once again Clifford was not particularly helpful. He justified the request for money by pointing out that the daily cost of the fleet ran to £1,500, and that it was necessary to send money to bolster the Triple Alliance, since the Swedes were a "mercenary" people. His enemy Henry Coventry, the former ambassador to Sweden, caught him up on this: such epithets might alienate the Swedes. Clifford had to explain away the objectionable word, which showed what he thought of the Triple Alliance; his explanation was lame. "*Merces*," he said, "being but 'a reward for a thing done,' though sometimes taken in an ill sense."[71] The rates on imported wines were set at a high figure; the government's spokesmen argued for lower rates on the ground that the higher ones would hurt receipts. They were met by the argument that at the lower rates it would take so long to raise the £400,000 that "the imposition would shade into a perpetuity."[72] The government made the best of it; in April Charles was asked in the foreign committee to thank Parliament "for having done all he desired and nothing that he would not have done," and "at coming down (a pretty ridiculous thing!) Sir Thomas Clifford carried Speaker and Mace, and all members there, into the king's cellar to drink his health."[73]

Clifford took a much larger part in the debates on supply in the session which ran from October, 1670, to April, 1671, a session which went well enough for the government to lead some modern historians to assert that it represented a success for the court party.[74] Success is a relative term, however. It is true that on this occasion the

[70] The crucial debate was that of November 26, 1669. Grey, *Debates* I, 186–89.

[71] *Ibid.*, pp. 176–77.

[72] Margoliouth, *Marvell* II, 92–94.

[73] P.R.O., S.P. 104/176, f. 231. Mar. 21, 1670, Marvell to Popple, Margoliouth, *Marvell* II, 301.

[74] Browning, *Danby* I, 82–83. D. T. Witcombe, "The Cavalier House of Commons: The Session of 1663," *Bulletin of the Institute of Historical Research* XXXII (1959), 181. D. T. Witcombe, "The Cavalier House of Commons: Court and Country Manoeuvres 1663–1674" (unpublished Ph.D. thesis, University of Manchester, 1963), pp. 182–217.

government's case was more carefully prepared than usual. On October 27, 1670, Clifford led off the debate with a speech which set out the government's financial plight in great detail and ended by asking for £800,000 for the fleet.[75] Six weeks later, on December 10, when the House showed signs of flagging, Charles himself called the members to Whitehall, informed them that Louis XIV planned to come to Dunkirk in the summer with 40,000 men to repair the fortifications there and "that he thought fit to tell them of it, to let them see the necessity of being well prepared, that we might owe our safety to our own strength and not to his courtesy," and asked again for the £800,000. Clifford had carefully laid the foundation for this speech the day before by pointing out that what they had agreed upon thus far would bring in but £400,000 a year.[76] The Commons were sufficiently impressed to try to raise the money, even by a land tax, although they quickly reversed themselves on this. An additional excise was levied as was a tax on legal proceedings which was the ancestor of the later stamp duties.[77] Furthermore, a subsidy was voted, which was levied on the basis of income and profits rather than on capital, with especially high rates on borrowed money kept on deposit by bankers. There was no tax on money lent to the government. Loans were to be sought on the security of this levy, at 7 per cent. This was a patent attempt to force down the interest rates for the benefit of the government. However well intentioned the Commons may have been, the government's position was not appreciably eased. By the time of the Stop of the Exchequer, according to Shaw, the subsidy had yielded £211,000, the legal duties £7,400, and the additional excise had been farmed for about £104,000 a year—a far cry from the £800,000 wanted for the fleet.[78]

---

[75] Grey, *Debates* I, 270–71.

[76] B. D. Henning, ed., *The Parliamentary Diary of Sir Edward Dering 1670–1673* (New Haven, 1940) , pp. 24–25, 27.

[77] For these duties see E. Hughes, "The English Stamp Duties 1664–1764," *English Historical Review* LVI (1941) , 234–42.

[78] Henning, *Dering*, pp. 36–38. Margoliouth, *Marvell* II, 119. Shaw, in *C.T.B. 1669–72* I, xxxiv. Among other things, the salaries of officeholders were taxed, a proposal warmly supported by Clifford, though most of the court party opposed it. Henning, *Dering*, pp. 39–40, 57. Clifford also supported an unsuccessful attempt to allow the transfer of some of the bankers' debts to the new subsidy bill, thus relieving the pressure on the other branches of the revenue. *Ibid.*, pp. 73, 78–79. It was also proposed in these debates that new building in London be taxed, a manifestation of rural jealousy of the metropolis. Clifford successfully

The protracted debate on these money bills was very revealing in many ways. For one thing, it showed a steadily mounting hostility to the bankers on the part of both government spokesmen and opposition. Sir John Duncombe, a treasury commissioner, said that the king's estate was mortgaged to these men; William Garroway, an opponent of the government, said that Genoese bankers had ruined the king of Spain, that the French king had made himself great by destroying the bankers, and that their English counterparts were "Commonwealth's-men that destroy the nobility and gentry." Clifford called them "necessary evils."[79] For another thing, the ostrich-like attitude of many members continued. In the opening phases of the debate after Charles's speech, it was said "that it was possible to supply the king out of his own, and that there was a million of money yet due the king of the former aids given him since his coming in, and this was in the receiver's hands." This moved the short-tempered Downing to exasperation. He said that not more than £110,000 was outstanding, of which £25,000 was due from the City of London and had been respited on account of the fire. Most of the rest, he added, was owed by M.P.s who could not be proceeded against owing to their privilege of freedom from arrest for debt. "These last words gave great offense to the House"; Downing was threatened with the Tower unless he named names, which he then proceeded to do.[80] The House was sufficiently mollified, or embarrassed, not to imprison Downing, but the trouble did not end there. In February, 1671, while one of the subsidy bills was before the Lords, Lord Lucas made a speech there, in the king's presence, complaining against the oppressive taxes burdening the kingdom. The speech was ordered burned by the common hangman, but it led the Lords to amend the bill and produced a row between the Houses over the Lords' right to do this, a row which was ended only by the prorogation in April.[81]

Most striking of all, however, was the hostility to France which

---

opposed this; it was beaten by one vote. *Ibid.*, pp. 8–9. Grey, *Debates* I, 301–2. For the working of the subsidy see W. Kennedy, *English Taxation 1640–1799* (London, 1913), pp. 43–44.

[79] Grey, *Debates* I, 272–75, 352–53.

[80] Henning, *Dering*, pp. 30–31.

[81] *History and Proceedings of the House of Lords from the Restoration in 1660 to the Present Time* (Timberland) (London, 1742) I, 106–10.

was revealed by the debates,[82] a hostility deliberately played on by the government at a time when the treaty of Dover had been signed and when the *traité simulé* was being negotiated. It was the danger from France which the government stressed in its requests for money, and it was to meet that danger that the House was prepared to be generous. The government's tactics in this business make it perfectly clear that Charles and Clifford had given up all hope—if, indeed, they had ever had any—of solving their financial problems by means of genuine cooperation with Parliament. And, indeed, these problems had not been solved or even greatly alleviated by Parliament. According to Shaw, the taxes voted in these three sessions of Parliament had produced, by the end of 1671, approximately £660,000, which was a mere drop in the bucket.[83] The majority of the House of Commons still held to the obsolete theory that the king ought to live of his own and that taxation was for emergencies. They would not vote to tax themselves directly by means of a land tax; they were afraid to raise the excise or to broaden its scope, lest Charles be able to govern without them;[84] the tales of the government's corruption, mismanagement, and extravagance gave them an excuse to be tightfisted. There was no hope to be had in Westminster.

So the peacetime years brought no improvement in the king's financial situation; it was as grim in 1671 as it had been in 1667. In October, 1670, it was estimated that the interest-bearing debt stood at over £2,000,000, and that some £3,000,000 would be required really to set the government on its feet again. Charles was far from frugal, and this did not help; far worse were what the commissioners called "great anticipations under a devouring interest."[85] The king could not even pay his servants; in March, 1670, Ralph Montagu, the ambassador in France, wrote to Arlington, "I have not yet, for my standing allowance from Michelmas last till Christmas, anything but an order from the commissioners, upon which nobody yet, my sister writes me word, will advance any money."[86] It was always difficult for

[82] See, for example, the speech of Sir Robert Howard on November 18, 1670, Grey, *Debates* I, 293.

[83] Shaw, *C.T.B. 1669–72* I, x, xxxiii–xxxiv.

[84] Kennedy, *English Taxation*, p. 62. On this point see also Pepys, *Diary*, July 7, 1667.

[85] Browning, *Danby* I, 108. Brown, *Shaftesbury*, p. 187.

[86] H.M.C., *Mss. of the Duke of Buccleuch and Queensberry* (London, 1899) I, 468.

ambassadors to get their money, but even the king's officials at home, even the treasury commissioners themselves, were often hard put to it to obtain their pay. "The officers of the works to stay a while for their exchequer salaries," reads an entry for December 10, 1667, and there are many such.[87] The government's difficulties were no secret, and its efforts to raise cash on its marketable assets were not very successful. Total sales of fee-farm rents, for instance, reached the high figure of £550,000 in 1671–72, but substantial blocks of these were simply transferred to important creditors, like the would-be customs farmers of 1671, whose advance was largely repaid in this way.[88] Debts had to be paid, of course, but the government's cash position was not improved.

Retrenchment, expansion of the hereditary revenue, Parliamentary grant—all had failed to alleviate the king's difficulties. And a war was being planned which would entail large initial expenditures which the French subsidy would not cover. In November, 1670, the Danish ambassador took note of the work on the fleet, which was progressing, but, he wrote, there was difficulty in finding crews. Men would not join because those who served in the last war had not yet been paid.[89] It was clear that the financial difficulty, if it was to be solved at all, had to be dealt with in the larger context of the king's political design.

III

Clifford's career as a financial expert was far from spectacular, and his ability to manage Parliament hardly entitled him to conspicuous reward. Yet he continued to grow in King Charles's favor and to maintain his position in the rivalry, chiefly with Ashley, for influence and control in the treasury commission, less for what he achieved than because he was honest and unswervingly loyal and because, as *The Alarum* put it, "in his nature he loveth absolute power"—because of his firm and publicly expressed belief in the overriding authority of the prerogative. He was ambitious, too, and

[87] *C.T.B. 1667–68*, p. 143. See also *ibid.*, p. 74; *1669–72* I, 139–40; II, 772.

[88] For the sale of fee-farm rents see D. C. Coleman, "Sir John Banks, Financier," in F. J. Fisher, ed., *Essays in the Economic and Social History of Tudor and Stuart England* (Cambridge, 1961) , pp. 221–22, and Shaw's introduction to *C.T.B. 1672–75*, pp. viii–xiii. See also *ibid. 1669–72* II, 932–33, 991–92, 997–98; P.R.O., S.P. 104/176, f. 245.

[89] Westergaard, *First Triple Alliance*, p. 331.

supremely self-confident. After his death Shaftesbury once remarked
that Clifford had said that his horoscope had told him, "while he was
only Sir Tho. Clifford and a Parliament man . . . 'My lord, I shall
be one of the greatest men in England; don't impute what I say
either to fancy or vanity; I am certain that I shall be a mighty man,
but it will not last long, I shall not hold it, but die a bloody
death.' "[90] Clifford evidently believed in horoscopes, and in this case
it was tolerably accurate.

These qualities in Clifford were not unique; he had yet more to
recommend him. He was Arlington's closest political ally, yet, unlike
his patron, he was anti-Dutch, so much so that when the war finally
came, he alone, of Charles's ministers, favored the total destruction
of the Dutch state, according to the French ambassador.[91] He could
therefore be enormously useful in the delicate business of managing
Arlington, which was indispensable to the king's central plan of
achieving independence of Parliament by means of an alliance with
France. It was no accident, therefore, that Clifford was one of those,
along with Arlington, whom Charles entrusted with the secret of his
"conversion." Clifford would wholeheartedly support the policy
which was to flow from that conversion, and he might well be
helpful in bringing Arlington around. And perhaps he was. Arlington ostensibly capitulated to the king's wishes in June, 1669, and
wrote the letter to Henrietta quoted above; in that same month
Clifford was officially admitted to the inner ring of the king's advisers by being appointed to the foreign committee of the privy
council.[92]

Charles had wrought better than he knew. Clifford embraced not
only the new policy but also the new religion. The problem of the
exact time of Clifford's conversion to Catholicism is a difficult one.
There is no evidence for Burnet's statement that Clifford was a
Catholic before the Restoration.[93] His biographer's view is that
Clifford's conversion came late in life and was the fruit of a good
deal of theological study. In 1669 he was buying books of Catholic
theology extensively; at this stage he may have hoped for some sort

[90] DeBeer, *Diary of John Evelyn* IV, 22.

[91] J. J. Jusserand, ed., *Receuil des instructions données aux ambassadeurs de France, Angleterre* (Paris, 1929) II, 104–5, n.

[92] See above, p. 105. Shaw, "Clifford," p. 141.

[93] Gilbert Burnet, *The History of My Own Time* (ed. Osmund Airy,
Oxford, 1897–1900) I, 402.

of reunion between the Church of England and Rome.[94] This was not such an absurdly unworkable notion, even for a House of Commons man, as it might seem. The most violent anti-Catholic postures of the Commons lay in the future; in the 1660's they had been at least as hostile to dissenters as to Papists. Clifford was deeply involved in the working out of the treaty of Dover; many of the original drafts are in his hand.[95] After it was signed, Clifford took the lead in urging upon Charles the implementation of the Catholicity clause. He even drew up a set of instructions for an embassy to the Pope. Charles kept stalling: first it was because the Pope was dying; then it was because various theological doubts had to be cleared up, and because these doubts had to do with questions of natural philosophy, the theologian who was to resolve them must also be a chemist—a difficult interdisciplinary combination to find. Finally Charles had to say straight out to Clifford that the time was not ripe and that nothing could be done.[96]

By 1671 Clifford's religious tendencies were becoming apparent to those who knew him best. It is true that in July of that year he had the chapel at his estate at Ugbrooke dedicated with Anglican rites, but he could hardly do anything else; two months earlier his friend John Evelyn wrote that he was "a little warping to Rome."[97] His drift into a close political alliance with the duke of York made his tendencies still more apparent. His enthusiasm may well have been quickened by the breaking of his health. At the beginning of 1672 he began to suffer from the stone; in the summer he had a savage attack of gout, "the old distemper," he called it in writing to Arlington. These diseases, coupled with the strain of the war and of his seven-month tenure of the treasury and the disappointment he suffered in the collapse of his plans and his hopes for his master, were to kill him in October, 1673. "These things" wrote Evelyn in his diary under date of July 25, 1673, "his high spirit could not support."[98]

[94] Hartmann, *Clifford*, pp. 12, 189–91.

[95] After her return from Dover, Henrietta wrote a note of thanks to Clifford, "the ferste letter I have ever write in inglis," as she said. Hartmann, *Charles II and Madame*, p. 318.

[96] Hartmann, *Clifford*, pp. 153, 160–65. Arthur Bryant, *King Charles II* (rev. ed., London, 1958), pp. 172–73.

[97] Hartmann, *Clifford*, pp. 203–4. DeBeer, *Diary of John Evelyn* III, 577.

[98] July 16, 1672, Clifford to Arlington, *C.S.P.D.* XIII, 347. On July 29 he wrote to Williamson, "I am ever in pain." *Ibid.*, p. 414. DeBeer, *Diary of John Evelyn* IV, 16.

Clifford's religious enthusiasm, which became steadily more obvious, his championship of the declaration of indulgence, and his violent and disastrous opposition to the Test Act, which probably prompted the epithet of "mad Cethegus," added considerably to Charles's difficulties and embarrassments when his designs collapsed in 1673. More important than these things, however, more important even than his support of the French alliance, which in the first instance was Charles's policy rather than his, was Clifford's contribution to the accomplishment of the design, a contribution which was peculiarly his own: the Stop of the Exchequer.

In the fall of 1671 the government's most pressing financial need was for ready cash to prepare for and then to fight the war. Parliamentary supply was inadequate. So, too, was the French subsidy; Charles, who thought in political rather than in economic terms, had given way on this point in the negotiations for the treaty of Dover. Matters were complicated still further by the decision in September, 1671, to end the customs farm. The transition to government-appointed collectors would take time, and meanwhile returns would be diminished, both by the bureaucratic adjustments entailed by the new system and by the proposed war itself, which would handicap trade for a while at least. The farmers could not be dealt with for an advance or for loans; in fact, their advance had to be refunded out of the fee-farm rents. It was impossible to borrow any more; the security the government could offer was insufficient, even at the prevailing high rates of interest, and the bankers simply would not lend.[99] In any case the government was not disposed to finance the war by borrowing from the goldsmiths. The last war had been so financed, and the results, from the government's point of view, were not good: a huge debt, very high rates of interest, and the necessity for accepting various unsatisfactory farming contracts.[100] Under these circumstances the king had only two choices: he could either abandon the war policy or he could turn to the one available source of cash, the hereditary revenue. This revenue was already pledged to the hilt—a year to eighteen months in advance—for the repayment of loans already contracted. What Charles could do was

[99] *C.T.B. 1669–72* II, 1033–35, 1255–56. Browning, *Danby* II, 27. Hughes, *Studies,* pp. 140–41. Hartmann, *Clifford,* p. 213.
[100] On this point see Clark, "Restoration Banking House," *Essays . . . in Honor of Wilbur Cortez Abbott,* pp. 23–30.

Charles II

John Maitland, duke of Lauderdale

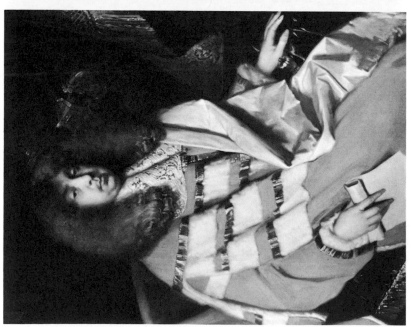

Henry Bennet, earl of Arlington

Thomas Clifford, Baron Clifford of Chudleigh

George Villiers, duke of Buckingham

Anthony Ashley Cooper, earl of Shaftesbury   *James II*

to suspend these repayments, postpone them until a later date, and use the cash thus liberated for the expenses of the war. This is essentially what the Stop of the Exchequer amounted to.[101]

It was the navy that needed the money. In 1670 the navy commissioners were having difficulty in borrowing for their current needs. With the signing of the treaty of Dover, it was ordered that naval preparation be speeded up and at the same time that the debt be held down—a difficult operation to manage.[102] In May, 1671, it was estimated that the debt for the current year would be £263,000, if only the minimal expenses of peacetime operation were met, but that, of course, was not enough for Charles. In that month Downing wrote to Ashley, "Both the king and the duke were this afternoon at the treasury chambers about more money for the navy, and the navy commissioners are ordered to bring a particular of what moneys they would have for this year's expense: the consequence whereof your lordship will easily conjecture." So the Stop was decided upon as soon as the decision was taken to set out the fleet on a war footing in the spring of 1672.[103]

The plan was Clifford's; he was, says Evelyn, the "sole adviser" of the Stop.[104] The idea was not new; it had been bruited about as early as 1667, and in 1669 Ashley and Clifford suggested that freeing the revenue of the anticipations upon it might solve the financial problem.[105] In its present form the plan was that of a politician not a financier; Ashley, who was a financier as well as a politician, now argued vehemently against it. He admitted that the goldsmith-bankers, on whom the loss would chiefly fall, were charging an exorbitant interest rate, but this measure, he argued, was against law and justice, would damage many poor people to whom the bankers would shift as much of the loss as possible, and would be harmful to trade and to the king's reputation.[106] This last was the essential point.

[101] For a detailed account of the technicalities of the transaction see Shaw, *C.T.B. 1669–72* I, xxxv ff. There are two useful articles on the Stop: Andrew Browning, "The Stop of the Exchequer," *History* XIV (1929–30), 333–37, and R. D. Richards, "The Stop of the Exchequer," *Economic History* II (1930–33), 45–62.

[102] *C.T.B. 1669–72* I, 450–51.

[103] *C.T.B. 1669–72* I, 422; II, 824. *C.S.P.D.* X, 205–6; XI, 267–69. Shaw, "Clifford," p. 166.

[104] DeBeer, *Diary of John Evelyn* III, 606.

[105] Shaw, "Clifford," p. 168.

[106] Brown, *Shaftesbury*, pp. 194–95. W. D. Christie, *A Life of Anthony Ashley Cooper, First Earl of Shaftesbury* (London, 1871) II, 59–60, 63. The high

Ashley, more than any other member of the Cabal, was in touch with the City and with the business mentality; he understood that the involved and delicate credit structure which had been erected was based primarily upon confidence and that, once that confidence was broken, as it would be by this measure, the gulf which would be created between the government and the business community would not be bridged for years, if at all.

Ashley's advice in this matter was very sensible, but the Devonshire squire and his royal master paid no attention. Admittedly what they were doing was a gamble, but it seemed to them to be a logical, indeed, an inevitable, gamble, and no one proposed any alternative.[107] They were betting on a quick and decisive victory in the war, a victory in six months; in October, 1671, Parliament was prorogued until October, 1672, and the war would start in the spring. The prorogation, the Venetian ambassador reported, caused surprise, since no one knew where Charles would find the money he needed for current expenses.[108] The risk was enormous: Charles and Clifford were betting not only on military victory in six months but also on financial returns sufficient to permit the process of repayment to begin before Parliament reconvened. They were not at all clear as to how this was to be managed. It could only be achieved by a windfall: this is probably why the war began with a sneak attack on the Dutch Smyrna fleet, which, if captured, would have realized a sizable sum in cash.[109] In the event, the stroke failed.

Ashley was by no means the only opponent of the Stop. The earl of Anglesey, a former treasurer of the navy, wrote in his diary under date of January 2, 1672, when the decision was formally taken, "An extraordinary council being summoned to, I went out of my bed to it, and gave the king faithful counsel against his seizing mens' moneys, etc., and so did most of the council but 'twas not followed.

---

rates charged by the goldsmiths were not entirely their fault; they in turn had to pay substantial interest to the private citizens whose cash they received and, in turn, lent to the government. On this point see A. E. Feaveryear, *The Pound Sterling* (Oxford, 1931) , p. 103.

[107] Even Sir William Temple, who had no love for Clifford, admitted this. *Works of Sir William Temple* II, 184–85.

[108] A. B. Hinds, *et al.*, eds., *Calendar of State Papers, Venetian* (henceforth *C.S.P. Venetian*) (London, 1864–1947) XXXVII, 111.

[109] DeBeer, *Diary of John Evelyn* III, 606–7.

God amend these [beginnings] of evil."[110] Charles, however, was quite impatient of opposition, unless it had some constructive alternative to offer. The king was not much interested in the details of finance. When the treasury commissioners began their service in May, 1667, he had promised that he would sit with them frequently, but it was a promise he had not kept. Not even the Stop and the crisis of the war could make him change his ways.[111] The king did not like to be cheated, and when he did attend meetings, he displayed his usual acumen. To him and to Clifford the basic solution to the financial problem was political in nature; it could be achieved by military victory over the Dutch. This would be popular in the country and make Parliament more tractable; it would, by ruining Dutch trade, so expand English commerce, and hence English customs and excise revenues, that the king would ultimately be financially independent of Parliament.

In one respect the king's luck was bad. In the mid-1670's an increased volume of business, coupled with Danby's skillful management, did increase the hereditary revenue sufficiently to allow him to make ends meet without recourse to Parliamentary grant. This has usually been explained by England's neutrality after 1674, while her rivals were still at war, but there is evidence that the revival began in 1673.[112] Charles, of course, had no way of knowing that his timing was fated to be unlucky, so he took the gamble of temporarily destroying his financial reputation by the Stop. It was a risk, but if it worked, his problems were solved.

The Stop was not a repudiation of the king's debts, as has sometimes been said. It was simply a postponement of repayment, and one which might well profit the creditors if they could weather the temporary shortage, since Charles promised 6 per cent interest on both principal and interest on the money thus withheld. Furthermore, not all exchequer orders were subject to the Stop; on January 20 letters patent were issued exempting most of the orders paid out directly to contractors and to servants for wages and salaries, unless

[110] H.M.C., 13th Report, appendix, pt. VI, p. 270. Payments had actually been halted unofficially on December 18, 1671.

[111] P.R.O., S.P. 28/231, f. 24. Baxter, *Treasury*, pp. 48–50. During Clifford's seven-month tenure as lord treasurer he held 114 meetings of the treasury board; Charles attended no more than seven. *Ibid.*, p. 22. n.

[112] Browning, *Danby* I, 130–31.

these orders had been assigned to a third party. This was the rub: the goldsmith-bankers were the third parties. They had made direct cash payments on the security of the orders.[113] When the Stop was announced, the goldsmiths promptly stopped payments to their own creditors, which caused widespread confusion and panic. "This hath made a great outcry in the City, and meeting with all other humors, hath begot a great deal of angry discourse," wrote Arlington on January 4. On the seventh the king met with the bankers, promised them their interest, and persuaded them to resume payments to their creditors; the next day, in the secretary's view, "discontent is already visibly appeased; so that we do not doubt, but in a few days, it will quite wear out," and ten days later everything appeared to be back to normal.[114] Although the bankers resumed payments—none of them was immediately ruined by the Stop—confidence was not restored, either at home or abroad. In February Ralph Montagu wrote another begging letter to his chief: "I have kept up my credit hitherto pretty well, but upon this noise of the bankers in England, I am torn a-pieces by all that I owe money to."[115]

One thing the Stop did accomplish: there was enough money to pay current expenses. Danby, then plain Sir Thomas Osborne and treasurer of the navy, found it impossible to negotiate the paper orders he had on hand at the moment of the Stop; "Sir Tho. Clifford then told me I should blame him if I was not supplied with money enough from time to time as fast as I had occasion for it"—and, indeed, he had £50,000 by January 17. Clifford assured the navy board that it would have the £800,000 it needed to set out the fleet for the year, and so, by Danby's own account, it did.[116] Naval officers were carefully instructed to use the money to cover current expenses, not old debts—easier said than done, as the victuallers kept clamor-

[113] Feaveryear, *Pound Sterling*, p. 104. *C.T.B. 1669–72* II, 1172.

[114] T. Bebington, ed., *The Right Honourable the Earl of Arlington's Letters to Sir Willam Temple, Bart.* (vol. I) , *and to the Several Ambassadors to Spain* (vol. II) (London, 1701) II, 347–50.

[115] Feb. 15/25, 1672, Montagu to Arlington, H.M.C., *Buccleuch and Queensberry Mss.* I, 512. The Stop led to a semi-permanent debt of about £1,000,000. Browning, *Danby* I, 112; III, 10–15. Clark, "Restoration Banking House," *Essays . . . in Honor of Wilbur Cortez Abbott*, p. 6, dates the decline of the greatest of the goldsmith-bankers, Sir Robert Vyner, from the Stop.

[116] B.M. Add. Mss. 28,040, ff. 16, 28, 31. *C.T.B. 1669–72* II, 1011–12, 1024.

ing for their arrears.[117] The basic financial problem was not solved, however. In June, 1672, the war being then three months old, the French ambassador reported that Charles was in financial trouble still, though "Clifford, who is one of the chief administrators, is incorruptible and does all that he can for the good service of his master."[118] To those around the king, Clifford's incorruptibility may have been apparent, but the opinion of the country at large was that expressed by Clifford's friend Evelyn, who hyperbolically declared that the exchequer's credit was ruined "forever," and by John Lacy, once the lover of Nell Gwyn, who, prompted perhaps by some feeling other than zeal for the public welfare, wrote:

> Stopping the Bank in thee was only great,
> But in a Subject it had been a Cheat
> To pay thy Debts what Sum canst thou advance,
> Now thy Exchequer is remov'd to France,
> T'inrich a Harlot all made up of French,
> Not worthy to be call'd a Whore, but Wench?[119]

IV

At the end of 1671, a few days before the Stop, the Venetian ambassador shrewdly deduced the direction of the king's policy. He also saw the risks involved: "If the king misses his stroke and does not render his authority absolute, he will greatly endanger that which he now exercises."[120] For about a year, until it became apparent that the stroke was indeed going to miss, no one was closer to the king than Clifford. In addition to the Stop, he was a prime mover in the issuance of the declaration of indulgence in March, 1672. By this time it was obvious that Charles would never declare himself publicly to be a Catholic; the declaration was the most that could be

---

[117] *C.T.B. 1669–72* II, 1188. *C.S.P.D.* XII, 498–99; XIII, 485. Clifford took an active interest in naval administration, especially with respect to cutting costs. In May, 1672, he catechized Pepys on this subject at a meeting of the foreign committee and at the treasury board, "Lord Clifford takes notice that when they [workers in navy yards] work task [piece work] they do one and a half days' work in a day and when they work for time a day for the king their tasks are small." P.R.O., S.P. 104/177, ff. 37–39. *C.T.B. 1669–72* II, 1071, 1090–91.

[118] Christie, *Shaftesbury* II, appendix ii, xix. Even before the war began the Scottish Council warned Lauderdale that the country could not afford even a regiment of 1,000 foot in the event of war. B.M. Add. Mss. 23,135, f. 132.

[119] DeBeer, *Diary of John Evelyn* III, 606–7. George deF. Lord, *Poems on Affairs of State* (New Haven, 1963) I (1660–78) , 427.

[120] *C.S.P. Venetian* XXXVII, 143.

achieved for the adherents of the ancient faith. Burnet remarks that with the declaration "Clifford began to show the heat of his temper and seemed a sort of . . . enthusiast for Popery."[121] However obvious his Catholicism may have been, it did not make him intolerant. He did what he could to forward the policy of persuading refugee Dutch families to emigrate to England after the war began,[122] which he would not have done if he had contemplated the imposition of Catholicism by force.

However close Clifford may have been to the king politically, temperamentally the two men were poles apart. The quick-tempered, stubborn, inflexible Devonshire squire was not at all like his devious, patient, supple, and rather cynical master, and there could have been very little of the easy sort of give-and-take that went on between Charles and Buckingham, or even Arlington, or Lauderdale. Clifford was much more like the duke of York—and, indeed, James, in his advice to his son, stated that Clifford was the only faithful minister his brother ever had.[123] Charles knew how to choose his instruments, however. The Arlingtons of this world are useful while one is making up one's mind. But now the course was set; what was wanted now was single-minded enthusiasm for the cause. This Clifford, and Clifford alone, of all the members of the Cabal, could supply.

Clifford shared in the general distribution of rewards in April, 1672, when he received a peerage and became Baron Clifford of Chudleigh; he acted as secretary during Arlington's abortive peace mission to the Continent in June and July; in November he reached the top of what turned out to be a very greasy pole when he received the white staff of the lord treasurer. Charles was aware that this appointment would cause trouble in his official family, but he had very little choice. For almost a year Clifford had been doing the work of the office; as soon as the policy of the Stop was decided on, both Ashley and Duncombe had dissociated themselves from the whole business of finding money and paying it out and had left it all to Clifford, although they had remained members of the treasury commission.[124] Ever since the appointment of the commissioners in 1667 there had been periodic speculation as to the appointment of a new

---

[121] Burnet, *History* I, 555.
[122] On this point see P.R.O., S.P. 104/176, f. 55.
[123] G. Oliver, *Cliffordiana* (Exeter, 1828), p. 24.
[124] Brown, *Shaftesbury*, pp. 194–95. B.M. Add. Mss. 28,040, f. 21.

lord treasurer. In 1668 there was a rumor that Arlington was to get the post and that Clifford was to be secretary—a reshuffle which Charles, if he ever contemplated it seriously, discarded in favor of the policy of Catholicity.[125] In the autumn of 1671 it was Ashley who was being considered, and Clifford was to replace him as chancellor of the exchequer. One report said that Ashley had declined the job because the financial situation was so chaotic.[126] After the Stop Ashley would certainly have declined the office; as it turned out, it was because Ashley, now earl of Shaftesbury, had to be transferred to another post that the treasury commission broke up and Clifford received the coveted appointment.

It was necessary in the fall of 1672 to replace Sir Orlando Bridgeman as keeper of the seal. Bridgeman had never been a member of the inner ring of Charles's advisers; since his appointment in 1667, which he may have owed in part to the fact that he was the only judge who had lent any money to the king during the second Dutch war,[127] he had stood as a pillar of Anglican and Cavalier respectability who served in some degree to mask Charles's real intentions. But now he was becoming a serious liability. He had refused to put the seal to the declaration of indulgence; he thoroughly disapproved of the Stop and would not issue the necessary injunctions to protect the goldsmiths from the suits begun by their creditors. Shaftesbury approved of the indulgence and sympathized with the goldsmiths, and so, in November, 1672, he was made lord chancellor. This entailed his departure from the treasury commission, which would now either have to be reorganized or replaced by a single lord treasurer. Clifford was the logical man for the latter position, since his was the financial policy now being pursued, and since he was in virtually complete control of the operations of the treasury anyway: "The king had a good deal of . . . French money lately, of which . . . Lord Clifford wholly disposes, as indeed of all, for he makes the lists what money shall be paid every Saturday himself."[128] The trouble was that Arlington wanted the post for himself and was

[125] Oct. 15, 1668, Lindenov to the Danish Chancery, Westergaard, *First Triple Alliance*, pp. 28–29. See above, pp. 102–3.

[126] Sept. 2, 1671, Richard Brockenden to Sir Robert Paston, H.M.C., 6th Report, pt. I (London, 1877), p. 369.

[127] *C.T.B. 1667–68*, p. 35.

[128] Nov., 1672, Sir Charles Lyttleton to Lord Hatton, E. M. Thompson, ed., *Correspondence of the Family of Hatton* (London, 1878) I, 100.

bitterly disappointed when he failed to get it. He felt that Clifford, his protégé, whose career he had made, had betrayed him and had shown the blackest sort of ingratitude. The long friendship between the two men, which had been severely strained by their differences over foreign policy, was now broken forever, and one more was added to the already long and impressive list of bitter rivalries within Charles's oddly assorted group of advisers.

Clifford's tenure of the treasury lasted only seven months and was dominated by the continuing problems of wartime finance. "Never would the philosopher's stone be more welcomed than in this juncture," wrote a contemporary when the appointment was announced.[129] The new lord treasurer was not unduly wasteful or extravagant; there is no reason to believe Sir William Temple's malicious allegation respecting "the bountys he used in the disposal of the king's moneys about six weeks before he left the staff."[130] Personally Clifford was not avaricious; he accumulated very little property while in office and always lived within his means, which he had learned to do during the lean years of his young manhood. Unlike Arlington, he did not have to hold on to office at any cost because he could not afford to quit it. He did secure appointments to places in the exchequer for two of his sons, but there was no unusual amount of wastage of public money under him. Secret service expenditure during his seven-month tenure came to £45,760, which in wartime was hardly excessive.[131] At the beginning of his tenure, indeed, there is some evidence of administrative vigor, of attempts, not always effective, to tighten up.[132] The trustees for the sale of the fee farms were ordered to prepare their accounts; their clerks would get no salary until they had done so. The accounts of the commissioners of customs were also called for: Clifford wished "an entire view of the

---

[129] Quoted in Shaw, "Clifford," p. 189.

[130] Sept. 8, 1673, Temple to Essex, B.M. Stowe Mss. 203, f. 18. A good deal of this letter is taken up with a report of an alleged criticism of Essex by Clifford.

[131] Baxter, *Treasury*, p. 18. *C.S.P.D.* XV, 414. Shaw, "Clifford," p. 196, and appendix, pp. 243–45. He spent far less secret service money than Danby, who used it to bribe M.P.s. Browning, *Danby* I, 274–75. Clifford's day book is printed in *C.T.B. 1672–75*, pp. 1–183.

[132] For example, in January a teller of receipt was dismissed for buying up orders on which payment had been halted by the Stop at discounts ranging up to 45 per cent, a practice which made the Stop look fraudulent. In April the man was reinstated. *C.T.B. 1672–75*, pp. 47, 104.

customs revenue."[133] By April, 1673, these efforts had slackened to almost nothing, because in February Parliament had met and on March 29 the Test Act had received the royal assent.

The Parliamentary session had been scheduled for October, 1672. It had been staved off for four months, partly by Clifford's ingenious proposal to keep the fleet at sea during the winter to avoid having to pay the seamen, and in the meantime the Stop was renewed. By February supply was imperative, to pay the goldsmiths if for no other reason.[134] Parliament showed very little concern over the Stop and the fate of the goldsmiths, though in later sessions the Stop was regarded as a fraud. Now Parliament was far more exercised about the declaration of indulgence, and as far as Clifford was concerned, the Test Act, which along with the canceling of the declaration was the *quid pro quo* of the essential tax money, was the handwriting on the wall. He would not renounce his newfound faith for the sake of office; he was too straightforward for that. He had never been one for devious courses. Furthermore, his health was rapidly worsening. In mid-May the rumors were rife that he would lay down his staff and be succeeded by Sir Thomas Osborne.[135] And so, indeed, a month later, it turned out. He survived his resignation only four months.

In 1675 there appeared a widely read pamphlet called *A Letter from a Person of Quality to his Friend in the Country*. It was written, if not by Shaftesbury himself—now in bitter opposition to Clifford's successor Danby—then by someone close to him, possibly John Locke. In it Clifford is described as "a man of a daring and ambitious spirit" whose purpose was to assist Charles to erect a despotism. Probably this is true, true in much the same sense as it was true for a back-country squire of another generation, Thomas Wentworth. Clifford, like Wentworth, began his career in the House of Commons; like Wentworth, he was convinced that the country's good could be achieved only by the king; like Wentworth he was to go to his grave with his hopes and dreams shattered. But there the parallel ends. Wentworth was a man of very great talent; Clifford, alone, among the Cabal, was a mediocrity. His rise to prominence was a matter partly of luck, partly of attaching himself to the right

[133] *Ibid.*, pp. 35, 38, 42.

[134] Hartmann, *Clifford*, p. 247. Christie, *Shaftesbury* II, 114. Brown, *Shaftesbury*, p. 207.

[135] May 18, 1673, Henry Ball to Williamson, W. D. Christie, ed., *Letters . . . to Sir Joseph Williamson* (London, 1874) I, 1–2.

man at the right time. Once arrived on top, he stayed there by dint of industriousness and loyalty to the king and because he was willing to take enormous risks in behalf of a policy he believed in, greater risks, in fact, than Charles himself was prepared to run. Like the king, he was a shortsighted gambler; the Stop of the Exchequer was a gamble, inevitable perhaps, but foolish in view of the odds against it. The year before his death Charles told the earl of Ailesbury that the Stop was a bad mistake, and added, "God forgive those vile persons that were the cause of that false step I made, to give it no worse a term."[136] Charles was being less than just here; given his objectives and the means he chose to implement them, there was very little choice.

Clifford never achieved any real influence over the king; he was no more than an eager and convenient instrument of Charles's policy. His financial advice turned out to be disastrous, not so much in and of itself but because it was part of a whole policy that failed. The government's inability to solve its financial dilemma was owing in part to the nature of the problem itself, in part to the king's constant habit of viewing his financial difficulties through political glasses, and most of all to Charles's inability to use the financial talent he had available. There were men around him—Ashley, Downing, Osborne—with real financial ability, but none of them could be entrusted with Charles's political designs. Two of them were ex-Cromwellians, after all, and the other was a protégé of the mercurial Buckingham. So Charles was left with Clifford. Financial failure substantially raised the odds against the king's grand design, but the storm which wrecked it was precipitated by religion, by the declaration of indulgence rather than the Stop of the Exchequer.

[136] W. E. Buckley, ed., *Memoirs of Thomas, Earl of Ailesbury, Written by Himself* (Roxburghe Club ed., Westminster, 1890) I, 92. Ailesbury did not admire Clifford, whom he called "haughty and aspiring," p. 12.

Chapter 5

The Religious Crisis

Buckingham

When in France and in Spain and in Holland 'tis known
What wonders our mighty statesman has done,
'Twill make them all tremble to hear his renown.
For he that can libel the Poets, and knows
How to mimick the Players in Gestures and Clothes
With ease may destroy all his Majesty's foes.
Now the Church he contemns as much as a Quaker,
The kingdom he'll ruin if the Parliament forsake her,
For he serves his King as bad as his Maker.
For he that forsook him in all his distress,
Kill'd the Husband and kept the Adulteress,
Like Judah would sell him, and sell him for less.
He hath mimicked the King and Duke o'er and o'er,
That merciful King, that hath pardon'd more
Than all our Kings e'er pardon'd before;
That king, that if e'er he committed a crime,
That to Church and to State may prove fatal in time,
It was in extending his mercy to him.
Now God grant his Majesty never may find,
What's fatal, to be to a Buckingham kind,
For his father was ruin'd by the first of the line.[1]

[1] *Poems on Affairs of State* (4th ed., London, 1702) II, 217–18.

George Villiers, second duke of Buckingham, has been
the delight of historians and literary men for three
hundred years. To the serious scholar he comes as a leavening joy;
to the sniffer after scandal he is a nonpareil. In his own lifetime he
was mercilessly attacked and satirized, and he gave as good as he
got, even against his most distinguished opponent, John Dryden:
Mr. Bays is as skillful a lampoon as Zimri and much more good-
natured.[2] To most writers Buckingham has epitomized all that was
evil in the regime of Charles II: frivolity, coldheartedness, extravagance, sexual license. "He had a great liveliness of wit, and a peculiar faculty of turning all things into ridicule," wrote Burnet.
"He had no principles, either of religion, virtue, or friendship.
Pleasure, frolic, and extravagant diversions, was all that he laid
to heart. He was true to nothing: for he was not true to himself."
And again: "He gave himself up to a monstrous course of studied
immoralities of the worst kinds. He was so full of mercury that he
could not fix long in any friendship or to any design." To Ailesbury
he was "flashy and vain, without judgement, and would rather lose
his friend (nay, the king) than his jest . . . living in such a dis-
ordered manner as in upwards of twenty years he ate up £26,000
yearly, and £40,000 in debt besides."[3] These verdicts could be multiplied many times over. The most recent biography of the duke is
entitled *A Rake and His Times*.

One more contemporary opinion is worth quoting, that of Roger
North. "While he was in affairs," wrote North, "he favored the true
enemies of the court, the fanatics: and when he was out he set up for
one of the heads of that faction." Burnet echoes this: "The duke of
Buckingham . . . set up for a patron of liberty of conscience and of
all the sects."[4] Buckingham was, indeed, full of mercury, but
throughout his eccentric and changeable public career he steadily
held to his belief in liberty of conscience and in the folly of a
doctrine of uniformity or conformity in religion. In his youth he
appeared to be—perhaps was—no more than a scoffer, surrounded

---

[2] The references are to Buckingham's play *The Rehearsal* and to
Dryden's *Absalom and Achitophel*.

[3] Gilbert Burnet, *The History of My Own Time* (ed. Osmund Airy,
Oxford, 1897–1900) I, 182, 477. W. E. Buckley, ed., *Memoirs of Thomas, Earl of
Ailesbury, Written by Himself* (Roxburghe Club ed., Westminster, 1890) I, 13.

[4] Roger North, *The Lives of the Norths* (ed. A. Jessopp, London, 1890)
I, 68. Burnet, *History* I, 454.

by people who were widely regarded as vicious and atheistic, and so
he was heartily disapproved of by the serious-minded Anglicans in
Hyde's entourage at the exiled court. As one of them wrote to
Secretary Nicholas in 1653, Buckingham was "after the old way, no
church or religion."[5] More than twenty years later, when his friend
of college days, Martin Clifford, published his *Treatise of Human
Reason,* Buckingham wrote to congratulate him. Clifford's tract was
an attempt to show that reason was man's only reliable guide in
religious questions; his arguments were based in large measure on
scientific analogies—they were genuinely deistic. Buckingham, the
amateur scientist, accepted the rationalist argument, and went on to
say, "Liberty of conscience . . . if once justly and firmly established, would open the door to that peace which the Gospel was
bestowed on us to introduce into the world. . . . To me it is very
unaccountable that they should pretend to tell us that we should
now freely consult the Word of God, and at the same time deny us to
understand it for ourselves; since that is but to fool us with the name
of Liberty, without letting us possess the thing."[6] In 1675, in a speech
in the Lords in opposition to Danby's nonresisting Test, he used an
argument that was becoming increasingly familiar: religious intolerance was bad for business and a violation of the property rights of
Englishmen:

There is a thing called property, which (whatever some men may think)
is that the people of England are fondest of . . . and it is that his majesty,
in his speech, has promised us to take a particular care of. This, my
Lords, in my opinion, can never be done without giving an indulgence
to all Protestant dissenters. It is certainly a very uneasy kind of life to any
man that has either Christian charity, humanity, or good nature, to see
his fellow subjects daily abused, divested of their liberty and birthrights,
and miserably thrown out of their possessions and freeholds only because
they cannot agree with others in some niceties of religion which their
consciences will not give them leave to consent to, and which, even by the
confession of those who would impose them upon them, are no ways necessary to salvation.[7]

And in 1685, two years before his death, and when his friend King
Charles was no longer alive to protect him, he was still holding to

[5] Dec. 23, 1653/Jan. 2, 1654, Hatton to Nicholas, G. F. Warner, ed., *The
Nicholas Papers* (London, 1886, 1920) II, 41. See also Mar. 11/21, 1652, Nicholas to
Hyde, *ibid.* I, 289.
[6] *The Works of His Grace George Villiers, Late Duke of Buckingham*
(London, 1715) II, 64–69.
[7] *Ibid.* I, 202–4.

the same position: "I have long been convinced . . . that nothing can be more antiChristian, nor more contrary to sense and reason, than to trouble and molest our fellow Christians because they cannot be exactly of our minds in all things relating to the worship of God. . . . If a serious consideration of the present state of this kingdom can sink deep enough into men's hearts, to make them endeavor now to promote a true liberty of conscience, I shall yet hope to enjoy happy days in England."[8] Buckingham simply could not understand how any reasonable man could so fly in the face of common sense as to believe in religious persecution on principle, and he never ceased to say so, even if his efforts to translate his conviction into practical results were sporadic at best.

The duke was a deist on principle, unlike his master, whose alleged deism was really indifference. Nor did he share the king's appreciation of the merits, political and otherwise, of Catholicism. The duke's principles made him decidedly anti-Catholic. In his *Commonplace Book* he wrote as follows, under the heading, *The Pope:*

> Tell me, my muse, (things past are known to thee)
> Thou every change of time's swift —— dost see,
> Tell me what age did first this monster nurse,
> What country's sins brought forth so dire a curse?
> Long did the servile world to Rome's pride bow,
> Their bodies once, their souls her captives now.
> The conquered earth seemed but a narrow praise,
> For bold usurping hands on heaven she lays,
> Unthrones she mighty God, and giant-like
> With her seven hills at the blest heaven does strike.[9]

Buckingham was not by nature a politician or a courtier, though he spent his life dabbling in politics and intriguing at court. He was a fashionable dilettante who was interested in all sorts of things, like chemistry and glass-making[10]—he was a member of the Royal So-

---

[8] Lord Somers, *A Collection of Scarce and Valuable Tracts* (2nd ed., ed. Walter Scott, London, 1812) IX, 13–14.

[9] The *Commonplace Book* is in the possession of the earl of Jersey and is quoted with his permission. I wish to thank Professor John H. Wilson for allowing me to use his microfilm copy of it.

[10] In 1663 he petitioned successfully for a patent for the manufacture of crystal looking glasses and various other sorts of glass, in order to cut into the Venetian monopoly of such products. M. A. E. Green, *et al.*, eds., *Calendar of State Papers Domestic, Charles II* (henceforth *C.S.P.D.*) (London, 1860ff.) III, 186–87. The result was a large and successful glass factory at Lambeth. H. W. Chapman, *Great Villiers* (London, 1949) , p. 125. See also Sept. 27/Oct. 7, 1672, Alberti to the

ciety—and whose real talents were literary. His attitude toward politics was, *mutatis mutandis,* rather like that of Mr. Gladstone with respect to the ace of trumps. He believed that, by virtue of his position as the greatest subject in England, he ought to be able to make his political weight felt—indeed, to have his way—and without much exertion. Unlike the other four members of the Cabal, he was unwilling to work steadily at politics, possibly because he did not take it seriously. As his friend Brian Fairfax put it, "When a dirty chemist, a foxhunter, a pretender to poetry or politics, a rehearsal should entertain him . . . a messenger to summon him to council could not be admitted."[11] This attitude was extremely disconcerting to his political allies. The future earl of Danby started his career as Buckingham's protégé; in 1669 he was driven to write to his patron, "I have called divers times again today to have spoke to your Grace about this [Irish problems] and other things which . . . I conceived to be of great importance, but since I cannot have that honor, nor can possibly bring myself to be of your Grace's opinion that such business as is now in hand will be done with so little time given to it as your Grace is pleased to afford, I must confess my despair of any future good."[12] Buckingham's condescension and his unwillingness to make use of the ordinary small change of politics were equally annoying. "Courtesies are never reckoned as anything with him," wrote the irritated Ralph Montagu to Arlington in 1671.[13] To the lighthearted duke, politics was an entertaining game, no more, but a game which he felt impelled to play because he disliked so many of its other practitioners. It is ironical, and yet, in a sense, typical of the career of this gifted man who frittered away his gifts, that he, the most deeply committed of the king's inner circle to

Doge and Senate, A. B. Hinds, *et al.,* eds., *Calendar of State Papers, Venetian* (henceforth *C.S.P. Venetian*) (London, 1864–1947) XXXVII, 299–300. The business had to be sold to Buckingham's creditors in 1674. *Ibid.* XXXVIII, 272.

[11] Brian Fairfax's *Memorial,* in E. Arber, ed., *The Rehearsal* (London, 1927), p. 9. His reputation as a rake eventually became so firmly established that, says Fairfax, "whenever he was shut up in his chamber . . . or in his laboratory . . . it was said to be with women." *Ibid.* Buckingham sometimes made deliberate use of his bad reputation, according to Pepys: when he was closeted with John Wildman and other ex-Commonwealthmen, he led the king to believe he was with his wenches. *The Diary of Samuel Pepys* (ed. H. B. Wheatley, London, 1926), Nov. 4, 1668.

[12] Dec. 18, 1669, Osborne to Buckingham, B.M. Add. Mss. 28,053, f. 28.

[13] H.M.C., *Mss. of the Duke of Buccleuch and Queensberry* (London, 1899) I, 495.

the principle of toleration, had very little to do with Charles's most serious attempt to implement that principle, the declaration of indulgence of 1672, on account of a temporary personal difference with the king over a military command to which Buckingham believed himself entitled.

King Charles, able judge of human nature that he was, knew very well with what sort of man he had to deal. Indeed, the king had always known Buckingham, who was born on January 30, 1628, some seven months before the death of his father at the hands of an assassin. Charles I immediately assumed responsibility for the children of his murdered favorite, and so the young Buckingham spent his boyhood at court, getting accustomed to a royal standard of living which in later years he would squander his enormous income to maintain and sharing the games and the tutors of the Prince of Wales, two years his junior, whom he treated, save on ceremonial occasions, as his equal. Charles was always genuinely fond of his boyhood friend, and as men they had much in common. Buckingham was always the favorite male companion of the king's leisure hours; he must have been extraordinarily good company. Even when the duke went into political opposition as an ally of Shaftesbury in the 1670's, Charles never showed more than an amused exasperation at "Alderman George," as he called him. The king knew that Buckingham was inconsistent and fundamentally lacking in seriousness, and so he never trusted the duke very far politically. Only once, in the months following Clarendon's fall, did Charles allow Buckingham to try his hand at serious political management, and the king was in part constrained to do so then because of the duke's great, if temporary, popularity. Buckingham failed utterly to achieve any positive results from the Parliamentary session of late 1667. The impeachment of Clarendon collapsed, and the government was unable even to raise the question of supply. What was worse, the duke supported the creation of the Parliamentary commission on accounts, which was most distasteful to Charles. Then, to cap all, Buckingham killed the hapless husband of his sleek and unpleasant mistress, the countess of Shrewsbury, in a duel. After this Charles never trusted Buckingham with serious political affairs again.

But Buckingham still had his political uses for the king. The objectives which Charles sought to achieve by means of the treaty of

Dover demanded secrecy, demanded that he make use of men of very different types whose policies were not compatible and who were united only in their willingness to serve him out of personal loyalty, Royalist conviction, ambition, or greed. It was the king's deliberate policy, in these years, to surround himself with men who did not agree with each other. "When rogues fall out," he remarked, "the master is like then to know the truth."[14] Buckingham was an unsettling influence by nature, with his princely contempt for most politicians, and he could be counted on to create disturbances because of his bitter hatred for Arlington—he would automatically oppose whatever the secretary favored. So Buckingham was held up to Arlington and the others as an alternative: if they did not fall in with the king's wishes, Charles might really do what he was always apparently threatening to do and make Buckingham his chief political adviser. At the same time, Buckingham was an admirable smoke screen for the king: how could any monarch who gave ear to such a man be taken seriously? Even Louis XIV, no mean judge of men himself, may have been partly taken in by Charles in this way: "I am told the fame of the duke of Buckingham's new play [*The Rehearsal*], has reached the French court, and that the king asked Monsr. Colbert when he would write him a play, who excusing his want of talents that way to serve him, the king told him he would be out of fashion, for the Chief Minister of State in England had gotten a great deal of honor by writing a farce; these tales *se non son veri son ben trovate.*"[15]

Buckingham did not fathom the depths of the game the king was playing, but he was by no means entirely taken in. He was intermittently aware of his lack of real power and occasionally gave vent to his exasperation, for instance in his poem *The Cabbin Boy:*

> Nay, he could sail a Yatcht both nigh and large,
> Knew how to trim a boat, and steer a Barge:
> Cou'd say his Compass, to the Nations Joy,
> And swear as well as any Cabbin-Boy.
> But not one lesson of the Ruling Art
> Cou'd this dull Block head ever get by heart.

[14] Quoted in John H. Wilson, *A Rake and His Times* (New York, 1954), p. 110.

[15] Dec. 16, 1671, S. Henshaw to Sir Robert Paston, H.M.C., 6th Report, pt. I (London, 1877), p. 368.

> Look over all the Universal Frame,
> There's not a thing the Will of Man can name,
> In which this ugly, perjur'd Rogue delights,
> But Ducks and loytering, butter'd Buns and whites.[16]

And, at the end of the Cabal period, when he was about to go into opposition, the duke remarked rather plaintively to Burnet, "Princes thought their favors were no ordinary things: they expected great submissions in return: otherwise they thought they were despised."[17]

The making of psychological judgments on historical figures is a doubtful business at best, but perhaps some of Buckingham's erratic behavior can be attributed to the vicissitudes of his adolescence during the civil war. In 1641, when he was thirteen, he and his younger brother Francis were sent off to Cambridge, where Buckingham spent a restless year and became a friend of the poet Abraham Cowley and the scholarly and rather eccentric religious radical Martin Clifford. In the spring of 1643 the brothers slipped away to join the king's army: the monotony of university life in a time of such excitement was not to be borne. Their relatives were not pleased with the boys' escapade and packed them off to the Continent in the summer of 1643. They spent most of the next three years in Italy, chiefly at Florence and Rome. In the spring of 1646 they were in Paris, where Buckingham met once more with Charles, now sixteen, whom, says Burnet, he proceeded to introduce to "all the vices and impieties of the age," including the wicked philosopher Thomas Hobbes. "So that the main blame of the king's ill principles and bad morals was owing to the duke of Buckingham"—a judgment we may take leave to doubt.[18]

In the spring of 1647 Buckingham and his brother returned to England, chiefly in order to try to keep the Villiers estates from confiscation by the triumphant Parliament. Whatever chance they might have had was ruined by a foolish military escapade in July, 1648, in which young Francis was killed. Buckingham escaped and returned to his friend, now at The Hague, whom the grim business outside the banqueting hall at Whitehall—by coincidence, on the duke's twenty-first birthday—was to turn into his king as well. The

[16] John H. Wilson, *The Court Wits of the Restoration* (Princeton, 1948), p. 129. "Buttered buns" are prostitutes; "whites," money.
[17] Burnet, *History* II, 34.
[18] *Ibid.* I, 183.

duke was in high favor with Charles, whose spirits needed reviving. Hyde and his friends were scandalized and disapproving and became more so when Buckingham supported the Scottish gamble proposed by Lauderdale. The duke accompanied Charles to Scotland; he "took all ways possible to gain Argyll and the ministers . . . his dissolute course of life was excessive scandalous; which to their great reproach they connived at, because he advised the king to put himself wholly in their hands."[19] Buckingham did not enjoy his stay in Scotland and, as usual, turned his annoyance into a witticism. "At dinners," he wrote, the Scottish clerics "lay about 'em as fiercely as in the pulpit."[20] He quarreled foolishly with the king because he wanted to be appointed commander of the army in England—he always had a hankering for military glory—but fought well at Worcester and, like his master, slipped out of the country after the rout.

After his return to The Hague Buckingham's behavior was, to say the least, tactless. He cast aspersions on the king's behavior at Worcester and paid court, in an idle sort of way, to Charles's sister Mary, the recently widowed princess of Orange. The disapproving Secretary Nicholas wrote in 1652, "I wish he may be half so wise [as his father] when he doubles his age. . . . Indeed he hath wit enough, but I doubt he wants ballast." A year later the secretary was even more concerned: Buckingham was in touch with "that rogue Lilburne."[21] This was an odd sort of combination indeed, and was the first obvious evidence of Buckingham's affinity for eccentrics and religious radicals which, after the Restoration, led him to surround himself with such people as the semi-professional conspirator John Wildman. Hyde's circle was more outraged than ever; Buckingham's behavior was regularly cited as an example of How Not to Behave. "The discourses of Lord Jermyn . . . are unsufferable concerning the king's person and affairs," wrote one of them in 1654, "and none can exceed them but the duke of Buckingham." They hoped and expected that his influence with the king would wane. "These great wits . . . may be good company for a time," wrote Secretary Nicholas to Hyde, "but they are uneasy to live with."[22]

Buckingham was never concerned about what people thought of his behavior. If Lilburne could be helpful in pulling down Crom-

[19] *Ibid.*, p. 93.
[20] Quoted in Chapman, *Great Villiers*, p. 65.
[21] Warner, *Nicholas Papers* I, 287; II, 13.
[22] *Ibid.* II, 72, 123.

well, he ought to be used. But "Free-born John" was a broken reed.
A turn at soldiering under Turenne proved equally unsatisfactory.
By the middle of 1657 Buckingham was thoroughly discouraged and
both irritated and bored by the life of the exiled court. So he decided
on an extraordinary sort of gamble. The Villiers estates had been
confiscated; the bulk of them had been given to Lord Fairfax.
Fairfax's heir was his only daughter Mary. Buckingham would go to
England, woo her and win her, and at one stroke recover his estates
and be in a position to help his master when the propitious moment
came: through Fairfax he would be able to influence the Presbyterians. This was a harebrained scheme, yet, astonishingly enough, it
worked. It was easy enough to win Mary's heart, once he got to know
her. Buckingham was handsome and charming and very difficult for
women to resist, and he had not yet acquired a reputation as a rake.
Her father was somehow won over also. Cromwell was less pleased by
Buckingham's return and in the spring of 1658 had him arrested; the
protector's death in September may have saved the duke's life. At
least Buckingham thought so. "If Oliver had lived for three days
longer," he wrote later, "I had certainly been put to death."[23]

The duke was released from the Tower after Cromwell's death
and rejoined his wife and father-in-law; on February 23, 1659, he
appeared at the bar of the House of Commons and promised "that
he should not abet any of the enemies of this Commonwealth."[24] He
was in Yorkshire when Monck began his march south; he helped
raise the county for Monck and accompanied the general to London,
where he did his best to prejudice Monck against Hyde, partly on
the ground that Hyde was hostile to the Presbyterians.[25] He also
accompanied Monck to Dover to greet the king when, on May 25,
1660, the long years of exile came to an end for Charles. The duke's
reception was chilly. He had not seen his master for three years and
had apparently turned his coat; for three years Hyde and his friends
had been filling the king's ear with their low opinions of the rene-
gade. Charles was in a generous mood, however—why should he not
be?—and within twenty-four hours, no one knows how, Buckingham
had talked his way back into the king's good graces. The feelings of
Hyde and his friends can be imagined; they were not improved by

[23] R. Bell, ed., *Memorials of the Civil War* (London, 1849) II, 253–54.
[24] Chapman, *Great Villiers*, p. 99.
[25] R. S. Bosher, *The Making of the Restoration Settlement: The Influence of the Laudians 1649–1662* (New York, 1951), p. 111.

the king's taking Buckingham's cousin Lady Castlemaine as his mistress. From now on, it was to be war to the knife between the king's friend and his principal minister.

It was a curious sort of war, fought, on Buckingham's part, in the king's leisure hours, at the parties given by Lady Castlemaine and by the beautiful Frances Stewart—Buckingham, along with Arlington, was on the famous committee to "get" her for the king.[26] Frances was found of card castles, so Buckingham built card castles for her and built them better than anybody else. The duke sang; he danced; he gave mock sermons; he did imitations of Clarendon and Arlington, so successfully that when the secretary, in his sober and rather pompous fashion, tried to persuade Frances to give in to the king, she burst out laughing at him. "Buckingham, as oft as he was admitted to any familiarities with the king," wrote Burnet, "studied with all his wit and humor to make Lord Clarendon and all his counsels appear ridiculous."[27] He was a wonderful mimic, but Clarendon survived. In these years the duke did not concern himself very much with politics. He was lord-lieutenant of the West Riding of Yorkshire and did his job there well enough; he favored the indulgence of 1662, but nothing came of that. Only with the war did he become really active politically, first going off to sea with the fleet and making a nuisance of himself, then raising forces in Yorkshire, and, in 1666, organizing a political faction among the Yorkshire M.P.s and beginning that Parliamentary campaign which was to play such a considerable part in pulling the chancellor down.[28]

Buckingham's campaign against Clarendon was neither systematic nor moderate. He got himself into silly scrapes: he knocked off the Clarendonian marquis of Dorchester's periwig; he allegedly "took the marquis [of Worcester] by the nose and pulled him about" at a committee meeting. On both occasions he and his opponent were sent to the Tower briefly to cool off.[29] The sobersided were half-amused, half-exasperated; William Coventry told Pepys that "he had wrought a miracle, which was the convincing the duke of

---

[26] Pepys, *Diary,* Nov. 6, 1663.

[27] Burnet, *History* I, 444–45.

[28] *C.S.P.D.* IV, 275–76, 301, 320, 360. Andrew Browning, *Thomas Osborne, Earl of Danby and Duke of Leeds* (Glasgow, 1951) I, 42.

[29] Pepys, *Diary,* Dec. 19, 1666. Dec. 22, 1666, Denis de Repas to Sir Robert Harley, H.M.C., *Mss. of . . . the Duke of Portland* III (London, 1894), 303.

Buckingham that something . . . he had intended to do was not fit to be done."[30] Many of the duke's maneuvers were purely opportunistic, but one at least represented a happy blend of political advantage and genuine conviction. As Clarendon said, "He had always held intelligence with the principal persons of the levelling party, and professed to desire that liberty of conscience might be granted to all."[31] Relief for Protestant dissenters was apt to be considered far more favorably by Anglican opinion now than it had been in 1662, owing in part at least to the London fire of 1666, which was widely believed to have been set by Papists. In October, 1666, Pepys reported that the Commons were made "mad" by the openness of the Catholics and were urging Charles to expel them from public office.[32] When, early in 1667, Buckingham was being sought on the trumped-up astrology charge, it was "reported that his chief offense is his activity against Papists, and in behalf of nonconformists, which makes him popular with some, though sober men believe otherwise."[33] Not all sober men thought otherwise; Richard Baxter deplored Buckingham's irreligion and private life but said that he was "of greater wit and parts, and sounder principles as to the interest of humanity and the common good, than most lords in the court. Wherefore he countenanced fanatics and sectaries, among others, without any great suspicion, because he was known to be so far from them himself."[34]

II

The few months which followed Clarendon's dismissal saw the apogee of Buckingham's political influence. "Things are done in a most foolish manner quite through," wrote Pepys sourly.[35] The duke quickly demonstrated his political incapacity by bungling the fallen chancellor's impeachment and his frivolity by his duel with Shrewsbury, but before the king withdrew his confidence, early in 1668,

---

[30] Pepys, *Diary*, Oct. 15, 1666.

[31] Edward, Earl of Clarendon, *A Continuation of His History of the Great Rebellion* (Oxford, 1857) II, 322.

[32] Pepys, *Diary*, Oct. 27, 1666. Three years earlier Pepys complained that too many Catholics held office. *Ibid.*, Feb. 19, 1663.

[33] Mar. 11, 1667, R. H. to Williamson, from Coventry, *C.S.P.D.* VI, 555. See also Mar. 18, 1667, Bower to Williamson, *ibid.*, p. 568.

[34] M. Sylvester, ed., *Reliquiae Baxterianae* (London, 1696) III, 21.

[35] Pepys, *Diary*, Sept. 25, 1667. See also the entries for November 15 and 17.

Buckingham helped set on foot a serious effort to benefit the dissenters. Clarendon's fall was followed by the release of many of them from prison; a rumor immediately began to circulate that an act was being prepared which would dispense with the Act of Uniformity.[36] At the same time the government ordered the judges to stiffen the enforcement of the laws against Papists. This was done to head off any new legislation against them in the forthcoming session of Parliament, and it succeeded.[37] Since Clarendon in his later years had been the supporter of the Anglican hierarchy, all those who benefited by his fall, even so staunch an Anglican as the new lord keeper, Bridgeman, were anxious to alter his religious policy, in order to make it more difficult for him ever to recover power. To accomplish this Buckingham was indispensable, because he alone, of the inner ring of Charles's advisers, could command the support of the dissenters. The group which collected around the duke in the years which followed Clarendon's fall has been called by one recent scholar the historical link between the republicans of the Interregnum and the exclusionists of the late 1670's.[38] The dissenters might have followed the future leader of the exclusionists as well as Buckingham, but at this point Ashley's influence with the king was negligible.

The hopes of the nonconformists were great, wrote Pepys in December, 1667. "They do expect to have their day now soon; for my Lord of Buckingham is a declared friend to them, and even to the Quakers."[39] Pamphlets arguing in favor of toleration began to appear, notably those of Buckingham's friend Dr. John Owen, who had been Cromwell's chaplain. Owen's arguments were not primarily religious, although he did say that persecution of dissenters was unscriptural. He stressed most heavily the civil advantages of toleration and the corresponding disadvantages of attempting to enforce conformity. The latter policy, he said, was bad for business: the trading classes were full of dissenters, "upon whose industry and endeavors . . . the trade and wealth of the nation doth much de-

[36] *C.S.P.D.* VII, 437.

[37] P.R.O., S.P. 29/231, ff. 53–54, 57. C. Robbins, ed., *The Diary of John Milward* (Cambridge, 1938), pp. 88, 104–5.

[38] M. Ashley, *John Wildman, Plotter and Postmaster* (London, 1947), p. 208. See also W. C. Abbott, "English Conspiracy and Dissent 1660–1674," *American Historical Review* XIV (1908–9), 710–11, and Dec. 19, 1667, H. W. to Sir Philip Musgrave, *C.S.P.D.* VIII, 89.

[39] Pepys, *Diary*, Dec. 21, 1667.

pend";[40] many of them were leaving the country to escape persecution. "The Hollander" wrote another pamphleteer, "have [sic] not
a better friend in Europe than Uniformity in England."[41] This was a
familiar argument by now. Dutch business success was equated with
their religious policy by the Dutch themselves, and English pamphlets on this subject steadily increased in numbers and in precision
of argument.[42] The prosperity of tolerant France and Holland and
the economic decay of Spain were repeatedly stressed. It was an
argument which the defenders of uniformity found difficult to meet
and which they usually passed over in silence. Their most widely
used argument was the political one: dissenters were seditious—had
not Cromwell been a dissenter?—and to tolerate dissent would simply invite a renewal of the late troubles. Owen and those who felt as
he did met this argument, which was usually couched in highly
emotional language, by replying that, on the contrary, it was persecution which led to civil disturbance; they pointed to the contrast
between the regimes of Henry IV of France and the duke of Alva.
Many people who were loyal subjects in every other respect differed
from the government only in this. There was one glaring logical
weakness in this argument, which the supporters of conformity
heavily stressed: the dissenters wanted toleration only for themselves, not for Catholics. Catholics, so the dissenters said, were politically dangerous—which was precisely the argument used by the
supporters of conformity against dissenters. The dissenters could
meet this argument only by stressing their own political loyalty and
by declaring that the arguments for conformity were essentially
Popish: the Catholics, as everyone knew, vehemently opposed liberty
of conscience.[43]

[40] John Owen, *A Peace-Offering in an Apology and Humble Plea for
Indulgence and Libertie of Conscience* (London, 1667) , p. 37.
[41] Sir Charles Wolseley, *Liberty of Conscience upon Its True and
Proper Grounds Asserted and Vindicated* (2nd ed., London, 1668) , p. 59.
[42] Charles Wilson, *Profit and Power* (London 1957) , pp. 15–18. H. G.
Plum, "The English Religious Restoration 1660–1665," *Philological Quarterly* XX
(1941) , 525.
[43] For Owen see the tract listed in note 40 above, *Indulgence and
Toleration Considered in a Letter unto a Person of Honor* (London, 1667) , and
Truth and Innocence Vindicated (London, 1669) . The antitolerationist arguments
are well summarized in Thomas Tomkins, *The Inconveniences of Toleration*
(London, 1667) , and Richard Perrinchief, *A Discourse of Toleration* (London,
1668) . There is a description of the theological arguments used on both sides in
John Hunt, *Religious Thought in England from the Reformation to the End of
the Last Century* (London, 1870–73) II, 1–28.

"The considerate Nonconformists will never promote their own liberty by such ways and means as would bring in a toleration of Popery: yea, they would rather help to bear up the present ecclesiastical state, than that Popery should break in"—thus a Presbyterian pamphleteer pointed to a way out, the way the Presbyterians had always favored: comprehension rather than toleration.[44] And, indeed, in December, 1667, a comprehension scheme was launched. The driving force behind the proposal was another of Buckingham's friends, John Wilkins, for whom the duke was soon to obtain the bishopric of Chester. Wilkins was a scientist, the first secretary of the Royal Society; he had had a distinguished academic career in Cromwell's day, he had married Cromwell's sister, and he shared Buckingham's rationalistic and deistic religious views.[45] In its original form the proposal was merely for comprehension of the Presbyterians, but in the conferences of January, 1668, with the Presbyterian leaders Wilkins introduced a plan for indulgence as well. Wilkins certainly favored indulgence; he may have been impelled to push for it at this stage by political considerations. The king had no interest in a solution which satisfied only the Presbyterians; only a general acceptance of the principle of indulgence would permit him to help the Catholics. It is true that the indulgence scheme worked out at the conferences by Wilkins and his associates specifically excluded Catholics from its benefits, but if Parliament accepted the principle of indulgence for Protestant dissenters, the chances of extending it to Catholics in time would be considerably improved.

Wilkins' plan had a good deal of support. The king was prepared to try it; Buckingham, naturally, backed it, as did Lord Keeper Bridgeman and Sir Matthew Hale, the chief baron of the exchequer and future chief justice; so, too, did some of the liberal-minded bishops. The rumors flew thickly that January; on the twentieth Pepys recorded in his *Diary*, "It seems there is a great presumption that there will be a Toleration granted: so that the Presbyterians do hold up their heads." A little while later Colonel Birch, who had planned to introduce a comprehension bill in the Commons in 1667 and had lost his nerve, told Pepys that Parliament would surely pass a toleration bill this time, in spite of the opposition of the bishops.

[44] John Corbet, *A Second Discourse of the Religion of England* (London, 1668). The quoted passage is on pp. 43–44.
[45] See his *Of the Principles and Duties of Natural Religion* (London, 1678).

The only problem would be that posed by the Catholics. Toleration could not be extended to them: "the sober party will be without it, rather than have it upon those terms."[46]

It was widely assumed that Buckingham was responsible for the new policy. "The great interest now driven on in the kingdom is by the duke of Buckingham, who heads the fanatics," wrote Viscount Conway in February. "The king complies with him out of fear; the Commons are swayed by him as a favorite and a premier minister; he himself thinks to arrive to be another Oliver, and the fanatics expect a day of redemption under him."[47]

The Commons were not swayed by Buckingham at all. The Shrewsbury affair did not help; Pepys's comment was, "This will make the world think that the king hath good councillors about him, when the duke of Buckingham, the greatest man about him, is a fellow of no more sobriety than to fight about a whore."[48] Probably this made little difference; Parliament was overwhelmingly against any religious bill, save one for rigid enforcement of the Conventicle Act. Wilkins unintentionally helped to seal the fate of his plan by revealing it to Bishop Ward of Salisbury, whom he knew to be opposed to both comprehension and toleration; he counted on his personal friendship with Ward to win the bishop over.[49] Ward instead revealed the details of the plan to Archbishop Sheldon and the other supporters of conformity, who were fully prepared when Parliament reconvened in February. On February 10 the king addressed the Houses and asked them to "think of some way how his Protestant subjects of all persuasions might be so provided for in matters of religion, as they might be induced cheerfully to contribute to the support of the government"; he linked this request with the announcement of the alliance with the tolerant Dutch. The popularity of the Dutch alliance made no difference; before the king had even made his speech, the Commons voted that no comprehen-

---

[46] Pepys, *Diary,* Jan. 31, 1668. W. G. Simon, "Comprehension in the Age of Charles II," *Church History* XXXI (1962) , 441. I have relied heavily on this article in the above account of the comprehension scheme.

[47] *C.S.P.D.* VIII, 258–59. See also Sylvester, *Reliquiae Baxterianae* III, 22–23.

[48] Pepys, *Diary,* Jan. 17, 1668. Curiously enough, Buckingham in April, 1668, became a member of the Lords' committee to consider a bill against duels—an indication of the vagaries of Restoration politics. *Lords Journals* XII, 232.

[49] Simon, "Comprehension," *Church Hist.* XXXI, 444.

sion bill be brought in without the particular leave of the House and that Charles be asked to enforce the Act of Uniformity and the other laws relating to church discipline. There was no debate on the question until early March; meanwhile the Commons' temper was further exacerbated by reports of fanatics who interrupted services and "pull[ed] the surplice over the parsons' heads."[50] On March 4 the Commons brushed aside the arguments of the supporters of toleration and asked Charles to issue a proclamation against conventicles and Catholics. Charles agreed to do so and said he hoped the House would consider the question of legislation for relief of dissenters. The Commons would hear of no change in the existing laws; they wanted neither toleration nor comprehension, and on April 8 they rejected a proposal that the king be requested to summon a group of dissenting leaders and receive suggestions from them by a majority of more than two to one. Instead they passed a new bill against conventicles and rather meanly instructed Colonel Birch to move the Lords to expedite it.[51]

The Commons' attitude convinced the king and Buckingham and everybody else who, for whatever reason, wished to see the existing religious situation altered that there was nothing to be hoped for from Parliament. The failure of the indulgence of 1662 might have been blamed on Clarendon, but now Clarendon was gone, and the temper of the House was no different. If the religious situation was to be altered, if there was to be legal relief for any group, it could come only through the use of the prerogative.

Practical relief for dissenters was a somewhat easier matter. It could be achieved in large part by nonenforcement of the law, and this was the policy the king followed for about a year and a half after his rebuff at the hands of the Commons. The Parliamentary session was ended before the bill against conventicles could be considered by the Lords, and the king's proclamation against such meetings was widely ignored. Conventicles, wrote Pepys, "are connived at by the king everywhere, I hear, in City and country." Wilkins got his

[50] P.R.O., S.P. 29/253, ff. 16–17. Pepys, *Diary*, Feb. 10, 28, 1668. Mar. 7, 1668, Andrew Marvell to Major Lambert, H. M. Margoliouth, ed., *The Poems and Letters of Andrew Marvell* (Oxford, 1952) II, 66–67.

[51] P.R.O., S.P. 29/253, f. 23. Robbins, *Diary of John Milward*, p. 293. The relevant debates are in *ibid.*, pp. 206, 214–22, 248–50, 282–83, and in A. Grey, *Debates of the House of Commons* (London, 1763) I, 103–6, 110–16, 126–32, 146–47.

bishopric in September, 1668, and rumor had him rising still higher: he is "a mighty rising man," wrote Pepys, "as being a Latitudinarian and the duke of Buckingham his great friend."[52] The duke's other friends were not forgotten either. His chaplain Thomas Sprat got a prebend in Westminster, and his Parliamentary supporter Sir Thomas Osborne became joint treasurer of the navy, along with Sir Thomas Littleton, who had made a "long and very impertinent" speech in favor of toleration in Parliament. Buckingham was anxious for a dissolution, on the assumption that a new House would be more favorable to dissenters, but this the king would not permit.[53] A House full of dissenters, ex-Commonwealthmen, would be more obstructive to his real designs than the Anglicans.

Charles had no particular interest in the welfare of dissenters as such, but for the moment it suited him to have the penal laws laxly administered. The project for union with Scotland looked hopeful until the end of 1669: its success would depend on the support of non-Anglicans on both sides of the Tweed. Furthermore, the king was officially the ally of the Dutch, and if he was to extract the maximum concessions from his cousin of France for abandoning them, he must demonstrate to King Louis that he could get along well enough without the French connection. There was also the question of the navy; many of the workers in the navy yards were alleged to be dissenters who would be disgruntled if the laws were rigidly enforced.[54] So violations of the penal laws would be winked at for the moment, but the laws themselves must remain on the books. It might be desirable to enforce them, so severely that when the day of indulgence came, the dissenters, in their relief, would accept relaxation for Catholics as well.

The Anglicans were not at all pleased with the king's attitude and kept complaining about the growth of conventicles. On April 15, 1669, the king put the matter to the foreign committee. Bridgeman felt that the dissenters were as quiet now as they ever had been since the Restoration; only if conventicles had increased in numbers should anything be done, a view which Arlington shared. Bucking-

[52] Mar. 20, 1668, Bower to Williamson, *C.S.P.D.* VIII, 300. Pepys, *Diary,* Aug. 11, 1668, Mar. 16, 1669.

[53] Pepys, *Diary,* Nov. 13, 1668. Burnet, *History* I, 504. Browning, *Danby* I, 61–62. *C.S.P.D.* IX, 191. The phrase about Littleton is in Robbins, *Diary of John Milward,* pp. 216–17.

[54] *C.S.P.D.* VIII, 376.

ham remarked that he was taken as a favorer of dissenters, but, he said, he favored them only because of English trade. He did not believe any declaration should be made against them without good reason, lest they all feel persecuted and aggrieved. A proclamation was issued against the dissenters in July, 1669, since they had abused "the tenderness his majesty had in his own private opinion expressed for the modest and misled part of them,"[55] but once again enforcement was lax. The king discharged a substantial fine levied on three nonconformists for their failure to attend the established church, "it being his judgement that no man ought to suffer merely for conscience' sake."[56] In September, 1669, one of Williamson's correspondents reported from Bristol that the new proclamation had had little effect. One preacher had been arrested, "but he preaches out of the grate to a numerous congregation."[57]

Early in November, 1669, the king had a long conversation with the French ambassador about his religious policy. The crucial phase of the Anglo-French negotiations was approaching, and Charles was making the most of his inspiration respecting the Catholicity clause. He assured Croissy that his declaration of Catholicism would not produce an upheaval: the Presbyterians hated Anglicans worse than they did Catholics, and if the other types of dissenters got toleration, they would be quiet. Croissy, who was anxious to sidetrack the Catholicity scheme, expressed his doubts. He felt sure, he said, that all the Protestants would combine against the Catholics and that a large-scale rebellion would result, which the Dutch would support—unless, that is, the French plan of fighting the Dutch first were adopted.[58] Charles saw this argument for what it was, but the problem of tactics began to disturb him. Parliament was now in session once more, as Anglican-minded as ever, and alarmed by rumors that London was full of Commonwealthmen and that dangerous conventicles were meeting in Westminster itself. The king resented its meddling in religious questions and expressed his an-

[55] P.R.O., S.P. 104/176, ff. 139–40; 29/253, f. 62. For an example of a typical Anglican complaint see June 5, 1669, Sir G. Shakerley to Williamson, *C.S.P.D.* IX, 354.

[56] Quoted in Arthur Bryant, *King Charles II* (rev. ed., London, 1958), p. 162, n.

[57] *C.S.P.D.* IX, 481.

[58] F. A. M. Mignet, ed., *Négotiations relatives à la succession d'Espagne sous Louis XIV* (Paris, 1835–42) III, 100–106.

noyance to Sir Robert Moray. The king "is now beginning to declare himself more vigorously against persecution of people for their religion," wrote Moray, "and says upon that subject things most pungent and unanswerable."[59] But there was no mistaking the temper of the Commons; they wanted a new act against conventicles. Clifford and some of the other believers in toleration did what they could, but some of the king's officials favored the bill, and it failed of passage only on account of a prorogation, which, rumor had it, was ordered by the king for precisely this reason.[60]

Parliament was prorogued in December, 1669; before it reassembled in February, 1670, the king had made his basic decisions. The plan for Anglo-Scottish union had been practically, if not officially, abandoned, and the crucial concession had been made on the financial clauses of the treaty with France. Toleration by the use of the prerogative would be tried again, and this meant that Charles now had no special objection to a new Conventicle Act, which was duly passed in the Commons. The supporters of toleration there did their best, but got nowhere; Clifford, the only member of the Cabal in the Commons, sat silent. When the bill was considered in the Lords, the king's supporters, possibly encouraged by Charles himself, who now began to attend the debates there,[61] inserted an extraordinary clause to the effect that "neither this act nor anything therein contained shall extend to invalidate or avoid his majesty's supremacy in ecclesiastical affairs or to destroy any of his majesty's rights, powers, or prerogatives belonging to the imperial crown of this realm, or at any time exercised or enjoyed by himself, *or any of his majesty's royal predecessors, kings or queens of England*" (italics mine). This would have effectively removed all limitations on the king's power. Andrew Marvell, who regarded the act as "the quintessence of arbitrary malice" and who expected the Lords to add what he called a "Scotch clause of the king's power in externals," was aghast at this proviso. "There never was so compendious a piece of absolute universal tyranny," he wrote. The great majority of the

[59] Nov. 20, 1669, Marvell to Mayor Tripp, Margoliouth, *Marvell* II, 89–90. Dec. 11, 1669, Moray to Lauderdale, Osmund Airy, ed., *The Lauderdale Papers* (London, 1884–85) II, 170.

[60] *C.S.P.D.* X, 13. The debates are in Grey, *Debates* I, 159–63, 174–75.

[61] *The Collection of Autograph Letters and Historical Documents Formed by Alfred Morrison: The Bulstrode Papers* (privately printed, 1897) I, 133–34.

Commons was equally horrified, and it took considerable skill on the part of Clifford and the other members of the court party to salvage a general statement of the king's supremacy in matters ecclesiastical.[62]

Charles now decided to enforce the new act, to increase the dissenters' taste for toleration: to Croissy he explained that he hoped to provoke them to forcible resistance, in order to have an excuse to call up troops, which would be necessary for his projected declaration of his Catholicism. So, in the summer of 1670, after the signing of the treaty of Dover, vigorous action was taken against conventicles. Exceptional severity was employed in London, where the militia was used.[63] Parliament was still dissatisfied. In February, 1671, the Commons expressed their alarm about the increase of Popery: the Mass was being publicly celebrated in London, and there was an alarming influx of priests and Jesuits into the capital. The king was requested to enforce the penal laws against Catholics and banish priests by proclamation. He agreed to do so, except against those who had been faithful during the civil war—a curious commentary on the treaty of Dover. Rather ironically, it was Clifford who was designated to convey the Commons' thanks to the king for his acquiescence in their wishes. The Commons then turned to the pleasant task of stiffening the Conventicle Act still further, but again their bill was lost by a prorogation.[64]

In 1671 the king changed his tactics once again. The enforcement

[62] Mar. 21, Apr. 14, 1670, Marvell to William Popple, Margoliouth, *Marvell* II, 301, 303. F. Bate, *The Declaration of Indulgence, 1672* (London, 1908), p. 67. The crucial debates took place on March 28 and April 4. Grey, *Debates* I, 245–50, 263–65. The "Scotch" reference is to the recently enacted Scottish Act of Supremacy; see above, pp. 61–62.

[63] Sir J. Dalyrimple, *Memoirs of Great Britain and Ireland* (Edinburgh, 1771–88) II, 59–61. *C.S.P.D.* X, 233–34, 236, 237, 239–40. June 4/14, 1670, Lindenov to Christian V, W. Westergaard, ed., *The First Triple Alliance* (New Haven, 1947), pp. 255–56. June 17/27, 1670, Mocenigo to the Doge and Senate, *C.S.P. Venetian* XXXVI, 215–16. A nonconformist tract of 1671 suggests that in some quarters the king's tactics had the effect he sought. *Somers Tracts* VII, 586–615.

[64] *Bulstrode Papers* I, 176–77. See also Mar. 17/27, 1671, Alberti to the Doge and Senate, *C.S.P. Venetian* XXXVII, 29. P.R.O., S.P. 104/176, f. 291. The debates are in Grey, *Debates* I, 406–9, 412–15, 417–23, and in B. D. Henning, ed., *The Parliamentary Diary of Sir Edward Dering 1670–1673* (New Haven, 1940), pp. 70–71, 80–81, 86–87, 94–95. The foreign committee discussed the possibility of getting a clause "for repressing ye insolencyes of ye Presse" into the bill, but apparently nothing was done. P.R.O., S.P. 104/176, f. 273.

of the Conventicle Act had been awkward and difficult. It was not always easy to get juries to convict nonconformists, especially in London, and the City's refusal of a loan to the king in September, 1670, may well have been prompted, in part at least, by religious irritation. Furthermore, there was some hope that the rigid hostility of the Presbyterians to the policy of indulgence had softened. Lauderdale's policy in Scotland had impressed them, despite its Erastianism; there was allegedly an offer to the king "to pay all his debt and advance him a considerable sum beside, providing the same liberty be granted to them."[65] The use of informers was unpopular, and enforcement had been ineffective anyway. "If the Savoy business had taken effect, there had not been a fanatic in England," wrote Joseph Williamson in September, 1671. "The people grow more fanatic; all the Presbyterians are growing to Independents."[66] By this time the laws were again being but feebly enforced, and rumors were again beginning to circulate that more than nonenforcement was intended: there would be a toleration.[67]

In this same month of September, 1671, Buckingham was hard at work on *The Rehearsal,* which was to burst on the world in December and give the duke a permanent, if minor, place in English literary history. In these years he continued his patronage of the dissenters, without concerning himself very deeply with their condition. His principal political purpose was to achieve influence, but it **was** influence for its own sake that he sought, not in order to implement any particular line of policy. This sort of influence could only be displayed by attacking those in power and pulling them down. He had two great successes in the early months of 1669. In February Ormonde lost his lord lieutenancy in Ireland. He and Buckingham were old enemies, and the world agreed with Pepys that Ormonde's fall was Buckingham's doing. Ormonde himself wrote angrily to his son of "that vile man": "I am confident he . . . hates the king's person and his brother's, and has designs apart, if not aimed at the ruin of them both."[68] Even more obviously Buck-

[65] D. Crawford, ed., *Journals of Sir John Lauder, Lord Fountainhall,* Scottish History Society publication XXXVI (Edinburgh, 1900) , p. 233. *Bulstrode Papers* I, 150. Abbott, "English Conspiracy and Dissent," *A.H.R.* XIV, 714.

[66] *C.S.P.D.* XI, 496–97. The reference is to the religious conference at the Savoy in April, 1661.

[67] Sept. 1, 1671, Bower to Williamson, *ibid.,* p. 464.

[68] Thomas Carte, *The Life of James Duke of Ormond* (Oxford, 1851) IV, 355. Pepys, *Diary,* Feb. 12, 1669.

ingham's doing was the ruin of Sir William Coventry. Buckingham wrote a play which included a scene satirizing Coventry, who was rather thin-skinned; Sir William complained to the king. Charles sent for the play, read it, and said there was nothing offensive in it, which was not surprising, since the scene in question was deleted before the play was shown to the king. Coventry was furious and challenged Buckingham. The duke told the king, who sent Coventry to the Tower and deprived him of his offices.

Buckingham's victories were far more apparent than real, however. Charles, as he often did, confided in his sister: "I see you are misinformed if you think I trust my Lord of Ormonde less than I did; there are other considerations which makes [*sic*] me send my Lord Robartes into Ireland. . . . I am not sorry that Sir William Coventry has given me this good occasion, by sending my Lord of Buckingham a challenge, to turn him out of the council. I do intend to turn him also out of the treasury. The truth of it is he has been a troublesome man in both places and I am well rid of him."[69] Buckingham provided the excuse for changes which Charles intended to make anyway. What he had written his sister almost exactly a year before was still true: "I assure you that my Lord of Buckingham does not govern affairs here."[70]

The fact that Buckingham did not govern is shown by his inability to bring down his chief enemy, Arlington. In these years Buckingham repeatedly attempted to interfere in foreign affairs, the secretary's special province, in an effort to ruin him, but without success. The duke got wind of the negotiations with France in 1669, and he had to be gulled, as the king explained to his sister. "It will be good that you write some times to [Buckingham] in general terms that he may not expect that there is [*sic*] farther negotiations than what he knows . . . he may suspect that there is something of [Catholic religion] interest in the case, which is a matter he must not be acquainted with, therefore you must have a care not to say the least thing that may make him suspect anything of it."[71] The duke was successfully taken in and became an enthusiastic supporter of the French alliance because he was sure that Arlington opposed it.

[69] Mar. 7, 1669, Charles to Henrietta, C. H. Hartmann, *Charles II and Madame* (London, 1934) , p. 236.

[70] *Ibid.*, p. 204.

[71] Apr. 25, 1669, Charles to Henrietta, *ibid.*, p. 245. Brackets indicate words in cipher in the original.

He preened himself on his success in negotiating the *traité simulé* in December, 1670, and revelled in the prospect of command of the English contingent of 6,000 men when the war began. Arlington, perhaps unwisely, balked him of this. Ralph Montagu, the English ambassador in France, persuaded the French government that Buckingham was untrustworthy, since he "desired to keep well with the Presbyterians and fanatic party, who were never well-affected to a French alliance."[72] So it was decided to reduce the English contingent and give its command to Monmouth, with Buckingham's enemy Lord Ossory, Ormonde's son, as second-in-command. The duke was enraged and had a furious scene with Charles, whose patience with his old friend at last snapped. The king was approaching the great crisis in his fortunes at the end of 1671, and Buckingham, for all his charm, was becoming a nuisance. The king reminded Buckingham that his factious behavior in the last session of Parliament over the peers' right to amend a revenue bill had cost the king money—a "million," the king said, hyperbolically—and that in the question of the army command he had to consider the national interest, not the duke's wounded vanity. Where the national interest was concerned, he would consider the duke no more than he would his dog.[73] For once Buckingham was without a reply. About his only genuine victory over Arlington in these years was his election to the chancellorship of Cambridge, a post which Arlington coveted but which, as an Oxford man, he had little chance of obtaining—"you know our academical humor," wrote one of his supporters sadly to Williamson on the day of Buckingham's election.[74]

The duke's other dabblings in high politics were no more effective than his campaign against Arlington. At the time of the Roos divorce case, early in 1670, he allegedly concocted the wild scheme of kidnapping Queen Catherine and removing her to one of the English colonies; his attitude, if not his plan, was bruited about and prompted Marvell's remark that he was talking to Charles of a new queen.[75] His attention to business was increasingly attenuated by his messy and complicated private life. In May, 1668, two months after

---

[72] Sept. 13/23, 1671, Montagu to Charles, H.M.C., *Buccleuch and Queensberry Mss.* I, 501–3.

[73] Oct. 30/Nov. 9, 1671, Croissy to Louis XIV, Dalyrimple, *Memoirs* II, 86–88.

[74] May 11, 1671, *C.S.P.D.* XI, 227.

[75] Burnet, *History* I, 473.

her husband's death at Buckingham's hands—he survived the duel two months—Lady Shrewsbury moved into Wallingford House, the duke's town residence. For about the only time in her life, his long-suffering wife protested: she could not live under the same roof with that woman. "Why, madam, I did think so," replied the duke, "and therefore have ordered your coach to be ready to carry you to your father's."[76] A long and tedious series of scandals followed this open cohabitation, climaxed by the duke's burial of his illegitimate son, who died an infant, in Westminster Abbey under the title of earl of Coventry, one of his hereditary titles. The king might ennoble his own bastards, but it was shocking to the sensibilities of the aristocracy as a class that Buckingham should try to imitate him. His extravagance continued to grow; by the summer of 1671, he was £140,000 in debt, according to Andrew Marvell, and the recent prorogation of Parliament would afford his creditors the opportunity "to tear all his lands in pieces." Some of this spending, according to the Venetian ambassador, was to gain popular support, but, said Mocenigo, "he does not hold tight the reins of government which Fortune offers him, to direct all the affairs of the crown."[77] Mocenigo described Buckingham and Arlington as the two chief men in England; thus it still appeared to the outside world. But the duke knew otherwise: he was aware of the waning of his influence. In July, 1671, he had dinner with Ashley, Trevor, and the earl of Anglesey and told the latter he hoped to see Anglesey replace Bridgeman as custodian of the Great Seal. He thought he could manage the intrigue, he said, as long as it could be kept secret from Arlington, who would prevent it if he learned of it.[78] If the duke reflected at all on his personal situation and his political standing as he coached John Lacy in Dryden's mannerisms preparatory to the mounting of *The Rehearsal*, he might well have been prey to gloom. The crisis of the Dutch war was approaching and with it the series of events

---

[76] Pepys, *Diary*, May 15, 1668.

[77] Margoliouth, *Marvell* II, 310. *C.S.P. Venetian* XXXVII, 66–67.

[78] July 19, 1671, Anglesey's diary, H.M.C., 13th Report, appendix, pt. VI (London, 1893), pp. 265–66. Three years earlier Buckingham had been contriving Anglesey's overthrow in collaboration with Bridgeman. Oct. 7, 1668, Osborne to Buckingham, B.M. Add. Mss. 28,053, f. 20. Buckingham's most remarkable social accomplishment in these years was his success in getting William of Orange drunk when that proper young man visited England in the winter of 1670–71. Andrew Browning, ed., *Memoirs of Sir John Reresby* (Glasgow, 1936), p. 82.

which would estrange him politically from his friend and master once and for all.

III

The impetus for a new attempt to provide toleration by the use of the prerogative came from many directions. For the king it meant, as in 1662, a chance to do something for his Catholic subjects and to assert his authority, the same authority wielded by his cousin of France. It was one policy on which all the members of the Cabal could agree, though for widely different reasons. Lauderdale, preoccupied with Scotland, believed in uniformity of polity in the two kingdoms and wanted to conciliate the bulk of the former Covenanters. Arlington was frightened by the risks involved in the forthcoming war; toleration, he hoped, would keep the dissenters quiet while England, in alliance with Catholic France, fell upon the Protestant Dutch.[79] For Clifford, a declaration of indulgence was part of his plan to implement the Catholicity clause of the treaty of Dover; when it became apparent that Charles would not declare himself a Catholic, Clifford became the most vehement advocate of the indulgence, as his own religious conviction deepened.[80] All three of these also favored it as a means of advancing the royal prerogative, especially Clifford, who once expressed the extravagant opinion that the king's power in ecclesiastical affairs was such that he had the legal right to ordain priests and administer the sacraments.[81] Ashley was less concerned about the prerogative, but he believed in toleration of Protestant dissenters on principle. He stressed the economic argument, and when the king asked him, Lauderdale, and Clifford to investigate the constitutional aspects of the proposed declaration, it was his secretary, John Locke, who drew up the memorandum which affirmed that Charles did indeed have the power to issue the declaration. The king's supremacy in matters ecclesiastical was unchallenged, said the memorandum, and had been recognized by

[79] Mar. 16, 1672, Arlington to Sir Bernard Gascoigne, Thomas Brown, ed., *Miscellanea Aulica* (London, 1702) , p. 66. See also John Stoughton, *History of Religion in England from the Opening of the Long Parliament to 1850* (4th ed., London, 1901) III, 382–83.

[80] Hartmann, *Charles II and Madame*, p. 344. See also E. S. DeBeer, ed., *The Diary of John Evelyn* (Oxford, 1958) III, 607–9, and the note on p. 608.

[81] Nov. 9, 1669, Moray to Lauderdale, B.M. Add. Mss. 23,132, f. 151.

Parliament as recently as 1670.[82] After the event Ashley used another argument: diversity of Protestant opinion would help to prevent the Church of England from becoming utterly conformist, which would be very dangerous in the event of the accession of a Catholic king.[83] Here was one of the many factors which led to the explosion of 1678.

As for Buckingham, his views were similar to Ashley's and were widely known. When he was being questioned by a hostile House of Commons in February, 1674, he put it this way: "I do not disown that I advised it, being always of opinion that something was to be done in that nature in matters of conscience, but no farther than the king might do by law."[84] In 1672 he was rather more forthright. In a pamphlet in which he supported both the indulgence and the Dutch war on economic grounds, he wrote, "It is the interest of the king . . . to make himself head of the Protestants, and . . . he should do it, not by being violent for any one sect, but by taking generally into his protection all Christians whatsoever, that will not submit to the government of the Church of Rome."[85] Yet the duke took little part in the discussions which led up to the issuing of the declaration. He was on bad terms with the king on account of his lost military command and stayed away from many of the meetings of the foreign committee, where the terms of the indulgence were worked out.

Discussions evidently began in November, 1671; in December there was some notion of having both toleration and comprehension, but the latter was quickly dropped as being too complicated.[86] In February, 1672, the king began to show his hand. There was a new lord lieutenant in Ireland, the pro-Catholic Lord Berkeley, who has succeeded the Presbyterian Robartes in 1670 after the latter had been in office only a year. On February 26 Charles instructed Berke-

---

[82] Louise F. Brown, *The First Earl of Shaftesbury* (New York, 1933). pp. 142–43, 195–96. M. Cranston, *John Locke* (London, 1957), pp. 143–44.

[83] *A Letter from a Person of Quality to His Friend in the Country* (London, 1675), pp. 4–6. The Tory Roger North, *Examen* (London, 1740), p. 44, states that the policy of indulgence and the Dutch war were part of a deep-laid plot of Ashley's to destroy the monarchy.

[84] *Works of . . . Buckingham* I, 200.

[85] *A Letter to Sir Thomas Osborn . . . Upon the Reading of a Book, Called, The Present Interest of England Stated* (London, 1672), esp. pp. 4–5, 7.

[86] Nov. 11, Dec. 13, 27, 1671, Williamson's notes, *C.S.P.D.* XI, 562–63; XII, 27–29, 44–46.

ley that Roman Catholics were to have the right to own property and pursue what business they chose, as in the days of Charles I, subject only to their taking the usual oath of allegiance.[87] This turned out to be a tactical blunder, as it rendered the indulgence far more suspect in the eyes of the English dissenters than it might otherwise have been. Early in March the final discussions took place in the foreign committee. There were several questions to be decided. Charles first raised the matter of his power to issue such a declaration, a point ultimately settled in his favor, thanks in part to Locke's memorandum. Then there was the question of what sort of declaration it was to be. Clifford argued in favor of a simple suspension of the penal laws; after some experience of the results, the rules for the conduct of non-Anglican worship could be fixed. No one else favored this; it would encourage disorders and conventicles. Lauderdale spoke in favor of a uniform policy including Scotland and Ireland and of the possibility of luring foreign Protestant immigrants. It was finally decided that the "Phanaticks" were to be allowed to worship in public, "Papists only privately in their houses and chapels, no Churches." The penal laws were to be suspended for now and repealed when Parliament met.[88]

Some support was evinced in the discussions for Clifford's idea that there should be a deliberate leak of the government's plans, so that public opinion would be prepared. There was no time for a propaganda campaign, however, since the indulgence had to precede the declaration of war. The final draft was approved in the foreign committee on the fourteenth of March; it went to the council on the fifteenth and was issued on the same day. Its purpose, according to the preamble, was to preserve the public peace and encourage foreign immigration—and, perhaps, although Charles did not say so, to help to reconcile to their fate those Dutch towns which were to fall to England's lot in the forthcoming war. The doctrine and discipline of the established church were not to be altered. The penal laws were suspended, but dissenters were to hold public worship only in

[87] *C.S.P.D.* XII, 166. Having served his purpose, Berkeley, who was not precisely honest, was dismissed and replaced in May by the Protestant earl of Essex.

[88] Minutes of the foreign committee, Mar. 6, 9, 11, 1672, P.R.O., S.P. 104/177, ff. 12, 14, 16. In September, 1672, Lauderdale, during his visit to Scotland as commissioner, extended his earlier policy of indulging deprived ministers. W. L. Mathieson, *Politics and Religion, a Study in Scottish History from the Reformation to the Revolution* (Glasgow, 1902) II, 249.

such places as the government indicated, and their ministers had to be licensed as well. Attacks on the established church would be severely punished. Catholics could worship in private houses only.[89]

"It is incredible," wrote the Venetian ambassador three days after the issuing of the declaration, "how much excitement the measure causes all over the country and in what different ways it is received."[90] The government knew that there would be no unanimity. Even some of the courtiers were uneasy. "I pray God they [the fanatics] make no ill return for this gracious declaration of his majesty," wrote one of them to Williamson on March 18, "which, it being his pleasure, I am highly satisfied with, but I know no other thing could have made it relished well with me."[91] The Puritan-minded earl of Anglesey recorded in his diary on March 15, "I was at council, where I spoke my mind freely to the declaration offered by the king for indulgence, observing the Papists are put thereby into a better and less jealoused state than the dissenting Protestants."[92] Catholics, after all, could begin their private worship at once, without having to wait on the process of licensing. It may be true, as a modern scholar says, that what the Catholics got "only legalized a state of things connived at for generations by successive governments";[93] it was still mightily unpopular. A Scottish diarist wrote that the declaration "appears to have been a deep popish design to procure indulgence to Presbyterians, that they might make way for toleration of Popery."[94] The open secret of the duke of York's Catholicism strengthened the popular belief and contributed to the declaration's unpopularity.[95] There were other difficulties as well.

[89] The text of the declaration is in Andrew Browning, ed., *English Historical Documents 1660–1714* (New York, 1953) , pp. 387–88.

[90] *C.S.P. Venetian* XXXVII, 186.

[91] *C.S.P.D.* XII, 215.

[92] H.M.C., 13th Report, appendix, pt. VI, p. 211.

[93] K. Feiling, *British Foreign Policy 1660–1672* (London, 1930) , p. 272.

[94] D. Laing, ed., *The Diary of Alexander Brodie of Brodie . . . and of His Son James Brodie of Brodie* (Aberdeen, 1863) , p. 327. The entry is dated March 29, 1672. See also the pamphlet by Francis Fullwood, *Toleration Not to Be Abused* (London, 1672), which makes clear the Presbyterian preference for comprehension. Lauderdale later told Burnet that the declaration was not popular in Scotland: *hinc illae lachrymae*. H.M.C., 5th Report, pt. I (London, 1876) , p. 317.

[95] May 26/June 5, 1672, Croissy to Louis XIV, Mignet, *Négotiations* IV, 42–43. In June Arlington told Croissy that the declaration had misfired and simply aroused the Protestants. It was in this conversation that the Catholicity scheme was finally buried, when Arlington said that the Pope would have to

The judges and the lord keeper had some doubts of the legality of the declaration, and many others were worried about its implications as to the power of the crown. It was, wrote one, "as great a prerogative act as has been done a good while."[96]

The government did its best to demonstrate to the country at large that the doubters were few and that the dissenters were happy with their new freedom. Addresses of thanks to the king from nonconformist ministers were organized. The plan was to have each group come to the king separately, for the maximum propaganda effect, and thank him as effusively as possible. "Few were so blind as not to see what was aimed at," wrote Burnet, but they complied. The first to be presented came from Devonshire, and may have been prompted by Clifford; that of the London ministers, presented by Buckingham's friend John Owen a week later, was, in part at least, Arlington's work.[97] Requests for licenses poured in, even from the Presbyterians; Richard Baxter himself, after considerable wavering, applied for and was granted a license in November. Large numbers of dissenters were released from prison, including John Bunyan, and pardons for past offenses were freely issued, especially to Quakers. The king even attempted, though in vain, to silence those Anglican clerics who were now preaching vehemently against Popery in an oblique attack on the declaration; he was met with the unanswerable reply that it was strange that a Protestant king should try to forbid preaching in defense of Protestantism.[98] And, indeed, the Anglican clergy and their supporters were the most vigorous opponents of the declaration. In some places, such as Bristol, the bishop paid no heed to the declaration and went on harrying noncomformists, and "threaten[ing] them with penalties and the Parliament"; in

---

concede communion in both kinds and the Mass in English before Charles could consider making an open declaration of his faith. Croissy replied that this would violate the Tridentine decrees, and the matter was dropped. Dalyrimple, *Memoirs* II, 83–84.

[96] Apr. 3, 1672, Daniel Fleming to Sir George Fletcher, H.M.C., *Mss. of S. H. LeFleming* (London, 1890) , p. 90. On the attitude of the judges see A. F. Havighurst, "The Judiciary and Politics in the Reign of Charles II," *Law Quarterly Review* LXVI (1950) , 72–73.

[97] Burnet, *History* I, 554. P.R.O., S.P. 104/177, f. 19. *C.S.P.D.* XII, 226. Bate, *Declaration of Indulgence*, pp. 92–93. Sylvester, *Reliquiae Baxterianae* III, 99.

[98] Bate, *Declaration of Indulgence*, p. 85. About all Charles could do was to prevent these sermons from being printed. B.M. Add. Mss. 40,860, f. 27.

others, the Anglicans complained that nonconformists claimed that the declaration protected them against penalties for any and all ecclesiastical offenses, including the fathering of bastards; in still others the justices of the peace either paid no attention to the declaration at all or else refused to interfere with unlicensed meetings of dissenters, claiming that the declaration forbade them to do so. The opponents of the declaration made good use of the situation in Ireland, where the government was chary of licenses to nonconformists and followed a policy very favorable to the Catholics. Just after the turn of the year the Venetian ambassador reported that members of Parliament were openly declaring that the whole country disapproved of the king's policy.[99] This was an exaggeration; those who hoped for widespread enthusiasm for the declaration may have been disappointed, but so also were those who hoped the dissenters would offer widespread resistance. At the end of September a Dutch agent received the gloomy report that "The fanatics, your best friends, rest quiet from the sweetness of their enjoyed toleration, and do not so much as mutter publicly."[100]

IV

For a supporter of the ostensible purpose of the indulgence, Buckingham took surprisingly little part in the discussions which preceded its promulgation. His relations with the king were very cool; even Charles's new mistress, Louise de Quérouaille, was more Arlington's protégée than his. This was partly his own fault. He had arranged to bring the lady over from France when he returned from the negotiation of the *traité simulé;* he was to send a yacht to Dieppe for her and forgot all about it. It was Arlington who sent the yacht, after Louise had cooled her heels for a fortnight in Dieppe, and she never forgave the duke for his negligence. Charles had good political reasons for keeping Buckingham at arm's length in 1672, however. The duke's talent for disruption and intrigue was the last thing that the king needed as he launched his grand design. Burnet put it

[99] *C.S.P.D.* XIII, 536–39, 543; XIV, 120–21, 332–33. P.R.O., S.P. 104/177, f. 70. June 22, 1672, Arlington to Orrery, *C.S.P.D.* XIII, 269–70. Aug. 31, Oct. 1, 1672, Arlington to Essex, B.M. Stowe Mss. 200, ff. 184–85, 326–27. *C.S.P. Venetian* XXXVIII, 3–4.

[100] Quoted in K. H. D. Haley, *William of Orange and the English Opposition 1672–4* (Oxford, 1953), p. 68.

rather extravagantly when he said that "the duke of Buckingham was alone, hated by all, and hating all the rest,"[101] but his isolation was evident.

When the war began, Buckingham tried once more to obtain some sort of position with the fleet. According to Burnet, he even tried to ingratiate himself with the duke of York by asking for a priest to reconcile himself with the Roman church. If this story is true, it seems more likely that Buckingham's real purpose was to try to discover the real nature of the king's policy, since he was too intelligent not to know that he was not fully in Charles's confidence. And, indeed, he may have learned the secret of the treaty of Dover from James at this time.[102] Partly in order to keep Buckingham from causing mischief, Charles made him Arlington's colleague in the peace mission which was sent to the Dutch in June, 1672.

This mission indicated that Charles was aware that his calculations were on the verge of going seriously wrong. The first few months of the war had brought but little success to the English fleet, which was not ready for war and, the Venetian ambassador reported, poorly officered: the king could not trust the common people and so had to rely on inefficient aristocratic commanders. "The monarchy would fall were it to rely on the people, who by nature and owing to circumstances are most bitterly hostile to it," he added. This was an exaggeration, but the acute shortage of naval stores was real. The king was very angry about this; as he put it in the foreign committee, "How can 25,000 men's victuals for three months be all gone in one? The question was asked," the minutes continue, "and it has not been yet answered."[103] The contrast with the triumphs of the armies of Louis XIV, which had conquered the better part of three Dutch provinces, was unfavorably noted by English opinion. The limited success of the declaration of indulgence and the stopgap nature of the financial remedy applied by the Stop of the Exchequer made a quick and profitable peace treaty more necessary than ever: hence

---

[101] Burnet, *History* II, 5.

[102] *Ibid.* I, 579. W. D. Christie, *A Life of Anthony Ashley Cooper, First Earl of Shaftesbury* (London, 1871), II, 86.

[103] May 24/June 3, 1672, Alberti to the Doge and Senate, *C.S.P. Venetian* XXXVII, 218. B.M. Add. Mss. 28,040, ff. 22–23. P.R.O., S.P. 104/177, f. 52. On the problem of English preparedness see H. A. Hansen, "The Opening Phase of the Third Dutch War Described by the Danish Envoy in London, March–June 1672," *Journal of Modern History* XXI (1949), 97–108.

the peace mission. Parliament, when it met again, must be presented with a *fait accompli* and a successful one.

Charles and Arlington hoped to find the Dutch demoralized and panic-stricken and therefore willing to accept the English demands, which were set high. The Dutch must pay for the cost of the war and an annual tribute for fishing rights off the English coast. The province of Zeeland, or at least three or four towns, must be ceded to England. The East India trade must be regulated in a manner favorable to the English. The cooperation of the young prince of Orange was to be secured by his being created hereditary prince of Holland. If these terms or those laid down in the treaty with France could not be obtained, the war would go on. The French would be kept informed: a separate peace was possible only with French consent since otherwise Louis might reveal the Catholicity clause of the treaty of Dover. Charles was not going to run the risk of alienating Louis by negotiating behind his back.[104]

The negotiations foundered on the cold, courageous, phlegmatic obstinacy of William of Orange, who would not panic and would not surrender. Buckingham's mercurial behavior made his colleague's task no easier. He was so moved by William's eloquent description of the danger to England which would follow from a French conquest of the United Provinces that he declared that he was prepared to sign an immediate peace treaty and had to be talked out of this mood by Arlington. After their failure with William, the envoys proceeded to the French camp, where Buckingham once more succumbed to the charm of Louis XIV and again became an ardent partisan of France. The envoys returned to England at the end of July with nothing accomplished.[105]

Arlington was still hopeful of an early peace when he and the duke came home. His hopes were raised still further by the murder of De Witt, whose restoration to power he had very much feared. William of Orange's resolution was showing some signs of cracking. He had made a peace offer at the end of July which involved an indemnity and the surrender of Sluys as a cautionary town; De Witt's murder might cause him to yield completely. So it was de-

[104] The discussion in the foreign committee on June 16, 1672, shows that this danger was very much in Charles's mind. P.R.O., S.P. 104/177, ff. 59–60.

[105] For an account of this embassy see V. Barbour, *Henry Bennet, Earl of Arlington* (Washington, D.C., 1914), pp. 188–99.

cided, on August 20, that the king should write a personal letter to William, renewing the offer of peace.[106]

This decision immediately raised the question of the forthcoming session of Parliament, which was supposed to begin in October. If the session were to be held as scheduled, the Dutch would delay the negotiations, in the hope that Parliament would compel the king to grant them easy terms. In the discussions in the foreign committee Bridgeman and Clifford pointed to the desperate condition of the treasury; Clifford, in particular, was worried about the attitude of the government's creditors if the session should be postponed. The king replied that, if the negotiations were going on, Parliament would hold up supply on the ground that peace was imminent, and Arlington added that no money bill would be passed before the holidays anyway. By the end of the year the result of the negotiations would be known. Furthermore, if the French discovered that English public opinion was hostile to them and to the war, they might make a separate peace. Charles put it thus: "If it should happen that the king of France should find 500 mouths infected to dog . . . the French and the alliance, why might he not look out to provide for himself on the other side?" So, on September 16, it was decided to postpone the Parliamentary session until February, 1673.[107] The secretary was still hopeful; he wrote of the prorogation as a great defeat for the Hollanders. Unhappily for his hopes, William of Orange was not yet prepared to admit defeat. In October Arlington wrote rather gloomily to Williamson that the king had received a cold letter from William.[108] The war would go on; nothing more than a truce could now be expected; the government would have to face a disgruntled House of Commons with empty hands and empty pockets.

On February 4, 1673, Parliament met. As Arlington expected, it focused its attention, not on the French alliance, not on the miscarriages of the war, but on the obnoxious declaration of indulgence. In his opening speech Charles attempted to forestall the anticipated criticism of his religious policy by minimizing the concessions to the

[106] July 15/25, 1672, Arlington to Charles, cited in H. C. Foxcroft, *The Life and Letters of Sir George Savile, First Marquis of Halifax* (London, 1898) I, 97. July 19/29, 1672, Alberti to the Doge and Senate, *C.S.P. Venetian* XXXVII, 261–62. P.R.O., S.P. 104/177, ff. 69, 70, 78.

[107] P.R.O., S.P. 104/177, ff. 77–78, 82–85.

[108] Sept. 20, 1672, Arlington to Gascoigne, Brown, *Miscellanea Aulica*, p. 80. Oct. 11, 1672, Arlington to Williamson, *C.S.P.D.* XIV, 37.

Catholics and by insisting that "I am resolved to stick to my declaration." The Commons would not be put off; the record of the House's proceedings of ten years earlier, at the time of Charles's first declaration of indulgence, was read, and it was voted on February 10 that the king had no power to suspend the penal statutes without the consent of Parliament. Four days later the Commons' resolution was embodied in an address to the king, after attempts to ask for the concurrence of the Lords and to express their intention to pass an act for relaxation of the laws against dissenters were beaten down.[109]

The ministry was badly divided on the proper course to pursue in the face of this determined stand. Henry Coventry, now secretary, Arlington, and the king himself were worried about supply. It was clear enough that there would be no supply without concessions. As one of the opponents of the declaration put it in debate on February 22, "a gracious answer from the king to the address would very much smooth the passage of the money bill."[110] Ashley, now earl of Shaftesbury, wanted to stand firm: "rather lose money than lose rights." Since the Commons kept asking for the opinion of the judges as to the legality of the declaration, Shaftesbury and Clifford advocated an appeal to the highest court in the land, the House of Lords; if the Lords supported the king's right to issue the declaration, a procedural wrangle might ensue which would redound to the king's advantage. Buckingham, for once, saw farther than his colleagues. No amount of wrangling would induce the Commons to vote supply: "they know, every man there, that as soon as the money bill is passed, their time is over." If the Commons get used to this practice of "selling their money bills," he went on, "take heed of what they may next ask." The duke favored a dissolution rather than a surrender; so did the other sympathizers with dissent, Shaftesbury and Lauderdale. Charles, however, was optimistic. The idea of promoting a procedural dispute appealed to the gambler's streak in his nature: he insisted that no one could tell what the result of such a row would be.[111]

On February 24, after considerable delay, the king replied to the

[109] Feb. 7/17, 1673, Alberti to the Doge and Senate, *C.S.P. Venetian* XXXVII, 13. Arthur Bryant, ed., *The Letters, Speeches, and Declarations of King Charles II* (London, 1935), pp. 260–61. Bate, *Declaration of Indulgence*, pp. 108–11.

[110] Henning, *Dering*, p. 128.

[111] Bate, *Declaration of Indulgence*, p. 115. The debates in the foreign committee took place on February 14 and 16, 1673. P.R.O., S.P. 104/177, ff. 144–48.

Commons, in a last attempt to mollify them before trying the admittedly risky policy of appealing to the Lords. He declared that the suspending power applied only in ecclesiastical matters. He did not claim that he had the right to suspend laws "wherein the properties, rights, or liberties of any of his subjects are concerned," nor was he planning to alter the doctrine and discipline of the established church. If Parliament would pass a bill "which shall appear more proper to attain the aforesaid ends," he would be happy to accept it.[112] The Commons, although they had begun the consideration of a bill in behalf of dissenters, would not take the bait. Within two days they had replied, reiterating their previous position. So the king played his last card and appealed to the Lords, attempting to create jealousy of the Commons by saying that the Commons' resolution, since it dealt with a question of law, in effect usurped the power of the upper house. Once more he was rebuffed; the Lords voted that the king's suggestion that the points in dispute be settled by Parliamentary legislation was "good and gracious, that being a proper and natural course for satisfaction." Clifford attempted to salvage something from the disaster by proposing a bill which would grant the king the power "if it be not in him already" to suspend the penal laws in matters ecclesiastical under certain specified conditions; the suggestion got nowhere.[113]

King Charles now stood at a crisis in his fortunes. His religious policy had been defied and his prerogative challenged by a solid Parliamentary opposition. There were only two choices open to the king, apart from the use of force, which Burnet alleges Buckingham and Lauderdale advocated,[114] but which would have been far too desperate a gamble for a monarch resolved never to go on his travels again. Charles could follow the advice of the majority of the Cabal and dissolve Parliament. This would mean abandoning the war, since there would be no hope of the tax money which was indispensable to its continuation. In the event of a new election the Commons, if it changed its composition at all, would change only in the direction of having a higher percentage of dissenters. Such a House might approve of the indulgence, but it would hardly be sympathetic to the theory of the suspending power in general, and it would

[112] Bryant, *Letters*, pp. 261–62.

[113] Bate, *Declaration of Indulgence*, pp. 121–22. H.M.C., 5th Report, appendix, pt. II, p. 25.

[114] Burnet, *History* II, 11.

be more hostile to the war and the French alliance than the present House. The king's other alternative was to give way on the declaration, get the Parliamentary grant, and continue the war. This was scarcely more attractive than the first alternative; it would be an open confession of defeat on the question of the prerogative. On the other hand, it was certainly the safer course to adopt. This was what the French wanted, and French military success might still enable the king to win in the end.[115] On March 7 Charles made up his mind. He broke the seal on the declaration with his own hands, and on the next day notified Parliament of what he had done. The news was received with joy in Westminster, in London, and in the country generally; bonfires were lit in the streets. Arlington, who had favored concession from the beginning, was much relieved. Now Parliament would vote supply, the Dutch hope of playing upon divisions within England would be shattered, and there would be a speedy peace. The Venetian ambassador scornfully reported that the king had given way to panic.[116]

The Commons' firmness in regard to the declaration was certainly due in part to their dislike of Charles's use of the prerogative virtually to nullify a statute. Far more important, however, was their fear of any concessions to the Catholics. They may not have been aware of the real purposes of the king's policy, but its general drift seemed plain enough to them, and it was the House which was close to panic rather than the king. There was far less hostility to dissenters now than ever before, and a bill to give them relief was started, although it was ultimately lost with the adjournment at the end of March; as one of the earl of Essex's correspondents accurately predicted, "when we have finished cooking it we shall throw it out of the window."[117] The state of mind which, five years later, was to make a national hero of the egregious Titus Oates was beginning to develop.

Buckingham was, naturally, disappointed by the failure of the

---

[115] Mar. 10/20, 1673, Croissy to Louis XIV, Dalyrimple, *Memoirs* II, 93–96. In this letter Croissy stated that Charles had virtually decided to dissolve Parliament and that French intervention tipped the scale in favor of concession. This is unlikely, although Charles may well have told Croissy so, in order to increase Louis' sense of obligation to him.

[116] Mar. 8, 1673, Arlington to Essex, B.M. Stowe Mss. 201, f. 237. *C.S.P.D.* XV, 24, 36–38, 41, 44, 49. *C.S.P. Venetian* XXXVIII, 28. *Bulstrode Papers* I, 263. The debates in the Commons are in Grey, *Debates* II, 12–92 and Henning, *Dering*, pp. 113–34.

[117] Osmund Airy, ed., *Essex Papers* (London, 1890) I, 57.

policy of toleration. His mood showed itself in a speech he made in the Lords on a bill to exclude Catholics from the armed forces. This, said Buckingham, would cause all sorts of difficulties for the press-gangs; their potential victims would avoid service by claiming to be Catholic. He suggested that a preaching minister with a basket of sacramental bread ought to follow the drummer, to offer the bread to all recruits.[118] In the spring of 1673 the duke's hopes of a military command rose again, and he went to Yorkshire to recruit for his regiment. He had a good deal of difficulty. His support of the declaration of indulgence led people to believe he was sympathetic to the Papists; even his ostentatious taking of the sacrament in most of the churches of his lieutenancy helped very little. "The people hearken as little to his devotions as (I believe) heaven to his prayers," wrote one of Williamson's correspondents. Another commented, "All men fear our officers of this army are not well picked out, for the most of them debauched profane persons and public atheists which they say openly they learn of the duke of Buckingham." The duke himself attributed his recruiting problems to the rumors circulating in Yorkshire that soldiers already in service were being badly treated.[119]

Buckingham was again disappointed in his hope of military glory, and as the year 1673 drew to a close, he prepared to play once more the game which had proved so successful in 1666 and 1667. He would build a Parliamentary party and use it to pull down the king's chief minister, the hated Arlington this time. He was trying to collect a following, wrote Sir Gilbert Talbot to Williamson, "the debauchees by drinking with them, the sober by grave and serious discourses, the pious by receiving the sacrament."[120] This time, however, the ploy would not work. It was the duke who was to be condemned by Parliament and to follow Shaftesbury into embittered opposition to his one-time protégé, the earl of Danby, to become "Alderman George," the defender of popular liberties and Parliamentary privilege as well as of religious toleration.

It is difficult to take Buckingham seriously as a politician—indeed,

---

[118] *C.S.P. Venetian* XXXVIII, 25. Nevertheless, on March 13, Charles ordered that all soldiers take communion according to the Anglican rite before being mustered. *C.S.P.D.* XV, 42–43.

[119] W. D. Christie, ed., *Letters . . . to Sir Joseph Williamson* (London, 1874) I, 58, 67. H.M.C., 9th Report (London, 1884) II, 448–49.

[120] Christie, *Letters to Williamson* II, 105–6.

it was difficult for his contemporaries to do so, possibly because, unlike most politicians, "he loved pleasure better than revenge."[121] Quite apart from his mercurial character, his devotion to his own pleasures, and his unwillingness to be bothered with routine, his incurable wittiness was also a handicap. Who could regard as a serious stateman a man who, in speaking in Parliament on behalf of the proposition that a statute of the reign of Edward III was still in force, remarked, "give me leave to tell Your Lordships that statutes are not like women, they are not one jot the worse for being old"?[122] John Dryden, when he took his long-delayed revenge in *Absalom and Achitophel,* summed it up for contemporaries and posterity as well:

> A man so various that he seemed to be
> Not one, but all mankind's epitome;
> Stiff in opinions, always in the wrong,
> Was everything by starts and nothing long;
> But in the course of one revolving moon
> Was chymist, fiddler, statesman, and buffoon;
> Then all for women, painting, rhyming, drinking,
> Besides ten thousand freaks that died in thinking.

It was only in the peculiar circumstances of the Cabal period that such a man could be a significant political figure. If Charles wished to give the impression that idleness and venery were his principal preoccupations, to conceal the fact that he really did have a policy, what better companion could he have had than the giddy duke? Buckingham's chronic dissatisfaction with those who wielded power was equally useful to the king. His ministers could be kept in line by the threat of Buckingham as an alternative, and the king could avoid the possibility of being coerced by the unanimous opinion of his ministers. Once the course was set, however, the duke became much less useful—in fact, he became a positive handicap—and the king gradually cut him loose.

It might have been better for the cause of toleration if Buckingham had not been associated with it, since his behavior made him suspect in so many other ways, but it is to his credit that he never wavered in his convictions on this point. The cancellation of the declaration did not mean that persecution was automatically resumed: the lax administration of the penal code continued, and the

---

121 The phrase is Marvell's. Margoliouth, *Marvell* II, 329.
122 Quoted in Chapman, *Great Villiers,* p. 233.

licenses to dissenting ministers were not recalled until 1675. And, indeed, the position of the dissenters was never again to be as bad as it was before 1672. As one contemporary put it, the indulgence "was the greatest blow that ever was given, since the king's restoration, to the Church of England, all sectaries by this means repairing publicly to their meetings or conventicles, insomuch that all the laws and care of their execution against these separatists afterwards could never bring them back to due conformity."[123] Catholics found things more difficult, to be sure. After the cancellation some of them began to sell their estates to avoid forfeiture, and in November a proclamation went out ordering the judges and magistrates to prosecute them with vigor.[124] Charles here was following one of his familiar tactical devices: wherever political pressure became especially acute, he attempted to relieve it by a show of anti-Catholic zeal.

A recent authority has characterized the cancellation of the declaration of indulgence as "the most important royal surrender of the century."[125] It was hardly that, but it was a major defeat for the king's plans. The elaborate scheme of achieving independence of Parliament by means of the war and the French alliance was on the brink of failure, and in a direct confrontation on the question of the prerogative, Parliament had forced the king to give way.[126] His attempt to emulate his cousin of France and to determine the fate of religious dissidents by prerogative action had failed, in large part because people believed that the action was taken in behalf of an unpopular and potentially subversive minority. Only now did Charles fully realize how visceral the average Englishman's hatred of Popery really was and that men who were devotedly loyal on every other issue would not follow him here. It was a lesson his brother James never did learn, and it would eventually cost him his throne. As Buckingham himself once said, "The king could see things if he would, and the duke would see things if he could."[127]

[123] Browning, *Memoirs of Sir John Reresby*, pp. 84–85.

[124] Christie, *Letters to Williamson* I, 146. *C.S.P.D.* XVI, 27. For the repression in Ireland see *ibid.* XV, 558–59.

[125] David Ogg, *England in the Reign of Charles II* (2nd ed., Oxford, 1955) I, 368.

[126] In June, 1673, the justices of Oxfordshire had to be instructed not to say publicly that the king had no power to suspend the laws. *C.S.P.D.* XV, 369–70.

[127] Burnet, *History* I, 295.

As for Buckingham, he and his old playmate were now at the parting of the ways.

> He laughed himself from Court; then sought relief
> By forming parties, but could ne'er be chief:
> For spite of him, the weight of business fell
> On Absalom and wise Achitophel.

The duke took service under wise Achitophel partly because of the similarity of their views on the religious question. It was Shaftesbury who was the central figure in the dissolution of the Cabal, in the last year of the war on which his master had gambled so heavily, and which was now his only hope.

Chapter 6

The Dissolution of the Cabal

Shaftesbury

Of these the false Achitophel *was first;*
A name to all succeeding ages cursed;
For close designs and crooked counsels fit:
Sagacious, bold, and turbulent of wit;
Restless, unfixed in principles and place,
In power unpleased, impatient of disgrace;
A fiery soul, which, working out its way,
Fretted the pigmy body to decay,
And o'er-informed the tenement of clay.
A daring pilot in extremity,
Pleased with the danger when the waves went high,
He sought the storms; but for a calm unfit,
Would steer too nigh the sands to boast his wit . . .
In friendship false, implacable in hate,
Resolved to ruin or to rule the state.

John Dryden was a Tory and a Catholic convert; yet such was the skill of his pen that his verdict on the motives and designs of "false Achitophel" has colored every account of the career of the object of his matchless invective. Anthony Ashley Cooper, first earl of Shaftesbury, was in many ways the most remarkable member of the Cabal, yet it is very doubtful that anyone would have thought so in the months which saw the protracted death agonies of that ill-assorted ministry. In 1673 the most spectacular part of Shaftesbury's career was still ahead of him. It was his activity in opposition to the government after the end of the Cabal which prompted Dryden's stinging verses and which, in the form of the party system, was to be his permanent legacy to his native land. Not all contemporary opinions were as hostile as Dryden's. The most common view was that he was ambitious. Ailesbury believed him to be a turncoat and a hypocrite, but he "might have been of a great support to his king and country, had not an unmeasured ambition blinded him."[1] And, of course, he had his admirers. His death occasioned the following lament:

> So 'twas when mighty Cooper dy'd,
>   The Fabius of the Isle.
> A sullen Look the Great o'erspread,
> The Common People lookt as dead,
>   And Nature droopt the while.
> Living, Religion, Liberty,
> A mighty fence he stood,
> Peers Rights and Subjects Property
> None stronglier did maintain than he
> For which Rome sought his blood.[2]

Shaftesbury's early career most nearly resembled that of Lauderdale, in that by the time of the Restoration he was already a prominent and experienced politician, though of a quite different sort from the Scottish earl. He was born in 1621, into a prominent, well-connected, and wealthy Dorsetshire family and was the heir to a baronetcy. He was a member of that segment of the gentry which had "risen" in Elizabethan days and which did not "decay" with the loss of public office. His father died when he was ten years old, which

---

[1] W. E. Buckley, ed., *Memoirs of Thomas, Earl of Ailesbury, Written by Himself* (Roxburghe Club ed., Westminster, 1890) I, 25.

[2] "An Essay upon the Earl of Shaftsbury's [*sic*] Death," *Poems on Affairs of State* (4th ed., London, 1702) I, 127.

meant that he passed under the jurisdiction of that engine of oppression of the landowning classes, the court of wards. His guardian had difficulties there with a granduncle, and young Anthony, by his own account, was cheated out of some £20,000 by the court.[3] In 1637 he entered Exeter College, Oxford, as his fellow west-country man, Thomas Clifford, was to do a decade later. His career at the university and at Lincoln's Inn, where he was also enrolled, was brief, for in February, 1639, at the age of seventeen, he got married.

The marriage was the sort that was to be expected of an ambitious and wealthy young man. His bride was the daughter of Lord Keeper Coventry, which meant that the young baronet was no longer a mere country gentleman, but the intimate associate of the court party. William and Henry Coventry were his brothers-in-law, and one of his wife's sisters was the mother of the future marquis of Halifax. It was probably this marriage which kept him from a seat in the Long Parliament. He had been elected to the Short Parliament and was returned to the Long Parliament for a Wiltshire borough, but the election was disputed, and the case was not reported out of committee. John Pym and his followers no doubt believed that they were thus eliminating one of the king's supporters from the House.[4]

Cooper's royalism was hardly perfervid, however. He was present at the raising of the royal standard at Nottingham in 1642, but he took no active part in the war during its opening months. Early in 1643 he had an interview with Charles I, during which he put forward a plan for settlement. The king was to empower him to promise the Parliamentary garrisons in Dorset a full pardon, a general amnesty, and a free Parliament to settle the nation's affairs, once peace had been restored. If the plan worked in Dorset, and Cooper was sure that it would, the idea would spread, and the war would soon be over. It was a rather unrealistic scheme, which reflected the optimism of youth. The king nevertheless gave him a certain amount of encouragement, no doubt calculating that such a rich and well-connected young man was worth having on his side. Within a year Cooper was thoroughly disillusioned with his royal master. He was not allowed a free hand in Dorset; worse still, he learned that the king was deep in negotiation with France and the

[3] Louise F. Brown, *The First Earl of Shaftesbury* (New York, 1933), p. 21.

[4] *Ibid.*, p. 38.

Papists, both of whom he disliked and distrusted all his life. He felt that he had been used. His advice was not followed, and the king had not been candid with him. And so he simply shifted sides. It was a pattern of behavior which he would repeat several times in the course of his long political career.

Early in 1644 Cooper went over to the Parliamentary party. He did some useful military work for Parliament in Dorset and in the process displayed that streak of ruthlessness which was to characterize his later political career. At the siege of a Dorset manor house he advocated giving no quarter to the garrison, in order to terrorize the other Royalist strongholds into prompt surrender. His advice was adopted, but at the last moment two of his fellow officers found that they could not stomach the prospect of watching their neighbors burn to death and offered quarter. Cooper did not approve.[5]

With the end of the fighting and the triumph of the New Model, Cooper went into temporary retirement on his estates, not to emerge until 1652, when he became a member of a commission for reform of the laws, probably because of his friendship with Matthew Hale, the future chief justice, who was the leading member of the commission. In the meantime his wife had died, and he married again, and again well: his bride was the sister of the earl of Exeter. He became a member, an important one, of Barebone's Parliament and was elected by it to the Council of State. By this time Cooper was an enthusiastic supporter of Cromwell, in whom he saw the only hope of stability for the new regime. Like many of the other legal-minded men around the new lord protector, he hoped that Cromwell would assume the title of king and thereby put an end to the legal anomalies in the existing situation. Cromwell's refusal to do this, his increasing dependence on the advice of General John Lambert, who was not in the least concerned with the legal problems which worried Cooper, and, possibly, Cromwell's refusal to have him as a son-in-law—Cooper's second wife had died after less than three years of marriage—sent Cooper into opposition once more. The exiled king felt that this was significant enough to warrant a friendly and hopeful letter.[6] And, indeed, Cooper's ideas may have begun to turn in the direction of a restoration. At least he took for his third wife, in 1656, a niece of the Royalist earl of Southampton. But he knew

[5] *Ibid.*, pp. 46–47.
[6] The letter is given in *ibid.*, p. 64.

perfectly well that no restoration was feasible while Cromwell was alive, and, indeed, it was always possible that the lord protector would regularize the situation by taking the crown. It seems likely that it was this hope which underlay his obstructionist attitude to the "other house" in Oliver's last Parliament: he wanted no halfway measures.

With the death of the lord protector in September, 1658, Cooper began to play a waiting game. It seems probable that he was now convinced that a restoration was inevitable, but when and how it would occur was by no means certain, and the matter of timing was all important: he must not commit himself too soon or to the wrong group of Royalists. He managed this extremely difficult and delicate problem with great skill. Monck's cousin Sir William Morice, on whom the general depended for political advice, was a friend and admirer of his, and through Morice Cooper became friendly with Monck and with Monck's wife, whose influence over her husband was considerable. Cooper's position on the Council of State, to which he was elected for the last time in the spring of 1660, receiving more votes than Monck, made the king and his advisers eager to win him over. So his former brother-in-law, Henry Coventry, brought him a friendly letter from Charles.[7] Cooper now, at last, took the plunge. On May 5 Coventry wrote to Hyde that he had had a long conversation with Cooper. He had assured Cooper that the king valued his talents and wanted to put them to use and had denied that Hyde had ever coveted his estates or asked the king for them. Cooper's reply was all that the king might have wished. Ever since he had broken with Cromwell, Cooper declared, he had been convinced that the king would return, and all his efforts since then had been dedicated to the promotion of governmental instability, so as to hasten that restoration. It was in order to maintain his influence and thus his ability to cause that instability that he had hitherto refrained from declaring himself: "the less he was thought to be the king's friend, the more he had the power of being it." Cooper also addressed himself warmly to Hyde. He had never believed the story about his estates, he said, and he promised to reveal to Hyde the nefarious designs of France upon England. He "can have no opinion that those that are too well with France should be too much in the

[7] The letter, dated March 15/25, 1660, is in *ibid.*, p. 94.

king's business"—an opinion he was to hold to steadily for the rest of his life.[8]

We may take leave to doubt that Charles and his lord chancellor believed Cooper's explanation of his behavior in the last half-dozen years, but they accepted it. So, in 1660, the Dorsetshire baronet was one of those, of whom Monck was the most prominent, who expected to be rewarded for making this bloodless restoration possible. Indeed, it was essential to reward many of these men and to take them into the government, not only because they had ability and experience but also to provide continuity of administration and reconcile the erstwhile partisans of the Good Old Cause to the change of regime. Twelve of the thirty members of Charles's privy council were ex-Parliamentarians, as were six of the twelve peers created at the coronation in April, 1661. Cooper was in both groups. A measure of the king's appraisal of his relative importance is afforded by the fact that Monck became a duke, Edward Montagu, Monck's counterpart in the fleet, an earl, and Cooper, a baron, Baron Ashley of Wimborne St. Giles, his ancestral estate in Dorset.

It was pleasant to be a peer, but political power was what the new Lord Ashley craved, and to obtain it he would have to walk warily for some time, curry favor with those who had the king's ear, and live down his Roundhead past. In the Convention Parliament he had done useful service; it was he who made the decisive motion to postpone any legislation on religion, which paved the way for the Cavalier Parliament to enact the Clarendon Code.[9] As might be expected, he was strongly in favor of abolishing the court of wards and of allowing the king to recoup financially by means of the excise,[10] measures which shifted a part of the tax burden borne by the landed classes onto the shoulders of other sections of society. Throughout his career Ashley was always in very close touch with business opinion in the City and did what he could to foster English trade, but never at the expense of the landed proprietors. Hence he, along with his fellow proprietor Buckingham, supported measures like the Irish cattle bill, which would reduce the amount of trade

---

[8] *Ibid.*, pp. 97–98. These paragraphs on Shaftesbury's career before 1660 are largely based on the account given by Miss Brown in the first six chapters of her excellent biography.

[9] W. Cobbett, *Parliamentary History of England* (London, 1808) IV, 83–84.

[10] *Ibid.*, p. 148.

between England and Ireland but would greatly benefit the cattle-raisers among the English landed classes.

The post which Ashley eventually obtained, in May, 1661, was one eminently suited to his interests and talents; he became chancellor of the exchequer. This appointment was, no doubt, chiefly owing to his uncle Southampton, the lord treasurer. Southampton was honest and faithful but not very competent, and a man of Ashley's energy and gifts was badly needed in the treasury. Clarendon, who did not like ex-Commonwealthmen, admitted that Ashley was well qualified for the position, "though some other qualities of his . . . brought no advantage to his majesty by that promotion." Clarendon hoped "that his slippery humor would be . . . restrained and fixed by the uncle."[11] Ashley was soon an immensely busy man, both at the treasury and on various committees of the privy council. His industry impressed even Samuel Pepys, who was prone to look down on most of the men around the king. He was reportedly "a very ready, quick, and diligent person"; one of Pepys's acquaintances told him that Ashley was the only man at Charles's pleasure-loving court who paid any attention to business.[12]

The busy bureaucrat thus had his feet on the ladder which would lead him upward to the policy-making position he craved, but he had not arrived there yet, so his behavior in the first few years of the reign was very circumspect. He was a believer in toleration for Protestant dissenters, principally on economic grounds, but he did not oppose the Corporation Act or the Act of Uniformity in Parliament. He did support the abortive indulgence of 1662—in fact, he was its principal spokesman in the Lords—because he knew the king wanted it. His principal concern was to ingratiate himself with Charles, to make himself useful, and to keep on good terms with both the Clarendonians and the opposition to the chancellor—the opposition within the administration led by Secretary Bennet rather than the backstairs opposition conducted by Buckingham. In May, 1663, Pepys reported that these three had "cast my Lord Chancellor upon his back past ever rising again," a report which turned out to be premature.[13] He covertly encouraged the earl of Bristol to attack

[11] Edward, Earl of Clarendon, *A Continuation of His History of the Great Rebellion* (Oxford, 1857) I, 278, 315.

[12] *The Diary of Samuel Pepys* (ed. H. B. Wheatley, London, 1926), May 27, June 6, 1663.

[13] *Ibid.*, May 15, 1663.

Clarendon, but, like everyone else, he quickly dissociated himself from the earl's foolish assault when it came. Not until the coming of the Dutch war did Ashley feel strong and secure enough to stand on his own feet politically and openly cut himself loose from the chancellor's faction.

Ashley supported the war, as did English business opinion generally, and in December, 1664, two months before the formal declaration, he was made treasurer of the prize commission. Clarendon was not at all pleased by this appointment, but Ashley and the rest of the commission justified the king's confidence in them and did a competent and honest job. Expenses and corruption were kept to a minimum, and the great bulk of the funds realized from the sale of prizes was spent on the war.[14] Ashley was very meticulous about this; he quarreled with William Coventry and, said Pepys, "did snuff and talk as high to him, as he used to do to any ordinary seaman." He also insisted on selling all the prize goods taken, even those that would have been useful to the navy, such as timber and hemp, possibly to avoid any hint of collaboration with the admiralty administration, which was generally regarded as corrupt and inefficient.[15] Pepys and his associates resented Ashley's attitude; they were convinced that, as one of them said, "my Lord Ashley will rob the Devil and the altar, but he will get money if it be to be got," but the diarist admitted that Ashley showed no favor to the man who allegedly bribed him.[16]

During the war Ashley continued to grow in Charles's favor; he was one of the few major administrative officials to emerge from the conflict with an enhanced reputation. During the plague summer of 1665, when the court was at Salisbury, he entertained his master at St. Giles at what was evidently a very convivial houseparty; that fall, at the Oxford session of Parliament, he felt sufficiently sure of himself to allow his religious convictions to show: he opposed the Five Mile Act and openly supported liberty of conscience in the

[14] M. A. E. Green, *et al.*, eds., *Calendar of State Papers Domestic, Charles II* (henceforth *C.S.P.D.*) (London, 1860ff.) IV, 122. W. A. Shaw, ed., *Calendar of Treasury Books* (henceforth *C.T.B.*) *1667–1668* (London, 1905), pp. xxii–xxiv, lviii–lix, lxii.

[15] Pepys, *Diary*, Mar. 21, 1666, Jan. 19, 1667. Pepys strongly disapproved of Ashley's policy. Arthur Bryant, *Samuel Pepys* (new ed., London, 1947) I, 321, opines that Ashley did this in order to feather his own nest.

[16] Pepys, *Diary*, Sept. 9, 1665, May 20, 30, 1666.

Lords. He was impatient with his uncle Southampton's inefficient administration of the treasury and caballed with Arlington and Coventry against him in 1665, according to Clarendon. He had serious doubts about Downing's financial scheme and said so, and no doubts whatever about the usefulness, to himself at least, of the Irish cattle bill.[17] He confidently expected to be rewarded for his wartime services, and he was: in May, 1667, following Southampton's death, he became one of the five commissioners of the treasury.

With this appointment the political power which was the great object of his ambition seemed to be within Ashley's grasp. He knew, none better, that finance was the most important and pressing of the government's domestic problems, especially in view of the disastrous outcome of the war, now limping to its conclusion, and he was very scornful of the abilities of his colleagues on the commission. Pepys reported that Ashley believed the commission would not last long, since his fellow commissioners "understand nothing."[18] He had also taken the measure of Clarendon; he knew that the chancellor was old and tired and that the king was less and less satisfied with him. Clearly, Clarendon would have to be replaced, but not yet, not until Ashley had had time to get a firm grip on the treasury machinery and thus make himself absolutely indispensable to his indolent and good-natured sovereign. Then he could combine the authority of Clarendon and Southampton and be the greatest man in England after the king.

The fact that his ambition could best be served by preservation of the *status quo* for the time being is the likeliest explanation of Ashley's behavior in the latter part of 1667, when he, alone of all the Cabal, opposed the dismissal of Clarendon. He did not fathom the intentions of the king, and, not for the last time, he underestimated Charles's tenacity and strength of purpose. His support of the chancellor was a serious miscalculation. The king was determined to be rid of Clarendon, and he gave his favor to those who helped him accomplish it and who could be useful in helping him to achieve his goal of independence of Parliament. On neither score, for the moment, did Ashley qualify. Charles never forgot that Ashley, now tarred with the epithet "Clarendonian,"[19] was an ex-Common-

---

[17] Brown, *Shaftesbury*, pp. 121–22. Clarendon, *Continuation* II, 96, 213–14. For Downing's plan see above, pp. 15–16.

[18] Pepys, *Diary*, May 31, 1667.

[19] He was so labeled by the French ambassador as late as November, 1668. K. Feiling, *A History of the Tory Party 1640–1714* (Oxford, 1924) , p. 122.

wealthman. But he was talented and efficient and anti-Dutch as well as anti-French, so he might have his uses in the future. So, contrary to Pepy's expectation,[20] he was not got rid of, the fate that befell his former brother-in-law, William Coventry, whose offense was actually less than Ashley's: Coventry opposed, not Clarendon's fall, but merely his impeachment. For the time being, however, the ambitious little man would have to wait.

Ashley was a patient man, though his patience was not inexhaustible, and he set himself to recover from this setback. It took him over two years to do so. When we read of "the Cabal" we tend to think of the five as competing with each other for influence on a more or less equal footing, but this was not in fact so. Ashley was not in the king's confidence in 1667; in fact, he never was in the king's confidence, even during his tenure as lord chancellor. Charles relied upon Arlington and Lauderdale from the beginning; he came to rely upon Clifford; but Ashley, like Buckingham, was a man to be used, though in an entirely different way from the giddy duke. Ashley's administrative and financial talents were helpful at the treasury; much more helpful was Ashley's past. Having an ex-Commonwealthman as a prominent member of his administration would provide Charles with another admirable piece of camouflage behind which his real designs could be pursued. It was a dangerous game to play with a man of Ashley's temperament; Charles might have taken warning from the circumstances surrounding Ashley's shift of sides during the civil war. The vehemence of the future earl of Shaftesbury's opposition to the government after the dissolution of the Cabal sprang in great measure from the bitterness of a self-confident and self-important politician who realizes that he has been had.

Ashley's campaign to recover the king's favor after the fall of Clarendon proceeded rather slowly and was interrupted by periods of ill health. In the summer of 1668 he was desperately ill with a liver complaint and was not expected to live. "My lord Ashley is not yet dead, but his friends have small hopes of his recovery," wrote Williamson in his journal on June 22.[21] His life was saved by John Locke, who had joined his household in the previous year as a combination secretary and medical adviser. Locke performed a successful operation, but the wound continued to discharge, and it was

[20] Pepys, *Diary*, Dec. 30, 1667.
[21] P.R.O., S.P. 29/253, f. 50. See also Sept. 8, 1670, Downing to Duncombe, *C.T.B. 1669–72* I, 661.

finally decided that it would be too dangerous to allow it to close. A tube was inserted in Ashley's side to provide drainage, and remained there for the rest of his life, a source of constant discomfort at the very least.

When his health permitted—he had recurring bouts of serious illness—Ashley diligently performed his duties on the treasury commission, and in the House of Lords he did his best to obtain revenue and to block any Parliamentary investigation of the accounts.[22] He was very cautious about committing himself in the perpetual tug-of-war between Buckingham and Arlington and shifted sides more than once. In the autumn of 1668 the French ambassador put him in Buckingham's camp;[23] a year later he was excoriated, along with Arlington and Clifford, in *The Alarum,* a pamphlet which, if Buckingham did not write it, certainly bears traces of his style. "Shall I forget my Lord Ashley? Good God! What a knave is here? The world calleth him an ingenious man; I suppose it is because he is not hanged, a thing he deserveth at least once a day. To speak truth, he hath some good nature, for he pitieth an honest man and wonders at his mistake. He is said to understand the king's revenue. No wonder, for he hath a share in every farm."[24] It may have been this pamphlet which prompted Ashley to write to his old friend Morice, whom Arlington had driven from office, "Those that hunted together now hunt one another, and at horse play the Master of the Horse [Buckingham] must have the better."[25] The year 1670 found him veering to the duke's side once again; he, like Buckingham, was an eager promoter of the divorce of Lord Roos. Andrew Marvell believed that he, Buckingham, and Lauderdale formed the nucleus of the governing clique, which indicates how skillfully the king, Arlington, and Clifford were masking the negotiations with France.[26] In May, 1670, Ashley was appointed to the foreign committee of the council: he was a member of the inner ring at last. His most recent biographer opines that he owed his appointment to his work on the treasury commission.[27] It is more likely that

[22] Pepys, *Diary,* Jan. 4, 1668.
[23] W. D. Christie, *A Life of Anthony Ashley Cooper, First Earl of Shaftesbury* (London, 1871) I, 312.
[24] Quoted in Andrew Browning, ed., *English Historical Documents 1660–1714* (New York, 1953) , p. 235.
[25] Brown, *Shaftesbury,* p. 186.
[26] Apr. 14, 1670, Marvell to Popple, H. M. Margoliouth, ed., *The Poems and Letters of Andrew Marvell* (Oxford, 1952) II, 303.
[27] Brown, *Shaftesbury,* p. 187.

this was one more of Charles's devices for concealing the real direction of his policy; it is more than coincidence that from this same month of May onward, Charles's attendance at the committee's sessions became much more regular. He was watching his servants and taking every precaution to prevent a leak.

Ashley was never very much interested in foreign affairs as such. His outlook was insular; when he did look beyond the shores of England, he did so through commercial spectacles. His attitude toward the Dutch was that which he was to express in his famous speech to Parliament in 1673: *delenda est Carthago*. So he reacted as the king hoped and expected he would and accepted the *traité simulé* of December, 1670. His attitude was not the same as that of the treaty's chief "negotiator," the duke of Buckingham, however; he did not become pro-French. He was always suspicious of France, but it was France as the right arm of militant Catholicism that he feared. He was not as concerned as Arlington was about France as a threat to England's European position. The treaty with France appeared to him to be what, indeed, in part, it was: an agreement by which France would help England to achieve what she had twice before sought in vain, the forcible destruction of Dutch commercial competition.

As the government steered slowly but surely toward war in 1671, Ashley's star still appeared to be in the ascendant. In August and September of that year it was rumored that he would be made lord treasurer, a rumor which, according to Ralph Montagu, the ambassador in Paris, caused alarm in France, since Ashley was regarded there as Buckingham's ally. Indeed, it was reported that he had been offered the post and declined it because the financial situation was so chaotic and the humor of the court so variable. In October Sir Charles Lyttleton wrote that Ashley's "credit I guess was never so high"; in December, Williamson wrote, "Lord Ashley will be the greatest subject the king has. All say so."[28]

It is unlikely that Ashley would have declined the treasury in September of 1671, but he probably would have done so four months later. The Stop of the Exchequer he regarded as a grievous mistake; he argued vehemently against it, and, when he was unable to block

[28] Sept. 13/23, 1671, Montagu to Charles, II.M.C., *Mss. of the Duke of Buccleuch and Queensberry* (London, 1899) I, 502. Sept. 2, 1671, R. Brockenden to Sir Robert Paston, H.M.C., 6th Report, pt. I (London, 1877), p. 369. E. M. Thompson, ed., *Correspondence of the Family of Hatton* (London, 1878) I, 71. *C.S.P.D.* XII, 46.

it, he virtually turned over all treasury business to Clifford. The king
was anxious to keep Ashley's support at this critical juncture; with
the war about to begin, Ashley's presence in the government would
be immensely helpful because of his connections with the City, the
dissenters, and the ex-Commonwealthmen. Therefore, Charles did
his best to mollify the little man; he made him lord-lieutenant of
Dorset in January, 1672, and in April promoted him to the dignity
of earl of Shaftesbury.[29] The declaration of indulgence must have
helped too: Shaftesbury was one of its strongest supporters.

II

Both the Stop and the indulgence were measures taken in anticipation of war. Shaftesbury favored the war, but he was worried
about public opinion, especially business opinion. The merchants
had had their fingers burned in the last Dutch war, and they had no
desire to repeat the experience. The appointment of Downing as
ambassador to the Netherlands they regarded as a portent, and it
made them nervous: "Our merchants are much troubled, fearing we
shall fall out with Holland."[30] The prospect that Spain might side
openly with the Dutch was even more alarming, especially to Arlington, who was disturbed by reports that Spanish officials in Flanders
were helping the Dutch and who told the marquis del Fresno, the
Spanish ambassador, that the Anglo-French treaty was so favorable
to Spain that it might have been drawn up by a Spaniard. Arlington
strove desperately to keep Spain neutral, not only by direct pressure
on the Spanish government but also by urging France to do nothing
to antagonize Spain.[31] It was not only the merchants who were
hostile to the war. "I cannot find the hearts of the common people
inclinable to hold with the French," wrote one of Williamson's
correspondents from Falmouth in February, 1672. Another reported
that "the malicious phanatick party" was spreading the report that

[29] *C.S.P.D.* XII, 80, 609.

[30] Sept. 28, 1671, Dr. W. Denton to Sir R. Verney, H.M.C., 7th Report,
pt. I (London, 1879), p. 489.

[31] T. Bebington, ed., *The Right Honourable the Earl of Arlington's
Letters to Sir William Temple, Bart.* (vol. I), *and to the Several Ambassadors to
Spain* (vol. II) (London, 1701) II, 356–57, 360, 363–64, 378–80. A. B. Hinds, *et
al.*, eds., *Calendar of State Papers, Venetian* (henceforth *C.S.P. Venetian*) (Lon-
don, 1864–1947) XXXVII, 199. K. Feiling, *British Foreign Policy 1660–1672*
(London, 1930), p. 350. P.R.O., S.P. 104/177, f. 21.

the Dutch were prepared to give in to all Charles's demands but that "nothing will satisfy but a war and Dutch ruin."[32]

The government was aware of the uneasy state of public opinion. "Pull down . . . coffee houses," wrote Williamson in November, 1671, "and nothing can be more to the establishment of the government."[33] Ashley would have preferred a meeting of Parliament to pave the way for the war, but this the king would not have: the Dutch must be taken by surprise. So a propaganda campaign was launched simultaneously with the war. Pamphlets were written excoriating Dutch ingratitude and treachery in the past; Dryden's play *The Massacre of Amboina* was revived; the commercial advantages to be reaped from the anticipated victory were heavily stressed, by Buckingham among others.[34] There was, as always, a good deal of bad verse:

> Proud Hogen Mogens, we will make you bow,
> Have at you, greasy Butter Boxes now,

one of these deplorable effusions begins. Another, almost equally bad, ends thus:

> Princes, beware to aid a growing state
> Lest thay be first that give you the check mate.
> Wealth and success turns humbleness to pride,
> Beggars on horseback to the Devil ride.[35]

Not all the propaganda was on one side, however. Particularly interesting is one long poem called *The Dream of the Cabal,* in which the five members of the Cabal advise Charles to destroy Parliament and the law and govern by means of a standing army, to be paid for by France and, suggests Clifford, the Papacy. Ormonde, also present, argues against this policy and is shouted down.[36] This was also the year of the quatrain quoted at the beginning of this book, in which Shaftesbury figures as the mole. More and more, the five were being thought of, by the opponents of the war and the policies that went with it, as a cabal linked together to undermine the foundations of church and state. This sort of opinion was suffi-

[32] *C.S.P.D.* XII, 122–23, 144.

[33] *Ibid.* XI, 581.

[34] W. de Britaine, *The Dutch Usurpation* (London, 1672), is a typical propaganda pamphlet.

[35] These poems are in P.R.O., S.P. 29/319, ff. 177–78.

[36] The poem is in *Poems on Affairs of State* (1702 edition) I, 136–47; it is given in full below, pp. 255–63.

ciently widespread for the government to issue a proclamation in
June, 1672, against the retailing of false news and licentious talk on
matters of state. Croissy reported to his government in the same
month that people were as much afraid of the fall of Amsterdam as
they would be if London were in similar danger.[37]

From the beginning Shaftesbury's attitude to the war was an
eminently practical one. He favored it as long as it promised any
commercial advantage; he also favored the negotiations with the
Dutch which Arlington undertook in the summer of 1672, as long as
they led to a settlement favorable to the English business classes. He
agreed with the secretary that war with Spain would be ruinous,
although he was more optimistic about being able to avoid it than
was Arlington. He argued, rather unrealistically, that Spain might
break only with France, in which case England could absorb the
trade of both. Whatever line the government took in dealing with
Spain, however, nothing must be done which would alarm the
merchants.

When the war began, Parliament had not met for a year. It was
scheduled to come together in October, 1672; Shaftesbury gave his
advice in favor of a further prorogation on the ground that, if it met
as scheduled, the Dutch would delay the peace negotiations and no
money would be forthcoming on account of the expectation of
peace.[38] When Parliament finally did meet, in February, 1673,
Shaftesbury greeted it from the lofty eminence of the woolsack. In
November, 1672, the king took the seals from Bridgeman and gave
them to the earl and also made him lord chancellor, which Bridgeman had never been. He became chancellor because of Bridgeman's
attitude respecting the legal aspects of the Stop and the indulgence
and also because Shaftesbury suggested that Chancery might legally
issue writs to fill up the vacancies which had occurred in the Commons during the long hiatus since the last session of Parliament.
There was some precedent for this, but it was not the sort of action
to commend itself to the conservative Bridgeman. The promotion
caused little surprise, even though Shaftesbury was not a lawyer; as
the Venetian ambassador put it, he "has caused himself to be

[37] *C.S.P.D.* XIII, 214. J. J. Jusserand, ed., *Receuil des instructions
données aux ambassadeurs de France, Angleterre* (Paris, 1929) II, 115.
[38] P.R.O., S.P. 104/177, ff. 82–84, 111–12.

deemed necessary for the government."[39] So, indeed, he had, although not in the way he expected or hoped.

Shaftesbury held his great office for a year. He performed its duties admirably, with the efficiency, clearheadedness, and dispatch which characterized all his administrative undertakings. Even Dryden paid tribute to his conduct on the bench:

> Yet fame deserved no enemy can grudge;
> The statesman we abhor, but praise the judge.
> In Israel's courts ne'er sat an Abethdin
> With more discerning eyes, or hands more clean,
> Unbribed, unsought, the wretched to redress;
> Swift of despatch, and easy of access. . . .

Shaftesbury did more than merely provide speedy and effective justice; he set out to reform the court's procedures. He considerably reduced the possibilities for error in the recording of decisions, and he had a plan of general reform ready when he was dismissed in November, 1673. John Aubrey remarked earlier in the year to Locke that Shaftesbury "seriously deserves a statue for the good he has already begun."[40] Had he been able to complete his contemplated reforms, it might even have been erected.

The earl took his position as chancellor very seriously and went in extensively for pomp and ceremony. Such things counted for little enough, of course; what Shaftesbury wanted was real political power. He may have thought that he was on the edge of achieving it. The king was following his advice with regard to the negotiations with the Dutch, the handling of the merchant community in the face of the threat of a possible war with Spain, and the problem of an unofficial Dutch agent named Gerbrand Zas, who had turned up in England unbidden in December, 1672, and had been sent home with a warning not to return without permission. Zas appeared again in January, 1673, ostensibly to negotiate a truce in the war at sea. He and his companion William Arton were arrested; on the day before they were due to be examined by the foreign committee a long report was read there, written by one William Howard, who was probably a double agent. This report indicated that Zas's real mis-

---

[39] Brown, *Shaftesbury*, p. 200. Nov. 22/Dec. 2, 1672, Alberti to the Doge and Senate, *C.S.P. Venetian* XXXVII, 318.

[40] The letter is quoted in Brown, *Shaftesbury*, p. 206.

sion was to spread propaganda against the war, the king's ministers, and the French alliance, especially among members of Parliament. Zas's explanations were rather limp and his offers unsatisfactory, since they made no concessions respecting Charles's major demand, the cautionary towns. In the ensuing discussion of Zas's fate, Lauderdale's view was brief and explicit: "First rack him and then hang him." It was pointed out that dead men were poor sources of information, and it was Shaftesbury's solution which was finally adopted. "Go as far to torment him as you can. Show him the rack, tell him of it, but not execute it." So Zas was spared, even though he turned out to be uninformative; he spent the rest of the war in the Tower.[41]

The men around William of Orange believed that Shaftesbury was an important man. Zas's companion Arton carried a letter to him from Peter Du Moulin, a Huguenot who had once been in Arlington's service and was now in William's. Du Moulin congratulated Shaftesbury on his new eminence and asked for a passport, since he wanted to confer privately with the earl and perhaps with Lauderdale too. The letter was full of harsh words for Arlington, who, said Du Moulin, hated him because he had opposed the Dutch war and the French alliance. It seems likely that Du Moulin's real purpose in this letter was not to flatter Shaftesbury or negotiate seriously with him—three months later Du Moulin was writing about the chancellor in bitterly sarcastic terms—but rather to sow suspicion among the members of the Cabal by writing the letter and then to reveal its existence by means of William Howard.[42] The advantages to be derived from such tactics were underlined by a newsletter of June, 1672, which stressed the unpopularity of the French alliance and went on to say, "He [Charles] begins to perceive his fault, in hearkening too much to the Cabal exclusively and contrary to the rest of his council."[43]

The Dutch hope of breaking down the fragile unity of the Cabal was closer to realization than they themselves knew at the beginning of 1673. The contradictions and deceptions inherent in Charles's

[41] For an account of the Zas episode see K. H. D. Haley, *William of Orange and the English Opposition 1672–4* (Oxford, 1953) , chap. 5.

[42] *C.S.P.D.* XIV, 325–26. On this point see Haley, *English Opposition*, pp. 75, 82–83, 86.

[43] H. T. Colenbrander, ed., *Bescheiden uit Vreemde Archieven omtrent De Groote Nederlandsche Zeeoorlogen 1652–1676* (The Hague, 1919) II, 125–27.

policy and methods were generating more and more tension as the conspicuous military success on which the king had gambled continued to elude him. The business community, shaken by the Stop and now very hostile to France on account of its fear of French competition and the unfavorable balance of trade with France,[44] was even less pleased by the impact of the war on its trade. People were pro-Dutch, wrote one of Williamson's correspondents in June, 1672, because of "our constant trade with them in peace." The grain and wool trade suffered from the beginning of the war; by the end of August the Venetian ambassador was reporting that the Zeeland privateers were doing considerable damage—enough so that Arlington fell to discussing convoys with Colbert in September.[45]

Under these circumstances the prospect of a war with Spain, which became increasingly likely as the months wore on, became a matter of great concern to Shaftesbury and a positive nightmare to Arlington. The French expected such a war from the beginning and were not greatly disturbed by the possibility.[46] Arlington, who knew what the reaction of the business community would be to such a war, continued alternately to cajole and to threaten Spain and to urge the French to do nothing which would give the Spanish government an excuse to go to war. When Spain did finally attack the French fortress of Charleroi, the secretary at once offered to mediate between Spain and France.[47] The Dutch, naturally, were working just as hard, by propaganda and direct pressure, to provoke Spanish intervention.[48] The Spanish government, and particularly del Fresno, played their few cards very skillfully. Spain was moving steadily toward an alliance with the Dutch, especially after the open intervention of the emperor against France in October, 1672, but she did not want to fight England. Del Fresno, who was unusual among Spanish ambassadors in London in his ability to

[44] See above, pp. 98–99, and the works there cited, and C. W. Cole, *Colbert and a Century of French Mercantilism* (New York, 1939) II, 561–69.

[45] *C.S.P.D.* XII, 236; XIII, 272. *C.S.P. Venetian* XXXVII, 274. P.R.O., S.P. 104/177, f. 86.

[46] Feb. 26/Mar. 7, 1672, Montagu to Arlington, H.M.C., *Buccleuch and Queensberry Mss.* I, 513.

[47] Dec. 26, 1672, Arlington to Godolphin, Bebington, *Arlington's Letters* II, 397–98.

[48] May 9, 1672, Sir John Frederick to Williamson, *C.S.P.D.* XII, 508. P. de Ségur-Dupeyron, *Histoire des négociations commerciales et maritimes du règne de Louis XIV* (Paris, 1863) I, 291–92.

gauge English public opinion, calculated that England could be coerced or persuaded into a separate peace by the prospect of Spanish intervention. So as early as April, 1672, he threatened Arlington with war and pointed out its disastrous commercial consequences for England.[49] It was a difficult game to play, and the attack on Charleroi made it no easier. Sir William Godolphin's report of his conversation with the queen regent of Spain seemed to indicate that Spain did not intend the attack on Charleroi to lead to a breach with England, but there was no disposition to accept the English offer of mediation.[50]

As the signs of Charles's failure multiplied, so did the evidence of dissatisfaction inside the court party. Even a good government man like Edward Seymour, the future speaker, wrote to Sir Thomas Osborne in July, 1672, that France would reap all the advantage of the war and that England will be "most damnably gulled."[51] The personal jealousies within the Cabal created further complications. To the hatred that had always existed between Arlington and Buckingham was added that between Arlington and Clifford as the secretary, assailed again by the gout, brooded over his failure to obtain the office of lord treasurer. Arlington, indeed, was almost isolated; according to the Venetian ambassador, it was Buckingham and Lauderdale who had supported Shaftesbury for the chancellorship.[52] Lauderdale was not precisely feuding with anybody, but he was not popular and was preoccupied chiefly with Scotland, where the war was disliked exceedingly and was to produce open opposition to Lauderdale in the Scottish Parliament. Indeed, only Shaftesbury was on tolerably good terms with all his colleagues, which was natural enough in a man who believed that he had arrived and was eager to consolidate his position. It was an extremely precarious unity which the government presented to the outside world, and Parliament was to shatter it for good.

As early as June, 1672, Arlington had told the French ambassador that there would be trouble for the government when Parliament

---

[49] Apr. 29/May 9, 1672, Alberti to the Doge and Senate, *C.S.P. Venetian* XXXVII, 207.

[50] Godolphin's report was discussed in the foreign committee on January 24, 1673. P.R.O., S.P. 104/177, f. 130.

[51] B.M. Add. Mss. 28,053, ff. 43–45.

[52] Nov. 22/Dec. 2, 1672, Alberti to the Doge and Senate, *C.S.P. Venetian* XXXVII, 318.

met. One source of difficulty was going to be one of the actions of the new lord chancellor; as Charles put it in the foreign committee on January 30, there would be "a great noise of ye Lord Chancellor issuing writs before ye Parliament meets." Yet, if the minutes of the foreign committee can be trusted, the government made no effort to decide in advance how to cope with the anticipated difficulties, except to approve, with minor alterations, Shaftesbury's opening address, the *delenda est Carthago* speech, justifying the war and putting the case for the subsidy.[53] With the opening of Parliament a blunder by the king gave the Commons the opportunity to attack the government on the matter of the writs. After the king's opening remarks, which reiterated his intention to stand by the declaration of indulgence, and Shaftesbury's speech, Charles unexpectedly spoke again. The writs were legal, he believed, but he would leave the question to the judgment of the House. The House, thus invited to express an opinion, promptly declared against the validity of the writs, not so much on legal grounds as because of the "inconveniences which might arise upon this power in the Chancellor," and the king gave way. Shaftesbury, who was prepared to argue the point, was very angry at this rebuff and at the king's failure to support him.[54] He was still further disillusioned by Charles's decision, against his advice, to withdraw the declaration of indulgence and to withdraw it in such a way as to suggest that he accepted the Commons' argument that it was illegal: it was Shaftesbury and his secretary, Locke, who had made the case for the king's suspending power in matters ecclesiastical. Here was another rebuff to the proud little chancellor. By March 7, 1673, when this decision was taken, it was apparent to Shaftesbury that, in spite of his exalted position, his influence was still nonexistent and his counsel unheeded. He allowed his irritation and disappointment to show by his open support of the anti-Popery bill which was to become the Test Act.

The problem of just when, and from whom, Shaftesbury learned the truth about the treaty of Dover and the full extent of the

[53] P.R.O., S.P. 104/177, ff. 136, 137, 140. See also Jan. 25, 1673, Francis Godolphin to Essex, B.M. Stowe Mss. 201, f. 107. The text of the speech is in *The Works of His Grace George Villiers, Late Duke of Buckingham* (London, 1715) II, 234–42.

[54] Haley, *English Opposition*, p. 91. Brown, *Shaftesbury*, p. 205. Gilbert Burnet, *The History of My Own Time* (ed. Osmund Airy, Oxford, 1897–1900) II, 8.

deception practiced upon him will probably never be solved. In November, 1673, Croissy guessed that he had been told of the treaty by Arlington, who never liked the Catholicizing policy anyway, in order to induce Shaftesbury to support the Test Act and thus ruin Clifford, whom Arlington now hated. This is possible, but it seems unlikely that Shaftesbury knew the whole truth before the end of the Parliament on March 29.[55] But he must have had his suspicions, and they became vehement suspicions when Clifford, who had been a member with Shaftesbury of the Lords' committee to confer with the Commons on the projected address against the growth of Popery, made a violently intemperate speech in the Lords attacking the Test bill. The speech horrified Croissy, who thought Clifford was a little bit mad. According to Burnet, the king's first reaction to the speech was favorable, but it soon changed when he saw its effect on the Commons. On March 22 Clifford was openly denounced in the House as a Papist, who had called the anti-Popery bill "dirty," and there was talk of an address to the king to remove him from office.[56]

Shaftesbury saw his opportunity, and seized it: he refuted Clifford point by point in the Lords, and thus committed himself publicly to the Test, though he favored some mitigations of the Commons' bill. The chancellor's speech caused great surprise inside the king's circle of advisers as well as outside, since he and Clifford had stood together in support of the indulgence. Shaftesbury's behavior has often been interpreted as indicating his decision to break with the king, who disliked the anti-Popery bill and hoped to head it off by giving way on the declaration of indulgence. This seems, on the whole, unlikely. Shaftesbury knew that without the Test Act there would be no supply and that with it the Commons were prepared to be generous. He still had hopes of a favorable outcome of the war, a war in which he believed: *delenda est Carthago* was an accurate

[55] F. A. M. Mignet, ed., *Négociations relatives à la succession d'Espagne sous Louis XIV* (Paris, 1835–42) IV, 233–37. Burnet's view was that "While he made a base complying speech in favor of the court and of the war, he was in a secret management with another party." *History* II, 6. C. H. Hartmann accepts Croissy's opinion. *Clifford of the Cabal* (London, 1937), pp. 264–65. Miss Brown, *Shaftesbury*, p. 209, suggests that his information may have come from Buckingham or Clifford.

[56] *Lords Journals* XII, 545. Hartmann, *Clifford*, pp. 263–64. Burnet, *History* II, 10–13. B. D. Henning, ed., *The Parliamentary Diary of Sir Edward Dering 1670–1673* (New Haven, 1940), pp. 148–49. A. Grey, *Debates of the House of Commons* (London, 1763) II, 147–54.

expression of his sentiments. If the popular fear of Popery could be laid to rest—and, incidentally, the duke of York driven from office —the nation might still bring the war to a successful conclusion. Shaftesbury knew Charles well enough to see that, as the Venetian ambassador put it, "policy, not zeal, led the king to favor the Catholic religion."[57] There had been no attack on the war in the Parliament, none on the French alliance, none, even, on the Stop of the Exchequer—only on the indulgence, and chiefly because it favored Papists. Shaftesbury knew that there was discontent with the war, but he was not yet aware of its extent.

The real test of the future, for Shaftesbury, would come after the end of the Parliamentary session. The earl had demonstrated his usefulness and ability to the king many times over; he had even shown a talent rare in Charles's inner circle, an instinct for the mood of Parliament, by preventing a major explosion over Clifford's *gaffe*. He had shown that he was no enemy to the prerogative. He believed in the legality of the suspending power in ecclesiastical matters, and in January, 1673, in administering the oath to a baron of the exchequer, he said, "Let not the king's prerogative and the law be two things with you. For the king's prerogative is law, and the principal part of the law, and therefore, in maintaining that, you maintain the law."[58] The ex-Commonwealthman had come a long way. If Charles would now turn to him and take his advice, if he now became in fact what he was in name, the king's chief minister, none would serve more loyally. The next few months would tell the tale.

III

On March 29, 1673, the Parliament was adjourned. There was a "great hum" when the king gave his assent to the Test Act, the hummers evidently being unaware that a veto would be political suicide. Charles reportedly said that he would get rid of all the Catholics in his entourage but his barber, "whom he meant to keep in despite of all their bills, for he was so well accustomed to his hand."[59] The king was hardly pleased with the session, but he had salvaged something. Supply in the amount of £1,260,000 had been

[57] Brown, *Shaftesbury*, p. 210. H.M.C., 5th Report, appendix, pt. II (London, 1876) , p. 29. *Lords Journals* XII, 557. Mar. 10/20, 21/31, 1673, Alberti to the Doge and Senate, *C.S.P. Venetian* XXXVIII, 27–28, 31.

[58] Quoted in Brown, *Shaftesbury*, p. 221.

[59] *C.S.P.D.* XV, 100–101, 126. P.R.O., S.P. 29/332, f. 192.

voted, the French alliance had not been attacked, and a successful campaign against the Dutch might enable him to win the game yet.

The impact of the Test Act on the Catholics in the administration was more spectacular than most people had expected. The purpose of the act may well have been no more than to compel an outward conformity;[60] on March 30, Easter Sunday, the day after Charles gave his assent to it, John Evelyn watched to see if the duke of York would take communion. His failure to do so gave "exceeding grief and scandal to the whole nation. . . . What the consequence of this will be God only knows, and wise men dread."[61] Clifford was even more vulnerable than the king's brother, especially after his public attack on the act. April passed, and Clifford made no sign. In May the rumors began that he would take communion on the eighteenth. He did not do so. The report was that he was ill, "which the people will have to be on purpose"; at once it was rumored that he would resign and be succeeded by Sir Thomas Osborne. Five days later the story was circulating that Clifford and a priest, Father Patrick, were riding in the treasurer's coach, which overturned, depositing them and embarrassing amounts of Romish vestments and whatnot in the street. By the end of the month everyone was sure; on June 1 Arlington told Croissy, no doubt gleefully, that both Clifford and James would resign. The Venetian ambassador wrote that the treasurer was stepping down because he feared an open attack at the next session of Parliament and the intrigues of his erstwhile patron.[62]

Clifford had indeed made up his mind. His health was deteriorating rapidly, the Catholicity scheme was dead, and financial strangulation would soon compel England's withdrawal from the war.[63] In mid-June, having stayed long enough to arrange an orderly transfer to his successor, he surrendered the White Staff. John Evelyn, always

[60] This is the opinion of Andrew Browning, *Thomas Osborne, Earl of Danby and Duke of Leeds* (Glasgow, 1951) I, 98.

[61] E. S. DeBeer, ed., *The Diary of John Evelyn* (Oxford, 1958) IV, 7.

[62] *C.S.P.D.* XV, 254–55. May 18, 23, 1673, Henry Ball to Williamson, W. D. Christie, ed., *Letters . . . to Sir Joseph Williamson* (London, 1874) I, 1–2, 6–7. Hartmann, *Clifford*, p. 279. *C.S.P. Venetian* XXXVIII, 56.

[63] Feb. 4, 1673, Francis Aungier to Essex, B.M. Stowe Mss. 201, f. 139. The financial situation was so acute that the speaker got only half of his accustomed fee for the recent session of Parliament. Sept. 26, 1673, Clifford to Osborne, B.M. Add. Mss. 28,053, f. 73. See also Browning, *Danby* I, 112; III, 10–15.

willing to think the best of his friend, attributed his resignation to "some promise he had entered into to gratify the duke [of York] than . . . any prejudice to the Protestant religion."[64] In July Clifford went to Tunbridge Wells to try to recover his health; Evelyn visited him there and saw him again, for the last time, on August 18, after Clifford's return to London. He found the ex-treasurer packing his belongings, including some large, violent paintings which suited his temperament.[65] By the end of the month he retired to his native Devon, "not like so great a man as he lived at Tunbridge," in William Temple's gloating phrase.[66] At the beginning of October he grew worse, and his death was momentarily expected by the gossips of London. On the day of his death, October 17, Henry Ball wrote to Williamson that he was dying opportunely, "for Parliament would talk with him."[67] For this reason, among others, the story spread that Clifford had committed suicide and was credited by Evelyn. This hypothesis had been convincingly refuted by Clifford's biographer: he died of the stone.[68]

Clifford's resignation did not cost him the king's friendship, and he was one of those, along with Buckingham and Lauderdale, who supported the appointment of Osborne as his successor. Arlington, still hankering after the post himself, argued vainly for a return to a board of commissioners.[69] Shaftesbury's views were not reported by the London gossips, but they came out clearly enough in the speech he made when he administered the oath of office to the new lord treasurer. The talents which enable men to obtain high office, he remarked, do not always serve to keep them there.[70] The chancellor was bitterly disappointed. He did not want the office himself, but Osborne was just the sort of man he did not want—an ambitious and able man with wide Parliamentary experience and considerable talent for financial administration, which he had shown as treasurer of the navy, and a man of impeccable Royalist and Anglican antecedents. Such a man would be a dangerous rival for the king's confi-

[64] DeBeer, *Diary of John Evelyn* IV, 14.

[65] *Ibid.*, pp. 16, 18–20.

[66] B.M. Stowe Mss. 201, f. 337.

[67] Christie, *Letters to Williamson* II, 46.

[68] DeBeer, *Diary of John Evelyn* IV, 20–23. Hartmann, *Clifford*, pp. 298–302.

[69] Hartmann, *Clifford*, p. 279. July 4/14, 1673, Alberti to the Doge and Senate, *C.S.P. Venetian* XXXVIII, 73.

[70] Browning, *Danby* I, 102.

dence, that elusive confidence which Shaftesbury had never yet succeeded in obtaining and which now looked further off than ever; Osborne's appointment had come on top of a scolding Shaftesbury received from Charles on account of his behavior over the Test Act.[71] The chancellor's drift away from the inner circle he had never really been part of was accelerated.

Part of the acceleration of that drift was owing to the change which came over English opinion in the spring and summer of 1673: it became pro-Dutch and anti-French and very much wanted a prompt peace. This shift was owing in some measure to the famous pamphlet, *England's Appeal from the Private Cabal at Whitehall to the Great Council of the Nation, the Lords and Commons in Parliament Assembled,* which was written by Du Moulin and was widely distributed in March, 1673. The pamphlet was a scathing attack on the present policy of the government. It pointed out very forcibly the political and economic dangers inherent in a French victory and in the war with Spain which was surely coming and accused the "private cabal" of taking French money to advise the king to adopt this ruinous course. Above all, the connection between the French alliance and the pro-Catholic policy of the government was heavily stressed. One recent authority has claimed that this pamphlet "did more than anything else to identify the French alliance in foreign affairs with the danger of Popery at home, and consequently to lead public opinion . . . to turn against the war."[72] This is something of an exaggeration, but the pamphlet's impact was certainly considerable and was increased by the resignations of York and Clifford, which only too clearly confirmed the charge of Popish influence in the government. Victory in the summer campaign of 1673 might have turned the tide, but no victory came. Indeed, victory was denied the English in a naval battle in August because the French admiral failed to obey the signals of Prince Rupert, who was the English commander. Rupert was furious and complained publicly of the French commander's behavior. "It was," he said, "the greatest and plainest opportunity ever lost at sea."[73] "To write town talk . . . is too dangerous," wrote one of Williamson's correspond-

[71] Shaftesbury retorted that the king had deserted him over the writs of summons. Apr. 11/21, 1673, Alberti to the Doge and Senate, *C.S.P. Venetian* XXXVIII, 37.

[72] Haley, *English Opposition,* pp. 97–98.

[73] *C.S.P.D.* XV, 520–22.

ents on August 22, "therefore I must credit what is printed, and believe the French fought bravely." A week later another wrote that public opinion now believed that the French alliance must be ended, in the national interest.[74] The frame of mind which, five years later, would allow Andrew Marvell[75] to proclaim that France was England's "hereditary, natural, inveterate enemy"—something she had not been for a hundred years—was rapidly developing.

Williamson was the recipient of so many letters in this difficult summer because he was out of the country at Cologne, engaged in a peace conference, which opened in June with the Swedes acting as mediators and which was destined to get nowhere. From the point of view of the English government, and particularly of Arlington, the purpose of the conference was to make peace if possible, but even more, to keep Spain out of the war by making it appear that a settlement was on the verge of completion.[76] Though he occasionally wavered, the secretary always returned to his position that England must not fight Spain and must get out of the war if Spain got in.[77] His hope of keeping Spain neutral crumbled rapidly as the months went by. The French, who had no objection to a war with Spain, made Arlington's task no easier. In April, 1673, under French pressure, Charles issued a declaration canceling his guarantees to Spain respecting the treaties of the Pyrenees and Aix, since Spain had violated them by attacking Charleroi. In May Louis recalled his ambassador from Madrid. Spain drew steadily nearer the Dutch and in August signed a treaty of alliance with the Dutch and the empire, binding the parties to joint action if the peace talks failed. The Dutch negotiators at Cologne remained intransigent, and the English failures at sea deprived Charles's government of its best hope of making the butterboxes "speak lower."[78]

The tactics of the Dutch were clear enough: they wanted to drive a wedge between England and France and force England to a separate peace by threatening her with a war with Spain. They came ap-

[74] *Ibid.*, pp. 507–8. Christie, *Letters to Williamson* I, 194–95.

[75] In his pamphlet *An Account of the Growth of Popery and Arbitrary Government in England.*

[76] See, for instance, Feb. 21, 1673, Arlington to Godolphin, Bebington, *Arlington's Letters* II, 406–7.

[77] See, for example, Nov. 8/18, 1672, Alberti to the Doge and Senate, *C.S.P. Venetian* XXXVII, 314.

[78] P.R.O., S.P. 104/177, f. 159. *C.S.P.D.* XV, 251. July 4, 1673, Secretary Coventry to Williamson, *ibid.*, pp. 419–20. Haley, *English Opposition,* p. 114.

preciably closer to success in July, when Charles dropped his demand for the cautionary towns. It would now be a simple matter to
agree on peace terms. The only obstacle now was Charles's unwillingness to make peace without France; Louis XIV was far from
ready to end the war or allow Charles to make a separate settlement.[79] On the other hand, it was increasingly clear that the English
business classes would never stand for war with Spain and would do
their best to compel the government to make peace, either by clamor
in Parliament or by financial pressure. The Dutch tactics were very
effective indeed. London opinion obviously favored peace and rejoiced at French failures in the field and at any sign of friction
between England and France—and there was such friction, over such
matters as prizes, even before the naval battle brought the discord
into the open.[80] As the prospect of war with Spain loomed larger, the
City merchants began to "clamor outrageously," as Arlington knew
they would. Since there were reports that Spain had seized an English ship, they had to cancel plans to send goods to Spain, which
meant heavy losses for them.[81] "They praise the king for the best of
men, but think not so of most of his servants," wrote Henry Ball to
Williamson. "God knows how long the war may yet last," wrote
Arlington's clerk, "which if his majesty were once well out of, I am
confident he would not be easily persuaded to another of that
kind."[82] This was Arlington's view exactly.

The secretary was becoming more and more nervous. At the end
of August he was talking of the possibility of a separate peace, which
had been on his mind almost from the beginning,[83] and his nervous-
ness increased as he witnessed his mounting unpopularity with the
public. "All shower curses on Arlington, for having been bribed to

[79] See, for instance, Louis' instructions, dated October 25/November 4,
1673, to Ruvigny, who was sent to England to "manage" Buckingham, to persuade
the mercurial duke to support in Parliament the continuation of the war.
Jusserand, *Receuil* II, 131–38.

[80] July 7, 1673, Ball to Williamson, Christie, *Letters to Williamson* I,
93. *C.S.P.D.* XV, 152–53. Sept. 30, 1673, William Bridgeman to Essex, B.M. Stowe
Mss. 203, f. 64. Bridgeman was Arlington's clerk.

[81] H.M.C., *Mss. of S. H. LeFleming* (London, 1890), p. 104. Oct. 3/13,
1673, Alberti to the Doge and Senate, *C.S.P. Venetian* XXXVIII, 137–38. Oct. 13,
1673, John Paige to Williamson, *C.S.P.D.* XV, 577.

[82] Christie, *Letters to Williamson* II, 45. Oct. 7, 1673, Wm. Bridgeman
to Essex, B.M. Stowe Mss. 203, f. 80.

[83] See, for example, Nov. 1/11, 1672, Alberti to the Doge and Senate,
C.S.P. Venetian XXXVII, 313.

sell the interests of king and country alike," wrote the Venetian ambassador on August 22.[84] Early in October the secretary's last hope of keeping Spain out of the war was shattered by Louis XIV himself, who declared war on Spain on October 5; this, wrote Arlington, meant the end of the Cologne conference. The ministry now almost unanimously wanted to abandon the French alliance; only the royal brothers still seemed to favor it.[85] The issue of a separate peace would now have to be squarely faced.

IV

"This year the Government begins to thrive marvelous well," wrote Sir Thomas Player to Williamson on July 29, "for it eats and drinks and sleeps as heartily as I have known it, nor doth it vex and disgust itself with that foolish, idle, impertinent thing called business."[86] In fact, it was on the verge of complete dissolution. The resignations of York and Clifford had an immense effect; the king had to order his busy censor, Roger L'Estrange, to suppress a book which was being planned, to list all those who complied with the Test Act, in order to distinguish them "from the troublers of Israel." Arlington, stricken by gout, his nerves strung up to the point that Lauderdale could describe him, in October, when Parliament met, as "almost dead with fear,"[87] disappointed again in his ambition to be treasurer, was thinking of retirement. He was fifty-five years old, and the strain was beginning to tell: he "seems weary of the fatigue of his place," wrote one of Williamson's correspondents in July. His plan was to purchase the office of lord chamberlain from its present holder, the earl of St. Albans, and pass on his secretary's post to Williamson: this would permit him to continue near the king, giving him advice on foreign affairs, without the burdens and responsibilities of office.[88] But Arlington, for all his timidity and ill health, would not quit under fire. The present storm had to be

[84] *Ibid.* XXXVIII, 100–101. Aug. 28, 1673, Arlington to Godolphin, Bebington, *Arlington's Letters* II, 425–27.

[85] Oct. 11, 1673, Arlington to Essex, B.M. Stowe Mss. 203, f. 87. Oct. 10/20, 1673, Alberti to the Doge and Senate, *C.S.P. Venetian* XXXVIII, 143–44.

[86] Christie, *Letters to Williamson* I, 133.

[87] *Ibid.*, p. 41. Burnet, *History* II, 37.

[88] Christie, *Letters to Williamson* I, 77. Sept. 3/13, 1673, Alberti to the Doge and Senate, *C.S.P. Venetian* XXXVIII, 114. The plan was that Arlington would buy the office of lord chamberlain for £10,000 and sell his post to Williamson for £4,000.

ridden out, and his good name vindicated; then he could find the rest that, by now, he was longing for.

The quarter from which Arlington expected to be attacked was the old familiar one: Buckingham. The duke, whose dreams of military glory had at last vanished, was more angry than ever at his ancient enemy; it was, he said, "hateful to him to act in concert with Arlington." The duke was "mad" at the rumor that he might be replaced as master of the horse; he planned to impeach Arlington at the forthcoming session of Parliament.[89] He "vows no less than ruin" to Arlington, "though most believe the bolt being shot, it will fall heaviest on himself." To Buckingham's chagrin the October session did not last long enough to allow him to launch his attack; he knew that he, too, would have suffered in reputation, but "like the envious man he could have been contented to lose an eye himself to leave his enemy none."[90] So he worked to prepare the ground more carefully for the next meeting of the Houses.

Lauderdale, too, was in danger of a Parliamentary attack; his reaction, unlike Arlington's, was one of mingled impatience, rage, and disgust. "My Lord Lauderdale is still at the Bath, and as angry as ever at somebody," wrote Henry Ball on July 25.[91] Lauderdale was irritated by what he regarded as weakness on the part of the government, especially in the matter of the cancellation of the indulgence, and his impulse was to take no more part in English affairs and concentrate on his Scottish satrapy. Only he and Clifford had stood by the king, he fumed to Burnet, and now Clifford was gone. He even sold his bedchamber post to Marshal Schomberg, the Huguenot general who received the military command Buckingham had coveted.[92] The Scottish secretary knew very well that the Parliamentary attack would come and from whom: "among the Lords his principal antagonist is the little one once his great confidant, who (though his Grace said he would crush the little worm with his great toe) most believe will wriggle from under him and trip up his heels."[93] In other words, from Shaftesbury.

[89] Aug. 29/Sept. 8, 1673, Alberti to the Doge and Senate, *C.S.P. Venetian* XXXVIII, 106. Aug. 1, Sept. 23, 1673, Sir N. Armorer to Williamson, *C.S.P.D.* XV, 475; Christie, *Letters to Williamson* II, 24.

[90] Oct. 3, 1673, Thomas Ross to Williamson, Christie, *Letters to Williamson* II, 29–30. Nov. 5, 1673, T. Derham to Williamson, *ibid.*, p. 62.

[91] *Ibid.* I, 130.

[92] *Ibid.*, pp. 73, 84, 88. Burnet, *History* II, 26.

[93] Oct. 3, 1673, Ross to Williamson, Christie, *Letters to Williamson* II, 29.

The lord chancellor was not at all pleased with the course of events in the summer of 1673. The king's tactics in negotiation with the Dutch he regarded as deplorable. As Shaftesbury saw it, there were two possible courses open to England: either to make a speedy separate peace with the Dutch—and there is some evidence that he was in touch with William of Orange to that end in May—or to fight on in order to get something substantial, like the cautionary towns.[94] But Charles was doing neither one. He had reduced his demands, but still he fought on; and why? Because Louis XIV insisted on it. Shaftesbury and his master now stood at the parting of the ways. He may well have known of the provisions of the treaty of Dover, but he did not need to know them to see that Charles was now sacrificing the national interest to a policy which, as Andrew Marvell was to say, would promote the growth of Popery and arbitrary government and the power of France, all of them anathema to Shaftesbury. From the beginning of his political career he had been anti-Catholic and anti-French, but for ambition's sake he had supported Charles's policy. Now, however, he saw, at long last, that he would never obtain the king's confidence, would never become the power behind the throne. If, for whatever reason, the king changed his policy, the man of the future was already in office: the new lord treasurer, Sir Thomas Osborne. In that respect the handwriting was already on the wall for Shaftesbury to read; as Henry Ball put it in July, the earl "does . . . not very well please the new great ones."[95]

So Shaftesbury began to contemplate the possibilities of opposition. The unhappy fate of the declaration of indulgence showed plainly enough that, faced with a determined Parliamentary opposition, Charles would climb down. Parliament had a veto over the king's actions; it remained to be seen whether Parliament could impose a policy—and, equally important, the men to carry out that policy—on the king. It was a difficult and dangerous game to play, but now, if ever, was the time to begin to play it. Public opinion was in a highly wrought-up state, thoroughly aroused over the events of the past twenty months, and leaderless. On September 1, 1673, it was put this way: the people are "ready to adore those they think oppose the French interest at Court, as that any great man might at a cheap rate make himself their darling."[96] Shaftesbury was prepared to make

[94] Haley, *English Opposition*, pp. 117–19. P.R.O., S.P. 104/177, f. 163.
[95] Christie, *Letters to Williamson* I, 99.
[96] *C.S.P.D.* XV, 524–25.

himself their darling, to give vent to his own political convictions, and he knew the most effective issue: Popery. In June he tested the ground and found it solid: a pamphlet which purported to be "a letter from the Chancellor to the duke of York dissuasive from Popery is showed about town and very much praised."[97] But the earl was cautious; he did not want to commit himself publicly to the anti-Papal cause and then find himself outmaneuvered by some spectacularly anti-Catholic stroke on the king's part which would cost him his following and leave him permanently in the wilderness, out of favor at court and without the means of marshaling an effective opposition. So he revived the idea of divorce for the king, surely the most effectively Protestant gesture Charles could make. Charles did not return an outright refusal, but his opinions were made clear enough by his sanctioning of the marriage of his Catholic brother to Mary of Modena, a Catholic bride picked out for James by Louis XIV himself. The proposed marriage was very unpopular in London. Shaftesbury had his issue.[98]

So the chancellor began, very cautiously, to play the Protestant and the popular champion, in preparation for the next session of Parliament. He broke with his old friend Lauderdale, who to many Englishmen was the embodiment of arbitrary government, and began to intrigue with the duke's Scottish enemies. He was seen much in the company of Prince Rupert, still smarting from the French behavior in the recent sea battle and from the bitter necessity of having to say publicly that the French admiral was a brave man; the chancellor and the prince "are looked upon to be the great Parliament men, and for the interest of Old England."[99] Shaftesbury was preparing to take advantage of and intensify the steadily mounting animosity toward France, to make unshakable the conviction later expressed by Burnet that with the French alliance, "the nation, and our religion as well as the king's faith and honor, [were] set to sale and sold."[100]

[97] Quoted in Haley, *English Opposition*, p. 117.

[98] June 20/30, 1673, Alberti to the Doge and Senate, *C.S.P. Venetian* XXXVIII, 68–69. Aug. 4, 1673, Ball to Williamson, Christie, *Letters to Williamson* I, 144. Oct. 25, 1673, Sir William Temple to Essex, B.M. Stowe Mss. 203, ff. 113–14.

[99] Sept. 10/20, 1673, Alberti to the Doge and Senate, *C.S.P. Venetian* XXXVIII, 121. Sept. 19, 1673, Ball to Williamson, Christie, *Letters to Williamson* II, 21–22.

[100] Burnet, *History* I, 554.

It was obvious to Charles and those still in his confidence, like Arlington, that the October session of Parliament would be stormy. All the members of the Cabal, including Clifford, got formal pardons for their official acts in the hope of forestalling any attempts at impeachment. As early as August 8 Williamson was informed that many people in the government favored peace as the only way to avoid very unpalatable concessions.[101] Buckingham's plan to impeach Arlington was common gossip in September. By October it was being reported that various M.P.s were saying that Parliament would not vote a penny of supply unless it was given a voice in the management of the war and permission to punish evil officials. Even Lauderdale, who was certainly not lacking in courage, was eager to be out of London when the Houses came together.[102] The French were apprehensive. Louis XIV correctly pointed out that the Dutch plans hinged on Parliament's forcing England out of the war and asked Charles to postpone the session. Charles replied that postponement would simply make things worse, and anyway he needed money. A short postponement would be necessary, however, for technical reasons. The last session had ended in adjournment, so that the new meeting did not mark the beginning of a new session. To prevent the argument that taxes should not be voted twice in the same session, it was decided that when Parliament met, on October 20, it would be prorogued for a week.[103]

The king's calculations were upset by the lord chancellor. When the Houses met, Shaftesbury insisted that the proper formalities be observed, which meant, in this case, the ceremonial induction of several new peers, including Osborne, now Viscount Latimer. This took time, and before it could be completed, the Commons voted an address to the king that the marriage not be consummated. Charles and James were very angry. They suspected that Shaftesbury had deliberately delayed the proceedings in the Lords, and there is little doubt that they were right. Shaftesbury knew the Parliament's temper; he was on his way to becoming the Protestant champion.

[101] Hartmann, *Clifford*, p. 287. Christie, *Letters to Williamson* I, 150–51.

[102] Aug. 25, Oct. 10, 17, 1673, Ball to Williamson, *ibid.*, pp. 187–88; II, 35–36, 46.

[103] Aug. 17/27, 1673, Louis to Croissy, Mignet, *Négociations* IV, 224–25. Sept. 1/11, 1673, Croissy to Louis, *ibid.*, pp. 225–26. Haley, *English Opposition*, p. 133.

On October 25, during the prorogation, Sir William Temple analyzed the situation for his friend Essex in Ireland. The Commons were very anti-Catholic, he reported, and determined to put an end to the war and the French alliance, but were not quite sure how to go about doing so. There were four major groups in Commons. One, headed by William Coventry, wanted to attack the ministers, especially Buckingham, Arlington, and Lauderdale; the second wanted simply to secure the Protestant religion and end the war, without attacking the ministers; the third was prepared to vote money, if the war was ended; the fourth, Shaftesbury's, was concentrating on the king's divorce. The king's party in Commons was very weak. The lord treasurer gave no lead in policy questions; only Arlington and James were supporting the king in wanting to go on with the war. The secretary, wrote Temple, will never desert France: "you will judge, I suppose, the reason."[104] On this point Temple's venomous dislike of his former patron misled him; Arlington's longing for peace was increasing every day.

Temple himself had helped to create the state of mind he described in this letter by means of a pamphlet, *Upon the Conjuncture of Affairs in October 1673,* which marshaled the now familiar arguments for peace, especially the economic ruin which would follow on a war with Spain, and added a new one: that France was now so poor that her subsidies were unlikely to continue. The government's financial situation was indeed desperate and an eloquent argument for peace; it was the only argument for allowing Parliament to reassemble.[105] If the king had any hope that the mood of the Houses had changed, he was soon to be undeceived. In his speech Charles stressed that his hope of peace had been wrecked by the intransigence of the Dutch negotiators at Cologne; Shaftesbury went on to develop this theme in his address, which was perfectly correct in its tone, but which ended in a most curious way. He hoped, said Shaftesbury, "that this session may equal, nay exceed, the honor of the last; that it may perfect what the last began for the safety of the king and kingdom; that it may be ever famous for having established upon a durable foundation our religion, laws and

104 B.M. Stowe Mss. 203, ff. 113–14.
105 H. E. Woodbridge, *Sir William Temple* (London, 1940), pp. 123–25. By the end of the year the situation was so bad that the king's servants were not receiving their salaries. Dec. 18, 1673, Ball to Williamson, Christie, *Letters to Williamson* II, 104.

properties."[106] This was certainly an open invitation to the Commons to pursue the anti-Catholic policy; they needed no urging to accept.

The session lasted less than ten days because the Commons got completely out of hand. The House immediately postponed consideration of the king's speech for four days, and the opposition promptly launched an unprecedented attack on the speaker, Sir Edward Seymour, because he was a privy councillor and a government man, and therefore unfit to be trusted with the secrets of the House. The motion to choose another speaker was voted down, but nothing could reveal more clearly the intensity of the House's suspicion of the king's policy. When the king's speech was debated, on October 31, the first proposal made was that no money at all should be voted. This was ultimately amended to the effect that there should be no supply until the eighteen-month grant voted the previous March had been collected—that is, for almost a year—"unless it shall appear that the obstinacy of the Dutch shall make a supply necessary," a phrase suggested by Sir William Coventry. To get even this meager commitment the government's spokesmen had to allow a debate on grievances first, and the principal grievances now were the war and the French alliance. It was not merely that the French were Popish and therefore a political and religious danger; they were an economic threat as well, and the possible war with Spain made matters worse. "You are letting the king of France be the merchant of the whole world," cried one speaker. "By falling out with Spain we spoil the best trade we have." There was talk of extending the Test Act to M.P.s, and that those who refused to take the Test be prohibited from coming within five miles of the court. There was another address against the duke of York's marriage. More ominous was the debate on November 3 on the standing army, whose commander was a foreigner who had an Irishman for his major-general. Almost unanimously the House voted that the army was a grievance —and this in wartime! The king had already planned to prorogue the session; this debate must have confirmed him in his decision. On November 4 the Commons had just begun the congenial task of attacking the king's ministers and had named Lauderdale when they were summoned by Black Rod. The king prorogued them for two months, after scolding them for their behavior and hoping that

[106] Quoted in Haley, *English Opposition*, p. 137.

when they reassembled in January they would apply themselves to
the problems of the nation rather more effectually than they had on
this occasion.[107]

The popular temper was shown clearly enough the next day, Guy
Fawkes Day. "This night," wrote Evelyn in his diary, "the youths of
the City burnt the Pope in effigy after they had made procession with
it in great triumph." Pope-burning became very popular; a month
later the pastime had spread to Scotland.[108] The lord chancellor took
careful note. He also took note of the intense interest in politics
shown by the lower classes, which a despairing supporter of the
government attributed to increasing sobriety. "Every carman and
porter is now a statesman," he wrote, "and indeed the coffee-houses
are good for nothing else. It was not thus when we drank nothing
but sack and claret, or English beer and ale. These sober clubs
produce nothing but scandalous and censorious discourses."[109]

Charles's decision to prorogue Parliament caused some surprise,
on account of his obvious need for money and his apparent intention to continue the war. As far as the outside world was concerned,
the situation was that described by Sir William Temple on Christmas day that "the court will upon no terms fall out with the French
alliance, and the nation will upon no terms fall in with it."[110] Insiders knew that the ministers were determined upon peace, especially Arlington, who was very depressed by the way the session had
gone and who now told Croissy that peace was absolutely essential.
"The poison of Parliament," he said, "has spread through all the
people and made them extremely suspicious of France."[111] The king
still put a bold face on it and talked of continuing the war, but in
fact he knew that peace was inevitable. He told Croissy that £1,400,-
000 would be necessary to fight the next campaign.[112] The money
would have to come from France, since clearly Parliament would not

[107] The debates for this session are in Henning, *Dering*, pp. 151–61, and
in Grey, *Debates* II, 182–223. There is a good account of the session in Haley,
English Opposition, pp. 136–42.

[108] DeBeer, *Diary of John Evelyn* IV, 26. Dec. 5, 1673, T. Derham to
Williamson, *C.S.P.D.* XVI, 44–45.

[109] Nov. 10, 1673, Player to Williamson, Christie, *Letters to Williamson* II, 68.

[110] Osmund Airy, ed., *Essex Papers* (London, 1890) I, 153–56.

[111] Nov. 3/13, 10/20, 1673, Croissy to Louis, Mignet, *Négociations* IV,
229–31, 233–37. Ségur-Dupeyron, *Histoire des négociations commerciales* I, 336.

[112] Mignet, *Négociations* IV, 243.

vote it, and Charles knew that Louis would give him no such astronomical sum as this, especially since he had added Spain to his list of enemies and was preparing a campaign in Flanders for the spring. But Charles had to play his cards carefully. The separate peace must be made with the French king's consent, to avoid any chance of Louis' disclosing the treaty of Dover, and this meant that Charles must avoid all appearance of wanting peace: he must be the victim of overwhelming pressure. So the king had to play a completely lone hand. Brother, ministers, opposition—all had to be deceived. The result was vividly described by the Venetian ambassador in December: ". . . the government is brought to such a state of confusion that the king calls a cabinet council for the purpose of not listening to it, and the ministers hold forth in it so as not to be understood."[113]

Further evidence that Charles had decided to liquidate his policy of the last five years and make peace was his dismissal of his lord chancellor on November 9. This step had been urged on him by his brother, who called Shaftesbury a "madman" for encouraging Parliament to oppose his marriage and who was generally held responsible for the king's action. Charles was not in the habit of taking James's advice, however. The king knew better than to believe, with James, that Shaftesbury's ability to make trouble would be lessened by his removal.[114] There was ample justification for getting rid of Shaftesbury, whose recent behavior had been ambiguous in the extreme, but it would have been a very foolish move if Charles had genuinely intended to try to continue the war, since public opinion would certainly react adversely. Williamson heard that this action, which caused some surprise, and the prorogation, caused "great jealousies and no less discontent."[115] Charles was astute enough to know that if he were to continue a manifestly unpopular policy, it was safer to have a politician like Shaftesbury partially immobilized by being in office, rather than free to attack the government, "which he did," says Burnet, "with as little reserve as decency."[116] Arling-

113 *C.S.P. Venetian* XXXVIII, 187.
114 *Ibid.*, pp. 175, 176. Burnet, *History* II, 42. Nov. 11, 1673, James to Lauderdale, Osmund Airy, ed., *The Lauderdale Papers* (London, 1884–85) II, 240.
115 Nov. 10, 1673, W. Bridgeman to Williamson, *C.S.P.D.* XVI, 12–13. Nov. 14, 1673, J. Paige to Williamson, *ibid.*, p. 18.
116 Burnet, *History* II, 43.

ton, who believed that Charles wanted to fight on, was very much disturbed, and hoped that Shaftesbury could be brought back into the government. But Charles's mind was made up. His policy had failed; he was preparing to liquidate it; Shaftesbury was neither useful nor desirable any more. Furthermore, he was untrustworthy. He was behind Lauderdale's troubles with the Scottish Parliament, or so the duke said, and anyway he was a Commonwealthman at heart.[117] Let him go; he would never see office again, if the king could help it.

Shaftesbury knew how Charles felt about him, and he could hardly have been very surprised at his dismissal. When Secretary Coventry came to him with the order to surrender the seals, the earl allegedly remarked that he was only laying down his gown and girding on his sword. Whether he made the remark or not, he certainly behaved as though he had and immediately began to play the role of the Protestant martyr. He knew now that his bid for the power and influence that he longed for had failed. That power and that influence would never be given to him willingly by Charles, who ordered him to leave London after his dismissal.[118] They would have to be seized.

Ten years of life were left to Shaftesbury after his dismissal in 1673. He was never again to be a great officer of state, yet it was during these last ten years that he left his mark indelibly upon the history of England. These were the years of the Green Ribbon Club, of the Popish Plot and the exclusion bill, of the Whig party— Shaftesbury's party—of organized electioneering and party platforms and the rest. They were also the years of Absalom. John Dryden was right. Shaftesbury was determined to rule in the state; he would be the power behind the throne. Twice before he had tried, and twice he had failed. Cromwell would not have him, and neither would Charles. And time was growing short; Shaftesbury was fifty-two years old in 1673, and fifty-seven when Titus Oates appeared on the scene with his providential pack of fairy tales. Mon-

---

[117] Christie, *Shaftesbury* II, 157, 180–81. Nov. 20, 1673, Lauderdale to Charles, Airy, *Lauderdale Papers* III, 16. In February, 1674, the Venetian ambassador reported that Charles was convinced that Shaftesbury was aiming at a republic. *C.S.P. Venetian* XXXVIII, 232.

[118] Shaftesbury refused to obey. Nov. 22, 1673, Conway to Essex, Airy, *Essex Papers* I, 141–42.

mouth was the only possible path to the power and influence Shaftesbury craved, because only Monmouth represented a shortcut. Shaftesbury's tragedy is the tragedy of disappointed ambition—a would-be *éminence grise* whose talents were destined never to be used.

Chapter 7

Liquidating the Grand Design

Epilogue

When the Seal's given to a talking fool
Whom wise men laugh att and the Women rule,
A Minister able only in his tongue
To make starcht empty Speeches two hours long.
When an old Scotch Covenanter shall be
The Champion of the English Hierarchye,
When Bishops shall lay all religion by
And strive by law to 'stablish Tyrany,
When a lean Treasurer shall in one year
Make him self rich, his king and People bare,
When the crown's heir shall English men dispise
And think French onely Loyall, Irish wise,
The wooden shoos shall be the English weare
And Magna Carta shall no more appeare,
Then the English shall a Greater Tyrant know
Then either Greek or Gallick Story shew.[1]

[1] "Nostradamus's Prophecy," quoted in H. M. Margoliouth, ed., *The Poems and Letters of Andrew Marvell* (Oxford, 1952) I, 171. The editor believes that the poem was probably not written by Marvell.

"Now there will be a new game played at court, and the designs and interests of all men will be different from what they were." So wrote Lord Conway to his friend, the earl of Essex, on February 24, 1674, some two weeks after the signing of the treaty which ended the war with the Dutch.[2] It was apparent to Conway and to all the political world that the era of the Cabal was over. Dating the rise and fall of seventeenth-century ministries is not always easy; indeed, it is often misleading to talk about a "ministry" at all. But if there is a date which marks the dissolution of the Cabal, whose popularity in certain quarters is indicated by the above lines of "Nostradamus," that date is not February, 1674, but rather November 9, 1673, the day of Shaftesbury's dismissal. On that date Clifford was dead and Buckingham in bad odor at court; only the two secretaries were left.

The duke of Lauderdale was increasingly preoccupied with the difficulties which the failure of the war policy had created in Scotland. Serious economic problems resulted from the cutting off of Scotland's principal overseas market; Lauderdale's increasingly tactless and overbearing methods and the constitutional implications of Charles's policy caused further trouble. Scottish politicians had divined the king's intentions. At the beginning of the war the marquis of Atholl informed the duke of Hamilton that "there was a settled design of having no more Parliaments in England. The king would be master, and would be no longer curbed by a house of commons."[3] Hamilton was disturbed by the prospect, not because he cared for English liberties but because he did not care for Lauderdale. In this same month of November, 1673, the opposition to Lauderdale broke into the open in the Scottish Parliament. Hamilton and others demanded a consideration of the nation's grievances, and among those others was Lauderdale's erstwhile ally Tweeddale. The duke was able to stifle the opposition temporarily by making concessions on the highly unpopular brandy, salt, and tobacco monopolies, but never again would he enjoy the quasi-unanimous if sullen acquiescence in his rule which characterized the Cabal years.[4]

---

[2] Osmund Airy, ed., *Essex Papers* (London, 1890) I, 179–80.

[3] Gilbert Burnet, *The History of My Own Time* (ed. Osmund Airy, Oxford, 1897–1900) I, 601.

[4] Dec. 6, 1673, Aungier to Essex, B.M. Stowe Mss. 203, ff. 237–38. For Lauderdale's handling of this crisis see W. C. Mackenzie, *The Life and Times of John Maitland, Duke of Lauderdale* (London, 1923), pp. 339–49.

As for the weary and discouraged Arlington, he now had to preside over the liquidation of a policy he never approved and to try to avoid impeachment if he could. His health was wretched; he was "tied to his chair" by gout, wrote the Venetian ambassador on December 19, 1673, and had been for a month. In spite of this he did not absent himself from court if he could help it: he dared not. "My Lord Arlington has not yet got his feet," wrote Henry Ball to Williamson on December 17, "but comes now to council, both yesterday and today."[5] He knew his master well enough to fear that Charles, if he were convinced that the secretary had outlived his usefulness, would not lift a finger to save him from his enemies. During his enforced absence from the council board, the king had silenced Buckingham once when the duke attempted to attack him, but Arlington could not be sure that Charles would do so again.[6] It did not matter that Arlington had never approved of the French alliance and the war. He was associated with them in the public mind, and Charles, if he were to benefit in the eyes of public opinion from a change of measures, must change men, too. Indeed, the king believed—or so he told Sir William Temple—that it was the bungling of his ministers which had caused the failure of his policy.[7] Arlington had no wish to avoid retirement. What he did wish to avoid was the fate of Clarendon, who had been the scapegoat of a policy he had disapproved.

The king saw clearly enough what he must do. The grand design had failed; he could not now, for the foreseeable future, be independent of Parliament. So, he must follow a policy which would command Parliamentary support, and this meant a policy of hostility to Catholicism and to France and of close alliance with the Anglican establishment—the policy of Danby. It was the alliance with the Church which differentiated Danby's policy from that of

[5] A. B. Hinds, et al., eds., *Calendar of State Papers, Venetian* (henceforth *C.S.P. Venetian*) (London, 1864–1947) XXXVIII, 190–91. W. D. Christie, ed., *Letters . . . to Sir Joseph Williamson* (London, 1874) II, 99. See also Dec. 18, 1673, Jan. 29, 1674, Arlington to Godolphin, T. Bebington, ed., *The Right Honourable the Earl of Arlington's Letters to Sir William Temple, Bart.* (vol. I) , and to the Several Ambassadors to Spain (vol. II) (London, 1701) II, 448, 465.

[6] Dec. 5, 1673, Derham to Williamson, M. A. E. Green, et al., eds., *Calendar of State Papers Domestic, Charles II* (henceforth *C.S.P.D.*) (London, 1860ff.) XV, 44–45.

[7] H. E. Woodbridge, *Sir William Temple* (London, 1940) , pp. 158–59. Temple replied that, on the contrary, it was the policy which was mistaken.

Shaftesbury, the patron of the dissenters, and the king decided to adopt it, not only because he felt that Danby was more trustworthy than Shaftesbury but also because the Anglican hierarchy was far more friendly to the prerogative, to the ideas of divine right and nonresistance, than were the dissenters, provided that the prerogative was not used, as it had lately been, in such a way as to favor the Papists. Hence Charles decided to dismiss his lord chancellor, while his lord treasurer became increasingly influential.

The king believed that he could launch this new course successfully because, oddly enough, his own personal position had not suffered overmuch from the collapse of his plans. The following lines, possibly written by Andrew Marvell, explain why:

> Great Charles, who full of mercy wouldst command
> In peace and pleasure this thy native land,
> At last take pitty of thy tottering throne,
> Shooke by the faults of others, not thine owne.
> Let not thy life and crowne togeather end,
> Destroyed by a false brother and false friend.
> Observe the danger that appeares soe neare,
> What all thy subjects doe each minute feare:
> A droppe of poisone or a papish knife
> Ends all the joys of England and thy life.[8]

Whatever his opponents may have thought of Charles—and Andrew Marvell did not think much; he once wrote a mock king's speech to Parliament in which Charles says, "if you do not make me rich enough to undo you, it shall lie at your doors"[9]—they infinitely preferred him to his narrow-minded Catholic brother. To them James was both foolish and dangerous, an opinion the king himself shared and occasionally gave vent to in his cups.[10] So most men in England were willing to give the king the benefit of the doubt.

Before the new course could be properly launched, however, it was necessary to liquidate the war. Here Charles had to be very cautious; Louis XIV must be convinced that Charles was making the separate peace very reluctantly and because he had no choice. As always,

---

[8] "Advice to a Painter to Draw the Duke by," Margoliouth, *Marvell* I, 200.

[9] A. Birrell, *Andrew Marvell* (New York, 1905), p. 201.

[10] See the French ambassador Barillon's letter of October 21/31, 1680, cited in J. Pollock, *The Popish Plot* (London, 1903), p. 69, n. 1.

when the king was faced with a concrete, short-run situation, he did a masterful job. The aura of governmental indecision was maintained.[11] The king continued to give the outward appearance of wanting to carry on the war. He replied to Dutch propaganda with propaganda of his own, but he told Croissy that without a Parliamentary subsidy it would be impossible to go on. Charles and the French and everyone else knew perfectly well that the reassembling of Parliament, in its present mood, would mean no such thing as a war subsidy; it would mean peace.[12] According to the gossip in anti-French circles, King Louis' minions went to considerable lengths to persuade Charles not to summon his refractory legislature:

> Before the meeting of the Parliament Madame Carwell sat upon him [King Charles] in the most efficacious manner with her coats up, for a dissolution, and he swore by Christ and by her —— (his new Sacrament) that it should be done. The next morning, she comes to him with an instrument ready drawn, which he refused to sign, alleging that he was drunk when he promised. But afterwards she came to him as he sat in his chair, took up her coats, and fell into his lap, and then again he swore to her as aforesaid to do it, but as before he was drunk with wine so now with his lust, and they have not yet been able to screw him up.[13]

As late as the end of the year there was still some doubt whether the session would be held, but then, "Captain Titus told the king that nobody doubted now of the sitting of the Parliament, because the duke of Buckingham was at Church twice upon Christmas day, and received the sacrament."[14] And, indeed, the king had decided by mid-December to go ahead with the scheduled January session. This was because the Dutch had finally made an offer, through the marquis del Fresno, which Charles felt he could accept. It was not very much of an offer: the Dutch would recognize England's claims with respect to the saluting of the flag and would pay England the sum of 800,000 patacoons, about £187,000, which did Charles little good, since much of it went to William of Orange in belated satisfaction of his claims respecting his mother's dowry.[15] Charles was now

---

[11] See, for instance, Dec. 5/15, 1673, Alberti to the Doge and Senate, *C.S.P. Venetian* XXXVIII, 184–85.

[12] Jan. 2/12, 1674, Alberti to the Doge and Senate, *ibid.*, pp. 195–96.

[13] This was written by one of Du Moulin's correspondents in January, 1674, and is quoted in K. H. D. Haley, *William of Orange and the English Opposition 1672–4* (Oxford, 1953), p. 159. "Madame Carwell" was what the English called Louise de Quérouaille.

[14] Dec. 30, 1673, Conway to Essex, Airy, *Essex Papers* I, 158–59.

[15] Woodbridge, *Temple*, p. 155.

prepared to accept any terms which would extricate him from the war without actual loss, since his real objective was beyond his reach. But he was in no hurry to close with the Dutch offer; he wanted to wait until Parliament met so that he could demonstrate to Louis XIV that he was yielding to irresistible pressure in making peace and so that he could associate Parliament with his acceptance of the meager offers of the Dutch.[16] So, to gain time, he referred the offer to the deadlocked Cologne conference and demanded that the Dutch also make concessions respecting the East Indian trade and the departure of English subjects from Surinam and acknowledge that they must pay for the right to fish off the British coast. Only on the second of these did the Dutch give any ground.

Parliament, when it reassembled, acted almost exactly as the king expected it would. The French alliance was its principal grievance, and it complained bitterly about the alliance and the policies which accompanied it, the indulgence and the Stop. Charles, on the advice of Danby and Buckingham, decided to demonstrate that there were no sinister religious overtones to the alliance by disingenuously showing the houses the *traité simulé*. "I know you have heard much of my alliance with France," said the king, "and, I believe, it hath been very strangely misrepresented to you, as if there were certain secret articles of dangerous consequence; but I will make no difficulty of letting the treaties, and all the articles of them, without any the least reserve, to be seen by a small committee of both Houses, who may report to you the true scope of them: and I assure you, there is no other treaty with France, either before or since, not already printed, which shall not be made known."[17]

According to Conway, the king at this point "fumbled" in his delivery, and well he might.[18] No one who knew of the treaty of Dover was going to expose him, however, and so, having laid the groundwork, he proceeded a few weeks later to wring the only advantage he could from Parliament's present mood by disclosing the Dutch terms and asking if he should accept them. "This bone," Conway remarked, "was cast before Parliament" by Danby's advice.[19] There were dangerous constitutional implications to this

[16] On this point see the Venetian ambassador's interesting dispatch of December 12/22, 1673, *C.S.P. Venetian* XXXVIII, 187.

[17] Quoted in Haley, *English Opposition*, pp. 160–61.

[18] Airy, *Essex Papers* I, 159–61.

[19] B.M. Stowe Mss. 204, ff. 114–15.

move, and Arlington, who was afraid of setting an unhappy precedent for the future, did not like it, but it served the king's immediate
purpose. The Commons in reply voted that the king be advised to
proceed to a speedy peace, without commenting on the terms, which
amounted to a tacit acceptance of them.[20] So Charles went ahead. In
the interest of speed, del Fresno was empowered to act for the Dutch,
and he was not disposed to delay: Spain had threatened to fight if
the Dutch offer was rejected, but she was as anxious as England to
avoid any possibility of war and had put pressure on the Dutch to be
reasonable. On February 9, 1674, the peace was signed. The French,
who had striven almost to the end to keep England in the war, were
not pleased, but they acquiesced. The king told Ruvigny, truly
enough, that he could not carry on the war without supplies, which
Commons would not vote, "and Lord Arlington had pressed him so
hard, that he had stood out till he was weary of his life.
. . . Ruvigny told him, what was done could not be helped."[21]

In England there was some dissatisfaction with the thinness of the
terms, but most people were content. One of Williamson's correspondents reported that everyone was pleased but the Catholics.[22]
There was even some optimism in government circles about the
future in foreign affairs. Arlington's fellow-secretary, Henry Coventry, put it this way in a letter to Essex in December: "God almighty
seemeth to have provided better for our security than our wisdom
could easily have figured to ourselves, whilst that exorbitant power
that appeared in our two neighbors, the one by sea and the other by
land, are already so far reduced and likely yet to be more by the
insupportable expense they put each other to, that a good union at
home, blest with a reasonable conduct, might establish the security

---

[20] The king made his disclosures on January 24; the House vote came
on the twenty-seventh. The debates are in A. Grey, *Debates of the House of
Commons* (London, 1763) II, 338–57.

[21] Burnet, *History* II, 49. Dec. 13, 1673, Wm. Bridgeman to Essex, B.M.
Stowe Mss. 203, ff. 259–60. K. Feiling, *British Foreign Policy 1660–1672* (London,
1930) , p. 359. Dec. 29, 1673/Jan. 8, 1674, Louis to Ruvigny, J. J. Jusserand, ed.,
Receuil des instructions données aux ambassadeurs de France, Angleterre (Paris,
1929) II, 143–46. Feb. 2/12, 1674, William Perwich to Arlington, M. B. Curran, ed.,
The Despatches of William Perwich, Camden Society, 3rd ser. V (London, 1903) ,
p. 287. Feb. 17, 1674, Conway to Essex, Airy, *Essex Papers* I, 175–76. Ruvigny was
sent to England late in 1673 in a last-ditch effort to keep England in the war; in
January, 1674, he replaced Croissy as ambassador.

[22] Christie, *Letters to Williamson* II, 152. Feb. 6/16, 1674, Alberti to
the Doge and Senate, *C.S.P. Venetian* XXXVIII, 215.

of his majesty's kingdoms upon a better foundation than your excellency's memory and mine ever knew."[23]

"A good union at home" seemed pretty remote early in 1674, however. Associating the Commons with the unsatisfactory peace was the only success the king was to have with his Parliament. Otherwise the session was notable chiefly for a series of attacks on the three members of the Cabal who still had some connection with the court. As one member of the opposition put it in debate, "The question is, whether a Cabal of seven, four, or five men shall take all business into their hands . . . to advise war, to the hazard of religion, laws, and all, and the king too."[24] Lauderdale was exceedingly unpopular, but there was no effective way for the Commons to get at him, since they had no shadow of jurisdiction over his official acts. All they could do was carry an address asking the king to remove him forever from his offices and the court, on all sorts of grounds, ranging from his alleged part in the death of Charles I to his penchant for violent measures and his belief in military despotism.[25] The duke was not worried. He was assured of the king's continued support, since he was still indispensable in Scottish affairs, and that was all that was necessary to him. He remarked when he heard of the Commons' attack—or so his enemies alleged—"that he had a dog in his a—— which could outbark all those curs."[26]

A far greater potential danger to the king, because of the revelations it might produce, was Buckingham's well-advertised assault upon Arlington. The duke was now clinging with his fingertips to the last shreds of his influence; what little weight he still carried was owing to his friendship with his former protégé Danby.[27] The duke's plan was to turn himself into a popular hero once again, as he had in 1667, by leading the attack on the man who was to be made the

[23] B.M. Stowe Mss. 203, f. 319.
[24] Grey, *Debates* II, 282–83.
[25] Burnet, *History* II, 44. Grey, *Debates* II, 236–44.
[26] This allegation is contained in a violently antigovernment pamphlet, possibly of Dutch origin, called *Verbum sapienti*, which appeared in January, 1674, and is interesting in that it contains one of the earliest references to exclusion, by asking if it were not more dangerous to have a Catholic king hereafter than a Catholic admiral now. *C.S.P.D.* XVI, 128–32.
[27] Danby, like most of Buckingham's associates, was a convivial sort. On November 29, 1673, Conway described a drunken supper party at Lady Shrewsbury's, which was graced by Buckingham, Danby, and Nell Gwyn, also a good friend of Buckingham. B.M. Stowe Mss. 203, f. 209.

scapegoat for the failures of the past few years, and thus force himself on the king. But his plans miscarried badly. For one thing, the king's position was quite different than it had been in 1667; Charles's sympathies now were with the prospective victim rather than the duke. For another, Arlington's friends were ready, and they got in the first blow, by an attack on the duke in the Lords, through the relatives of the late earl of Shrewsbury.[28] Buckingham's scandalous private life was thoroughly aired. The facts were bad enough; where fact was absent, conjecture suggested worse things still. "He has attempted a horrid sin not to be named; not to be named at Rome, where their other practices are horrid."[29] The duke did what he could, but he could hardly deny his liaison with Lady Shrewsbury, and ultimately they each had to post bond of £10,000 that they would no longer cohabit. Buckingham's wife stood loyally by him throughout this sordid episode, and they were seen at church together; the duke, wrote one of Essex's correspondents, had become "a great convert."[30]

The circumstances were hardly propitious for an attack upon anyone else, but the duke plunged on. He requested a hearing in the Commons, ostensibly to defend himself against charges of favoring the French alliance, calling the king an arrant knave who was unfit to govern, and, oddly enough, being popishly inclined. He did not make a good impression. His statements were rambling and rather incoherent; he was not believed when he tried to blame everything on Arlington and exculpate himself—". . . if I am a grievance, I am the cheapest grievance . . . that ever this House had"—and he infuriated the king by comparing him and James to a brace of lobsters. The Commons voted, as they had with Lauderdale, to petition the king to remove him from all his employments and from his presence and councils forever.[31] Charles was happy enough to comply. Buckingham, whose finances were in desperate condition, was afraid that Charles would simply dismiss him

[28] Sir Gilbert Talbot's letter of January 2, 1674, to Williamson, shows that the plan was known in advance to Arlington's friends. Christie, *Letters to Williamson* II, 105–6.

[29] Quoted in H. Chapman, *Great Villiers* (London, 1949) , p. 206.

[30] Jan. 27, 1674, Aungier to Essex, Airy, *Essex Papers* I, 167. See also his letter of February 7, and Conway's of January 10, *ibid.*, pp. 160, 173–74.

[31] Buckingham's appearances in the Commons, and the debates which culminated in the vote, occurred on January 13 and 14, 1674. Grey, *Debates* II, 244–70.

without allowing him to sell his offices and wrote his master a humble letter recounting his past services, concluding, "my whole estate being at present mortgaged, and I having lived to this age without being acquainted with any way of getting money." Charles finally gave him permission to sell and provided him with an annuity of £1,500 and various other financial *douceurs*.[32]

Arlington profited from his enemy's blunders. On the day after Buckingham's fiasco he too made a request to be heard by the House, which was readily granted. He made a surprisingly effective speech; he did not deny his share in the unpopular policies of recent years, but he took the position that the entire ministry was responsible for them. The House, which had apparently regarded him as just another courtier, was favorably impressed by his evident capacity and grasp of affairs. The secretary's eloquence was not the only reason for his success, however. The charges against him appeared to be even more baseless than those against Clarendon, and they collapsed when the only witness to his alleged treason turned out to be a servant of Buckingham's who failed to appear. So, when the motion for his removal was made, it was beaten, on January 20, after some days' debate, by thirty-nine votes. Even Shaftesbury was disconcerted, and Buckingham's state of mind can be imagined.[33]

The secretary was saved, but the Commons quickly demonstrated that they did not intend the vote as an endorsement of the policies of the government. The debate on the Dutch peace terms revealed their furious enmity toward France, and, once more, it was moved that the standing army be voted a grievance. Their hostility to Catholics was not abated by Charles's customary ploy of enforcing the recusancy laws. The government's spokesmen in the debate on the King's Speech had to accept a clause that the king would have

[32] Mar. 7, 1674, Aungier to Essex, Airy, *Essex Papers* I, 181. John H. Wilson, *A Rake and His Times* (New York, 1954), pp. 250–51. Buckingham's letter is in R. Bell, ed., *Memorials of the Civil War* (London, 1849) II, 249–53.

[33] Jan. 13, 17, 1674, Aungier to Essex, B.M. Stowe Mss. 204, ff. 38–39, 57–58. Jan. 21, 1674, Temple to Essex, *ibid.*, ff. 92–93. V. Barbour, *Henry Bennet, Earl of Arlington* (Washington, D.C., 1914), pp. 235–36, says that Shaftesbury's friends supported Arlington. It is true that in December one of Conway's correspondents put Arlington and Shaftesbury in the same faction at court. Christie, *Letters to Williamson* II, 92. But in January Conway himself, as well as Aungier and Temple, stated that Shaftesbury and Buckingham were working together. See, in addition to the letters cited above, Jan. 27, 1674, Aungier to Essex, and Conway to Essex, B.M. Stowe Mss. 204, ff. 112, 114–15. The course of events can be followed in Grey, *Debates* II, 270–329.

the London militia ready to suppress meetings of Papists, and a bill was prepared which would bar Catholics from Parliament.[34] The situation was even worse in the Lords, where Shaftesbury was making the first of a long series of successful efforts to whip up anti-Catholic hysteria. He made an impassioned speech about a popish plot and brought in a bill on the education and marriage of royal children. The Lords voted, with only three dissenting voices, to ask the king to banish all Catholics except peers' servants from London while Parliament was in session. Other bills were brought in to remove the sons of Catholic peers from their control and to exclude from the succession any member of the royal family who should marry a Catholic in the future. Shaftesbury explained that this was not an *ex post facto* measure, but his target was obvious to everybody. The Lords, wrote the Venetian ambassador, voted the removal of James's daughters from his charge because of his Catholic wife, "after making audacious speeches against the duke's succession." Coming events were casting their shadows. The Lords also undertook the consideration of measures directed against French trade.[35] So Charles, who suspected that the opposition in the two houses was working in concert, decided late in February to put an end to the session. He caught people by surprise. There was no subsidy and no legislation; people reproached each other "that they had sat so long upon eggs and could hatch nothing."[36]

If the metaphor be pardoned, one thing had been "hatched": the final public dissolution of the Cabal. Arlington lingered on in office until the autumn of 1674 and then demitted his post to Williamson and retired to the position of lord chamberlain, as he had planned. He never lost his master's goodwill, in spite of occasional flirtations with Shaftesbury's party, but his political influence was gone, and he ultimately resigned himself to the role of an elder statesman. He followed his master's example to the end and on his deathbed sent for a priest. Lauderdale's race was not yet run, but he, too, eventu-

---

[34] Grey, *Debates* II, 235–36. *C.S.P.D.* XVI, 136–37.

[35] Haley, *English Opposition*, pp. 187–88. Jan. 10, 1674, Conway to Essex, Airy, *Essex Papers* I, 159–61. Feb. 13/23, Feb. 27/Mar. 9, 1674, Alberti to the Doge and Senate, *C.S.P. Venetian* XXXVIII, 220–21, 232. See also *C.S.P.D.* XVI, 176, and Louise F. Brown, *The First Earl of Shaftesbury* (New York, 1933), pp. 221–23.

[36] Feb. 24, 1674, Conway to Essex, Airy, *Essex Papers* I, 179–80. Feb. 28, 1674, Talbot to Williamson. Christie, *Letters to Williamson* II, 156–57.

ally fell from grace, and his death in 1682 prompted this bit of Biblical moralizing: "The wise man dies, and so does the fool: they who have been a terror in the land of the living, how easily are they brought down to the grave in a moment!"[37] As for Shaftesbury and Buckingham and their careers as leaders of the Country Party, the witty duke summed it up, rather inaccurately, when all was over, Shaftesbury dead, and James II apparently firmly seated on his throne:

> If, by my deep contrivance, wit and skill
> Things fall out cross to what I mean them still,
> You must not wonder; 't'is the common fate
> Of almost all grave governors of late:
> And one would swear, as every plot has sped,
> They thought more with their elbows than their head;
> Yet they go on as brisk and look as well,
> As if they had outwisdom'd Machiavel:
> So curs will wag their tails and think they've won us,
> At the same instant they make water on us.
>   .   .   .
> Yet, faith, the little Lord, when hence he ran,
> Did compass one thing like an able man:
> For since he could not living act with reason,
> 'T'was shrewdly done of him to die in season.[38]

II

Roger North, in looking back on these confused years, concluded that

the king was beset by a double-visaged ministry, half papist and half fanatic, who co-operated in mischief, the former to favor their party and the other to ruin the king. The Lords Clifford and Arlington of the former and Bucks and Shaftesbury of the latter party. And the game lay by soothing up the king and pushing him on in designs of advancing his prerogative. . . . But these parties had different aims, the popish really to enhance the king's power in order to have the sway of it on their side; the other, to loosen the king from the affections of his people and so directly to destroy him.[39]

[37] D. Laing, ed., *The Diary of Alexander Brodie of Brodie . . . and of His Son James Brodie of Brodie* (Aberdeen, 1863), p. 473.
[38] Quoted in Chapman, *Great Villiers*, p. 167.
[39] Roger North, *The Lives of the Norths* (ed. A. Jessopp, London, 1890) I, 114.

North misread the significance of the Cabal in most respects, but on one point he was absolutely right: its members were constantly working at cross-purposes. And this circumstance, which Charles had counted upon to further his designs, was one of the major factors in his failure.

These incompatible men, who could agree on almost nothing save their willingness, for different reasons, to serve the king and their dislike, again for different reasons, of the Anglican monopoly, were chosen by Charles as the instruments of his grand design. Some of them—Lauderdale, Arlington, then Clifford—were to be the active promoters of the king's policy; Buckingham and Shaftesbury were there *pour encourager les autres* and to act as a sort of camouflage. When Clarendon fell, the king did not know just how he would go about achieving his independence of Parliament, but he did know that, whatever scheme he finally pitched on, he must not appear to be doing what he actually was doing, or Parliament could and would stop him. Hence the necessity for concealment, camouflage, a divided ministry. What Charles failed to realize was that a divided ministry is useful only for the purpose of doing nothing. It is of no use in the implementation of a positive or controversial policy, especially one which involves substantial change in the *status quo*. It is a still greater handicap if that policy demands the utmost secrecy, as the agreement with France most emphatically did. The treaty of Dover was the key to the Cabal years. Its purpose was to achieve the king's domestic objectives; Charles's principal intended victim was Parliament and only secondarily the Dutch. The treaty was the king's doing. Of his advisers only the mediocre Clifford and the obtuse James were enthusiastic; Arlington had serious misgivings, and the others did not know all that was involved. The odds against the king's success were enormous, owing chiefly to the financial stringency which precluded military preparations adequate for the swift and overwhelming victory which was indispensable to Charles's purposes. And, when things began to go wrong, Parliament did what the king feared it would: it stopped him.

By 1674, then, the king had not succeeded in making himself independent of Parliament; in fact, he had lost ground, if anything. In the one open confrontation over the scope of the royal prerogative, it was Charles who had to give way, by canceling the declaration of indulgence. Even more than in 1667, an all-out assault on the ministry in Parliament was thought to be the ladder to power and office; Shaftesbury's conduct was so analyzed by the Venetian ambassador in February, 1674.[40] The financial situation was as bad as it had been in 1667, and Charles's financial reputation, which was poor to begin with, was compromised still further by the Stop of the Exchequer, which by now was very critically regarded in the Commons.[41] The king's grip on foreign policy had weakened owing to his financial dependence, and he had taken the unprecedented step of asking Parliament's advice regarding the provisions of a peace treaty. His grip had also been weakened by the treaty of Dover itself. The Catholicity clause gave Louis XIV an ideal weapon with which to blackmail his English cousin. It was a weapon which had to be used cautiously, as both Louis and Charles knew; it would do Louis no good to precipitate a revolution in England which would bring to power the militantly Protestant and anti-French elements in English society. But it did mean that Charles could never put himself at the head of those elements and lead an anti-French crusade, as his new chief minister Danby would have preferred.

Charles learned a great deal from the collapse of his grand design. The indolent exterior would remain, but the king meant to keep control of his government: Danby would not be another Clarendon. Charles was no Merovingian even before 1667, although Pepys, among others, believed that he was: "My grief," wrote the diarist on October 31, 1666, "being that the king do not look after his business himself, and thereby will be undone both himself and his nation." Pepys might have known better; he had been told by Anglesey that nothing got done in committees unless Charles was present, a situation which was still truer after 1667 than before.[42] The major political fact that was borne in upon this astute royal politician by his recent experience was that he could never be truly independent of Parliament; he could not create in London a docile body like that in Edinburgh, on which he could absolutely impose his will and the recognition of his prerogative. Parliament would have to be man-

[40] *C.S.P. Venetian* XXXVIII, 228.

[41] See, for instance, Buckingham's hasty disclaimer of responsibility, with the statement that he had lost £3,000 by it, during his interrogation by the House. Grey, *Debates* II, 263.

[42] *The Diary of Samuel Pepys* (ed. H. B. Wheatley, London, 1926), Feb. 27, 1665. As one example among many for the Cabal years see Apr. 19, 1670, Downing to Williamson, *C.S.P.D.* X, 170.

aged, and this meant that Parliament's prejudices, rather than his own, must be catered to. This in turn meant a policy of narrow Anglicanism at home and hostility to Louis XIV abroad, the policy of Danby, coupled—and this was Danby's special contribution—with the creation of a dependable bloc of government votes by bribery. Support of the Anglican church posed no problem, and in the autumn of 1674 Charles, for the first time in his reign, began to call on his bishops for advice.[43] Genuine hostility to Louis XIV was impossible, however, and it was the contradictions involved in an ambivalent foreign policy which eventually led to Danby's ruin and which contributed so heavily to the panic of the Popish Plot. Out of that panic there emerged the last and perhaps the most brilliant of Charles's devices for accomplishing his goal of ruling as well as reigning: the remodeling of the House of Commons itself in the interest of a political faction of which he was the leader.

So, in the final analysis, the story of the Cabal is that of a disguised attempt at a veiled absolutism, an attempt which went wrong. Because it was so carefully disguised, the king survived it and went on through greater perils to greater success. For his five collaborators, the last word should go to that most gifted dealer in words, the duke of Buckingham, words written when the other four, and the king himself, were dead. They are autobiographical words, but they apply to each of the five:

> Perhaps he wished it might have been his fate
> To lend a helping hand to rule the state:
> Though he conceives, as things have lately run,
> 'Tis somewhat hard at present to be done.[44]

[43] F. Bate, *The Declaration of Indulgence, 1672* (London, 1908), pp. 139–40.

[44] Quoted in Chapman, *Great Villiers,* p. 167.

Appendix

The Royal Game: or, A Princely new
Play found in a Dream, &c. 1672.

PROLOGUE

Whoever looks about and minds things well,
And on Affairs abroad doth take a View,
May think the Story which I here do tell
Was never dreamt, it falleth out so true.
I do confess it's something hard to find
A crooked Path directly in the dark;
And while a Man's asleep, you know he's blind,
And cannot easily hit on a Mark.
Well, be it so; yet this you know is right,
What's seen i' th' Day is dreamt again at Night.
A Dream I hope will no wise Man offend,
Nor will it Treason be (I trow) to lend
A Copy of my Dream unto my Friend.
Cabal, beware your Shins,
For thus my Tale begins.

The Dream of the Cabal: *A Prophetick Satyr,*
Anno 1672.

As t'other Night in Bed I thinking lay,
How I my Rent shou'd to my Landlord pay,
Since Corn, nor Wool, nor Beast would money make;
Tumbling perplex'd, these Thoughts kept me awake.
What will become of this mad World, quoth I?
What's its Disease? what is its Remedy?
Where will it issue? whereto does it tend?
Some ease to Misery 'tis to know its end.
Till Servants dreaming, as they us'd to do,
Snor'd me asleep, I fell a dreaming too.
Methought there met the Grand Cabal of Seven,
(Odd numbers some Men say do best please Heaven)
When sat they were, and Doors were all fast shut,
I secret was behind the Hangings put:
Both hear and see I could; but he that there
Had plac'd me, bad me have as great a care

Of stirring, as my Life: and e'er that out
From thence I came, resolv'd shou'd be my Doubt;
What would become of this mad World, unless
Present Designs were cross'd with ill Success.
An Awful Silence there was held some space,
Till trembling thus began one call'd his Grace.
Great Sir, your Government for first twelve years
Has spoil'd the Monarchy, and made our Fears [*Buck.*
So potent on us, that we must change quite
The old Foundations, make new, wrong or right.
For too great mixture of Democracy
Within this Government allay'd must be;
And no Allay like nulling Parliaments,
O' th' Peoples Pride and Arrogance the Vents;
Factious and saucy, disputing Royal Pleasure,
Who your Commands by their own Humours measure.
For King in Barnacles (to the Rack-staves ty'd)
You must remain, if these you will abide.

So spake the long blue Ribbon: then a second,
Tho not so tall, yet quite as wise is reckon'd, [*Orm.*
Did thus begin. Great Sir, you are now on
A tender Point much to be thought upon,
And thought on only; for by antient Law,
'Twas Death to mention what my Lord foresaw:
His trembling shew'd it, wherefore I'm so bold
T' advise its standing, lest it shou'd be told
We did attempt to change it; for so much
Our Ancestors secur'd it, that to touch,
Like sacred Mount, 'tis Death, and such a Trick,
I no ways like my Tongue shou'd break my Neck.

Thus said, he sat. Then Lord of Northern Tone, [*Laud.*
In Gall and Guile a second unto none,
Inraged rose, and Col'rick, thus began:
Dread Majesty, Male Beam of Fame, a Son
Of th' hundred and tenth Monarch of the Nore:
Dee'l split the Weam of th' Loon that spoke afore;
Shame faw the Crag of that ill-manner'd Lord,
That 'nent his King durst speak so faw a Word:
And aw my Saul, right weel the first Man meant,
Dee'l hoop his Lugs that loves a Parliament.
Twa Houses aw my Saul are too too mickle,
They'l gar the Leard shall ne'er have more a Prickle;
Ne Mony get to gee the bonny Lass,
But full as good be born without a T——
Ten thousand Plagues light on his Crag, that gang
To make you be but third part of a King,

Dee'l take my Saul, I'll ne'er the matter mince,
I'd rather Subject be than sike a Prince.
To hang, and burn, and sley, and draw, and kill,
And measure aw thing by my awn gude Will,
Is gay Dominion: a Checkmate I hate,
Of Men, or Laws, it looks so like a State.
This eager well-meant Zeal some laughter stir'd,
Till Nose half Plush, half Flesh, the Inkhorn Lord
Crav'd Audience thus: Grave Majesty Divine [*Arling.*
(Pardon that *Cambridg* Title, I make mine)
We now are enter'd on the great'st Debate
That can concern your Throne and Royal State.
His Grace hath so spoke all, that we who next
Speak after, can but comment on his Text:
Only 'tis wonder, at this sacred Board
Shou'd sit 'mongst us a *Magna Charta* Lord,
A Peer of old rebellious Barons breed,
Worst, and great'st Enemies to Royal Seed.
But to proceed; well was it urg'd by's Grace,
Such Liberty was giv'n for twelve years space
That are by-past, there's no necessity
Of new Foundations, if safe you'l be.
What Travel, Charge, and Art, before was set
This Parliament, we had, you can't forget;
Now force, cajole, and court, and bribe, for fear
They wrong should run, e'er since they have been here.
What Diligence, what Study, Day and Night,
Was on us, and what Care to keep them right?
Wherefore if good you can't make Parliament,
On whom such Costs, such Art and Pains were spent,
And Monys, all we had for them to do;
Since we miss that, 'tis best dismiss them too.
'Tis true, this House the best is you can call,
But in my Judgment, best is none at all.
Well mov'd, the whole Cabal cry'd, Parliaments
Are Clogs to Princes, and their brave Intents.
One did object, 'twas against Majesty
T' obey the Peoples Pleasure: Another he
Their Inconvenience argues, and that neither
Close their Designs were, nor yet speedy either.

Whilst thus confused chatter'd the Cabal,
And many mov'd, none heard, but speak did all;
A little bobtail'd Lord, Urchin of State, [*Chan. Shafts.*
A *Praise-God-bare-bone* Peer, whom all Men hate;
Amphibious Animal, half Fool, half Knave;
Beg'd Silence, and this purblind Counsel gave.

Blest and best Monarch that e'er Scepter bore,
Renown'd for Vertue, but for Honour more:
That Lord spake last, has well and wisely shown,
That Parliaments, nor new, nor old, nor none
Can well be trusted longer; for the State
And Glory of the Crown hate all Checkmate.
That Monarchy may from its Childhood grow
To Man's Estate, *France* has taught us how:
Monarchy's Divine, Divinity it shows;
That he goes backward that not forward goes.
Therefore go on, let other Kingdoms see
Your Will's your Law, that's absolute Monarchy;
A mixt Hodg-podg will now no longer do,
Caesar or nothing you are brought unto:
Strike then, Great Sir, 'fore these Debates take wind,
Remember that Occasion's bald behind.
Our Game is sure in this, if wisely play'd,
And sacred Votes to th' Vulgar not betray'd:
But if the Rumour shou'd once get on wing,
That we consult to make you abs'lute King,
The Plebians head, the Gentry forsooth,
They straight would snort, and have an aking Tooth.
Lest they, I say, should your great Secrets scent,
And you oppose in nulling *Parliament,*
I think it safer, and a greater Skill,
To obviate, than to o'ercome an Ill:
For those that lead the Herd are full as rude,
When th' Humour takes, as th' following Multitude;
Therefore be quick in your Resolves, and when
Resolv'd you have, execute quicker then.
Remember your great Father lost the Game
By slow proceeding, mayn't you do the same?
An unexpected, unregarded Blow
Wounds more than ten made by an open Foe.
Delays do Dangers breed; the Sword is yours
By Law declar'd, what need of other Powers?
We may unpolitick be judg'd, or worse,
If we can't make the Sword command the Purse;
No Art, or Courtship can the Rule so shape
Without a Force, it must be done by Rape.
And when 'tis done, to say you cannot help,
Will satisfy enough the gentle Whelp.
Phanaticks they'll to Providence impute
Their Thraldom, and immediately grow mute:
For they, poor pious Fools, think the Decree
Of Heaven falls on them, tho from Hell it be;
And when their Reason is abas'd to it,

They forthwith think 'tis Religion to submit;
And vainly glorying in a passive Shame,
They'll put off Man to wear the Christian Name.
Wherefore to lull them, do their Hopes fulfil
With Liberty, they're halter'd at your Will;
Give them but Conventicle-room, and they
Will let you steal their Englishman away;
And heedless be, till you your Nets have spread,
And pull'd down Conventicles on their Head.
Militia then and Parliaments cashier,
A formidable standing Army rear;
They'll mount you up, and up you soon will be,
They'll fear, who ne'er did love your Monarchy:
And if they fear, no matter for their Hate,
To rule by Law becomes a sneaking State.
Lay by all Fear, care not what People say,
Regard to them will your Design's betray:
When bite they can't, what hurt can barking do?
And, Sir, in time we'l spoil their barking too,
Make Coffee-Clubs talk of more humble things
Than State-Affairs, and interest of Kings.

Thus spoke the rigling Peer: when one more grave,
That had much less of Fool, but more of Knave,
Began: Great Sir, it gives no small content, [*Cliff.*
To hear such Zeal (for you) 'gainst Parliament
Wherefore, tho I an Enemy no less
To Parliaments than you yourselves profess:
Yet I must also enter my Protest
'Gainst these rude rumbling Counsels indigest;
And, Great Sir, tell you, 'tis a harder thing
Than they suggest, to make you abs'lute King.
Old Buildings to pull down, believe it true,
More danger in it hath, than building new.
And what shall prop your Superstructure, till
Another you have built that futes your Will?
An Army shall, say they. (Content) but stay,
From whence shall this new Army have its Pay?
For easy gentle Government a while
Must first appear i' th' Kingdom, to beguile
The peoples Minds, and make them cry up you,
For razing old, and making better new.
For taxes with new Government all will blame,
And put the Kingdom soon into a Flame:
For Tyranny has no such lovely Look
To catch Men with, unless you hide the Hook;
And no Bait hides it more than present Ease;

Ease but their Taxes, then do what you please.
Wherefore, all wild Debates laid by, from whence
Shall Mony rise to bear this vast expence?
For our first thoughts thus well resolved, we
In other things much sooner shall agree.
Join then with Mother-Church, whose Bosom stands
Ope to receive us, stretching forth her Hands:
Close but this Breach, and she will let you see
Her Purse as open as her Arms shall be.
For, Sacred Sir, (by guess I do not speak)
Of poor she'll make you rich, and strong of weak.
At home, abroad, no Money, nor no Men,
She'll let you lack, turn but to her agen.

The *Scot* cou'd here no longer hold, but cry'd, [*Laud.*
Dee'l take the Pape, and all that's on his side:
The Whore of *Rome,* that mickle Man of Sin,
Plague take the Mother, Bearns, and aw the Kin.
What racks my Saul! must we the holy Rood
Place in God's Kirk again? troth 'tis not gude.
I defy the Loon, the Dee'l and all his Works,
The Pape shall lig no mare in God's gude Kirk.

The *Scot* with Laughter check'd, they all agreed,
The Lord spoke last shou'd in his Speech proceed, [*Clif.*
Which thus he did: Great Sir, You know 'tis Season
Salts all the Motions that we make with Reason;
And now a Season is afforded us,
The best e'er came, and most propitious.
Besides the Sum the Cath'licks will advance,
You know the Offers we are made from *France;*
And to have Money and no Parliament,
Must fully answer your design'd Intent.
And thus without tumultuous Noise, or Huff
Of Parliaments, you may have Money enough;
Which if neglected now, there's none knows when
Like Opportunities may be had agen:
For all to extirpate, now combin'd be,
Both Civil and Religious Liberty.
Thus Money you'll have to exalt the Crown,
Without stooping Majesty to Country Clown.
The Triple League, I know, will be objected,
As if that Ought by us to be respected:
But who to Heretick or Rebel pay'th
The Truth ingaged to by solemn Faith,
Debaucheth Vertue; by those very things
The Church profaneth, and debaseth Kings:
As you your self have admirably shown

By burning solemn Cov'nant, tho your own;
Faith, Justice, Truth, Plebeian Vertues be,
Look well in them, and not in Majesty.
For publick Faith is but a publick Thief,
The greatest Cheat in Nature's vain Belief.
The second Lord tho check'd, yet did not fear,
Impatient grew, and could no longer bear,
But rose in Heat, and that a little rude,
The Lord's Voice interrupts, and for Audience su'd.

Great Majesty, authentick Authors say,
When Hand was lifted up *Croesus* to slay,
The Father's Danger on th' dumb Son did make
Such deep Impressions that he forthwith spake.
Pardon, Great Sir, If I, in imitation,
Seeing the Danger to your Land and Nation,
Do my resolv'd-on Silence also break,
Altho I see the Matter I shall speak,
Under such Disadvantages will fall,
That it, as well as I, exploded shall.
But vainly do they boast they loyal are,
That can't for Princes Good, Reflections bear;
Nor will I call Compurgators to prove,
What Honour to the Crown I've born, with Love:
My Acts have spoken, and sufficient are,
Above what e'er Detractors did or dare.
Wherefore, Great Sir, 'tis Ignorance, or Hate,
Dictates these Counsels, you to precipitate.
For say't again I will, not cat my Word,
No Council's Power, no nor yet the Sword,
Can old Foundations alter, or make new;
Let Time interpret who hath spoken true.
Those Country Gentry with their Beef and Bacon,
Will shew how much your Courtiers are mistaken:
For Parliaments are not of that cheap rate,
That they will down without a broken Pate;
And then I doubt you'll find those worthy Lords
More Brave, and Champions with their Tongues than Swords.
Wherefore, Dread Sir, incline not Royal Ear
To their Advice, but safer Counsels hear;
Stay till these Lords have got a Crown to lose,
And then consult with them which way they'l chuse.
Will you all hazard for their Humours sake,
Who nothing have to lose, nothing to stake;
And at one Game your Royal Crown expose,
To gratify the foolish Lusts of those
Who hardly have Subsistance how to live,

But what your Crown and Grace to them does give?
And one of those (Bag-pudding) Gentlemen,
(Except their Places) wou'd buy nine or ten.
Then, why they shou'd thus slight the Gentlemen,
I see no Reason, nor think how they can:
For had not Gentleman done more than Lord,
I'll boldly say't, you ne'er had been restor'd.
But why of Armies now, Great Sir, must we
So fond (just now) all on the sudden be?
What faithful Guardians have they been to Pow'rs
That have employ'd 'em, that you'd make 'em yours?
Enough our Age, we need not seek the Glory
Of Armies Faith in old, or doubtful Story.
Your Father 'gainst the *Scots* an Army rear'd,
But soon that Army more than *Scot* he fear'd:
He was in hast to raise 'em, as we are,
But to disband 'em was far more his Care.
How *Scotish* Army after did betray
His Truth and Person both, I need not say.
Rump-Parliament an Army rear'd, and they
The Parliament that rais'd them, did betray:
The Lord Protector they set up one hour,
And next pull'd down the Protectorian Pow'r.
Your Father's Block and Judges the same Troops
Did guard, same Tongues at Death of both made hoops:
And will you suffer Armies to beguile,
And give your Crown and them to Cross and Pile?
What if, as *Monk,* both shou'd swear, lye and feign,
Till he does both your Trust and Army gain,
And you believe his Oath and Faith is true,
But serves himself instead of serving you?
Pardon, Great Sir, if Zeal transports my Tongue,
T' express what e'en your Greatness don't become
Expose I can't your Crown and Sacred Throat,
To the false Faith of a common Red-Coat.
The Law your All does fence secure from Fears;
That kept, what trouble needs of Bandileers?
Consider, Sir, 'tis Law that makes you King,
The Sword another to the Crown may bring;
For Force knows no distinction; longest Sword
Makes Peasant Prince, Lacquey above his Lord.
If that be all that we must have for Laws,
Your Will inferior may be to *Jack Straw's,*
If greater Force him follow; there's no Right
Where Law is failing, and for Will Men fight.
Best Man is he alone, whose Steel's most strong;
Where no Law is, there's neither right nor wrong.

That Fence broke down, and all in Common laid,
Subjects may Prince, and Prince may them invade.
See, greatest Sir, how these your Throne lay doun,
Instead of making great your Royal Crown
How they divest you of your Majesty:
For Law destroy'd, you are no more than we.
And very vain would be the Plea of Crown,
When Statute Laws, and Parliaments are down.
This Peer proceeded on, to shew how vain
A Holy League would be with *Rome* again,
And what Dishonour 'twould be to our Crowns,
If unto *France* give cautionary Towns.

He's interrupted, and bid speak no more
By's enrag'd Majesty, who deeply swore
His Tongue had so run over, that he'd take
Such Vengeance on him, and Example make
To after-Times, that all who heard should fear,
To speak what wou'd displease the Royal Ear;
And bid the Lord that spoke before, go on,
And silence all should keep till he had done;
Who thus his Speech resum'd. If Lord spake last,
To interrupt me had not made such hast,
I soon had done; for I was come, Great Sir,
T' advise your sending *Dutch* Embassador.
But much it does concern you whom to trust,
With this Embassy: for none true, or just,
Wise, stout, or honourable, nor a Friend,
Should you in any wise resolve to send,
Lest any unseen, or unlucky Chance
Shou'd in this War befal to us or *France*.
We may that loathed Wretch give to the Hate
Of th' Peoples Fury, them to satiate.
And when all's done that can be done by Man,
Much must be left to Chance, do what we can.
And if you'l make all *Christendom* your Friend,
And put to *Dutch-land League* an utter end;
Then surely you may have of Men and Treasure,
Enough of both to execute your Pleasure.

This Speech being ended, five of six agree,
France shall be lov'd, and *Holland* hated be.
All gone, I wak'd, and wonder'd what should mean
All I had heard, methought 'twas more than Dream.
And if Cabal thus serve us *Englishmen*,
'Tis ten to one but I shall dream again.

Index

IE